Asian Americans

Emerging Minorities

Third Edition

Harry H.L. Kitano
University of California, Los Angeles

Roger Daniels
University of Cincinnati

Prentice
Hall

Upper Saddle River, New Jersey 07458

Library of Congress Cataloging-in-Publication Data

Kitano, Harry H. L.
    Asian Americans: emerging minorities / Harry H.L. Kitano, Roger Daniels.—3rd ed.
    p. cm.
    Includes bibliographical references (p. 225) and index.
    ISBN 0-13-790486-X
    1. Asian Americans. I. Daniels, Roger. II. Title.

E184.06 K57 2001
973´.0495—dc21

00-058901

For Lynn and Judith

VP, Editorial director: Laura Pearson
AVP, Publisher: Nancy Roberts
Managing editor (editorial): Sharon Chambliss
Managing editor (production): Ann Marie McCarthy
Project liaison: Fran Russello
Editorial/Production supervision: Pine Tree Composition, Inc.
Prepress and manufacturing buyer: Mary Ann Gloriande
Cover director: Jayne Conte
Cover designer: Bruce Kenselaar
Cover photos: David Young-Wolff/PhotoEdit (t/l); Nathan Benn/Woodfin Camp &
Associates (t/r); Don Smetzer/Stone (m/l); Stewart Cohen/Stone (b/r); Michael
Newman/PhotoEdit (b/l)

Extract on pp. 161–162 from *American Mosaic: The Immigrant Experience in the Words of Those Who Lived It,* by Joan Morrison and Charlotte Fox Zabusky. © 1980 by Joan Morrison and Charlotte Fox Zabusky. Reprinted by permission of the John A. Ware Literary Agency. Currently available from the University of Pittsburgh Press.

Printed in the United States of America
10 9 8 7 6 5 4 3 2 1

ISBN 0-13-790486-X

PRENTICE-HALL INTERNATIONAL (UK) LIMITED, *London*
PRENTICE-HALL OF AUSTRALIA PTY. LIMITED, *Sydney*
PRENTICE-HALL CANADA INC., *Toronto*
PRENTICE-HALL HISPANOAMERICANA, S.A., *Mexico*
PRENTICE-HALL OF INDIA PRIVATE LIMITED, *New Delhi*
PRENTICE-HALL OF JAPAN, INC., *Tokyo*
PEARSON EDUCATION ASIA PTE. LTD., *Singapore*
EDITORA PRENTICE-HALL DO BRASIL, LTDA., *Rio de Janeiro*

Contents

3 The Chinese: The Early Years 21

4 The Chinese: After 1943 38

5 The Japanese: The Early Years 57

6 Japanese Americans: After 1946 72

Preface

This third edition came about because of both the continuing immigration of relatively large numbers of Asians and because of the growing consciousness of many Americans about the increasingly multicultural nature of American society and the increasing self-consciousness and assertiveness of Asian Americans and other long-ignored American ethnic group members.

We have again added new material to reflect developments in the last years of the millennium, updated the bibliographies, provided new demographic and economic data, and incorporated suggestions and corrections offered by some readers. We welcome such input.

H. H. L. K.
R. D.

Chapter 1

INTRODUCTION

Asian Americans, in common with all Americans, have faced good times and bad times. In the nineteenth and the first half of the twentieth century they were pariahs, excluded from meaningful participation in American society, viewed as racially and culturally inferior, and often compared to monkeys. But in the second half of the century, the image had largely changed so that they were labelled the "model minority."

To use examples only from the history of the two earliest groups of immigrants from Asia and their descendants we can observe the following:

- The Chinese Americans were the first immigrant group to be excluded in 1882, yet they were better treated during World War II when China and the United States were allies, but viewed with suspicion again after 1949 when the emergence of what was then called "Red China" increased anti-Chinese hostility.
- The Japanese Americans were restricted by the Gentlemen's Agreement of 1907–1908, totally barred from immigration in 1924, forcibly incarcerated behind barbed wire during World War II (1942–1946), yet in 1988 they were granted redress, including a formal apology and a cash payment of $20,000 to each survivor of the wartime camps.

It is important to recognize the peaks and valleys of the Asian American experience, which means analyzing both the past and the present. The constant variable in this picture is one of dynamic change. Therefore, in any coverage of groups it is important that we provide a longitudinal, historical analysis, a snapshot of the present, and take a tentative peek at the future.

The purpose of this third edition is to discuss the following groups: Chinese, Japanese, Filipinos, Asian Indians and other South Asians, Koreans, Pacific Islanders, and Southeast Asians. Each of these groups is different in terms of history, culture, time of entry in the United States, and reception by the host society. Yet, because of a number of factors they are often combined under groupings such as Asians and Asian Americans. Note that one almost never hears people talk about European Americans.

Populations isolated by geography and culture are especially likely to be characterized by symbols and stereotypes. Asian Americans are one such group; they are relatively few in number and are clustered primarily in Hawaii, along the West Coast, and around New York City, so to the general public they remain a largely invisible population. In addition, knowledge about their ancestral homelands is often based on wartime and colonial experiences, so stereotypes abound. Who has not heard "masses of people," "life is cheap," "sly and tricky," or, somewhat less negatively, "hardworking and industrious" and "good at math"? It would be refreshing if we could go beyond such simple "one-liners," especially the hostile and negative ones, even though the more benign images also distort reality.

THE IMMIGRANT IMAGE

One common image associated with immigrants is of crowded boats, the Statue of Liberty, Ellis Island, poverty, hard work, night school, and the Americanization of succeeding generations. This process, often referred to as the "European model" or "straight-line" theory,[1] includes voluntary immigration, acculturation, integration, assimilation, and eventual absorption into the dominant society. This theory assumes that given sufficient time, anyone can become a part of the American mainstream by working hard, learning English and the American way, participating in the community, and blending into the mainstream. Those who do not are looked on as somehow lacking the motivation to become American.

But this scenario is a narrow one and may reflect an idealized vision of the past, reserved primarily for those of "proper" Caucasian background. Not all immigrants were welcome; many did not possess the desired attributes or background for easy blending, and many came with different notions of the meaning of America. Black slaves did not come freely, nor were they given unconditional welcome; the native inhabitants were already here, then conquered, while those who had settled in the Southwest became Americans through treaties and land acquisition.

The Asian experience provides another image of immigration. Until after World War II, for example, many immigrants from Asia were kept not on Ellis Island, in the shadow of the Statue of Liberty, but in the detention barracks on Angel Island, near San Francisco's Alcatraz, a notorious prison.

In the wooden prison buildings, which can still be visited, some Chinese detainees whiled away the time by carving poems in Chinese characters into the soft wood of the walls. One poem read:

> There are tens of thousands of poems composed on these walls,
> They are all cries of complaint and sadness.
> The day I am rid of this prison and attain success,
> I must remember that this prison once existed.
> . . .
> All my compatriots please be mindful,
> Once you have some small gains, return home early.
>   *By one from Xiangshan*[2]

So the image of Ellis Island is only one of a variety of images and symbols representing different immigrations. Present-day migration provides different symbols and images. Some newcomers simply walk across the border, while others arrive in jet aircraft; the new ports of entry include overcrowded border cities in Texas and California. But despite these differences, a number of similar questions may be asked about both the older and present-day immigrants, no matter how they arrived.

Why and how did they come to the United States? What skills, resources, values, cultures, and lifestyles did they bring with them? Did they have family and community support? And—most important for peoples who have faced much discrimination—how were they received by the host society? Were they made to feel welcome or unwelcome?

Asian migration to the United States provides a rich source of data regarding these questions. Some Asians came as contract laborers and as sojourners with the expectation of returning to their home country; others arrived with the hope of permanent residence. Many came for economic and educational opportunities and ready to participate in the American dream. Others fled for personal and political reasons. Some Asians carefully planned their move to the new country; others, forced to flee at a moment's notice, arrived as refugees.

They came to America at different times. After a period of "free immigration," the early immigrants faced steep barriers that virtually forced a separatist and less than equal existence. But at other times the barriers were lowered, and Asians integrated and acculturated more fully. It is the interaction between the dominant society and the immigrant group that determines outcomes. The direction of change is controlled largely by the group with greater power and resources.

We perceive a relationship among the motivations for migration, the reactions of the host society, and the adaptive patterns of the migrants. The state of an immigrant group is the result of the interaction of factors within the ethnic group and the reactions of the host society. In addition, relationships among ethnic groups are significant.

Certain factors are internal to the ethnic group, including:

Historical circumstances, including motivations for migration, goals, and expectations

Demographic factors, such as number, age, sex ratio, education, training, and skills

Cultural factors, including language, values, social class, urban or rural experience, religion, and lifestyle

Family and community cohesion, resources, power, and alternative opportunities

Home-country factors, such as power, stage of development, and status of the mother country

The host society provides the context for immigrant adaptation through factors including:

Government policies
Barriers, including prejudice and discrimination
Relations between the host nation and the mother country
Reactions of other ethnic groups
International, national, and local economic factors

WHO IS AN AMERICAN?

One of the critical factors affecting the ability of immigrants from Asia to participate as equals in American society has been the varying definitions of who is an American. If being an American is defined in terms of race, the question of Asians' belonging becomes difficult.[3] If being an American is determined by nationality and country of origin or by religion and culture, all who do not fit into the white, European Protestant or Catholic mode will again face difficulty. However, if being an American is defined on the basis of a belief in the American system or by the needs of the economy or by relatives already in residence, Asians will find an easier fit. At different periods of our history, the question of who could become an American has had different answers. Asian immigrants were deeply affected by these changes in definition, as reflected in our national policies. The question of who could become an American is analyzed in Chapter 2.

For example, in the mid-nineteenth century (1840s–1870s) there was no formal immigration policy—anyone willing to work was welcome. Chinese laborers filled a critical labor gap, working the mines and building the railroads, but when their labor was no longer needed, their race and nationality became an issue. In 1882, Chinese laborers were no longer allowed to immigrate to this country. Race and nationality as criteria for becoming

"American" were reinforced in 1917 and 1924, when immigration policy extended discrimination to almost all Orientals (as they were known in those days).

There was little immigration from Asian countries from then until World War II, when China was an American ally. To defuse Japanese arguments about a race war, it was felt that it would be politically sound to grant a token immigration quota and the right of naturalization to "friends" of the United States. Current immigration legislation gives preferences to immigrants with special skills or capital: Qualified Asian immigrants are welcome. The history of U.S. immigration policy reflects changes in orientation toward immigrants.

Philip Gleason indicates that although colonial America was populated primarily by immigrants from Britain, the early American identity was based more on abstractions such as liberty, equality, and a belief in the republic rather than on any particular language, religion, nationality, or ethnic background.[4] But in spite of these idealistic abstractions, a two-tiered system developed in America. One tier was free and open to all whites; the other, a step below, was for American Indians and blacks. A belief in liberty and justice was insufficient for Indians and blacks to participate in the society; "pure" Caucasian ancestry was required to become a part of the mainstream. Asians were soon to join other "nonwhites" in the second-class section of the social structure.[5]

WHO WANTS TO BE AN AMERICAN?

Another related but often unasked question is "Who wants to become an American?" This apparently simple question turns out to be complicated because it involves different "Americas." If becoming an American means full acceptance and the chance for equal participation in the mainstream, most immigrants would answer with a resounding yes. If becoming American means giving up one's cultural heritage in order to participate in the mainstream, the affirmative responses of some immigrants might be less enthusiastic. And if it means domination and a second-class role, many immigrants would not wish to become Americans.

Some Asians prefer to retain strong ethnic ties, and hence their definition of being American is based on a pluralistic model. They may see themselves primarily as Asians, believing that the meaning of America lies in its recognition of diversity. Others may prefer to live their lives within ethnic boundaries because they feel that America will never accept people of color as equals.

These various definitions are not static. There is constant change, in both the immigrant group and the host society. American society is and has been characterized by change. Present-day America is significantly different from the nation that existed at the beginning of the twentieth century. For example, a book about Asian Americans in 1910 or even 1950 might have dealt with only two groups, the Chinese and the Japanese. They would be seen as "problem minorities"; they did not fit into the prevailing definition of who could become an American. The solution to the problem was simple: Discriminatory legislation would prohibit further immigration and erect barriers to equal participation for those already here.

MODELS OF IMMIGRANT GROUPS

Because we are a nation of immigrants, much attention has been paid to the experiences of immigrant groups. One widely used model was developed by Milton Gordon, who sees different stages in the assimilation of various groups.[6] Cultural assimilation, or acculturation, means taking on the ways of the host society in such matters as dress, diet, and lifestyle; other types of assimilation extend to the structural, marital, identificational, and civic. The critical entry for minority groups is structural assimilation. Once a group enters the social clubs, groups, and institutions of the core society at the primary level, it will inevitably lead to marital assimilation. According to Gordon:

> If children of different ethnic backgrounds belong to the same play group, later the same adolescent cliques and at college the same fraternities and sororities; if the parents belong to the same country club and invite each other to their homes for dinner; it is completely unrealistic not to expect these children, now grown, to love and marry each other, in spite of ethnic extraction.[7]

Gordon also predicts that all of the other types of assimilation will follow once structural assimilation is achieved. The price of such assimilation is the disappearance of the ethnic group as a separate entity and the loss of its distinctive values. Given this perspective, different groups can exist at different stages of the assimilation process. Blacks are culturally but not structurally assimilated; Jews still retain some cultural and structural distinctiveness. Asians may also have acculturated but many remain structurally separate. The basic criticism of Gordon's model is that it is based on a majority-group perspective and overemphasized acculturation and integration.

A model proposed by Robert Blauner provides a contrasting perspective.[8] Not all groups have followed the immigration–acculturation–assimilation path. The key points in his model include:

Forced involuntary entry

Impact of interaction that is much more dramatic than the natural pace of acculturation

Rule by outsiders
Racism against the group

Blauner refers to his model as domestic or internal colonialism and likens the relationship between the dominant society and America's racial minorities to the practices of the European colonial powers over their conquered populations in Africa and Asia. The conquered population is forced to participate in someone else's society, whether it wishes to or not. The people are subjected to a wide number of restrictions in their social, economic, and political mobility; and their culture and social institutions are attacked, often to the point where they are forced to give up their own "inferior" ways and to accept the ways of their "superiors."

Asian experiences lie somewhere between the assimilation model of Gordon and the domestic colonial model of Blauner, especially since Asian immigration has covered a wide span of years and faced a number of different Americas. For example, many early Asian migrants came as contract laborers intending to return at the end of their contract period. Thus they were not striving to assimilate into the dominant society, nor was their migration totally voluntary. Early Asian immigrants to Hawaii lived on separate ethnic plantations ruled by "outsiders."[9] For the majority, acculturation was primarily functional—they learned enough about the new culture to survive, but most retained their Asian cultural ways, reinforced by the hostility of the American society. Restrictions were placed on their social, economic, and political mobility, and racism was prevalent.

One progressive and well-educated California editor put it this way early in the twentieth century:

> Race counts more than anything else in the world. It is the mark God placed on those whom he put asunder. . . . An educated Japanese would not be a welcomed suitor for the hand of any American's daughter, but an Italian of the commonest standing would be a more welcomed suitor than the finest gentleman of Japan. . . . If we deal with the Japanese question now, our descendants will have no race questions to deal with. If not, they, like antebellum South Carolinians, will leave a race question which their descendants will have to deal with, and against which they will be helpless.[10]

But at other times, Asian experiences were different; no one model can encompass the experiences of all Asian groups. Racism is most effective if the dominant group is successful in convincing the dominated group that there are "superiors" and "inferiors." It is to the credit of America's racial minorities and to the American system that its racial minorities have never fully accepted a permanent inferior position.

Most generalizations concerning Asians concentrate on the male population. Very little information on the role of Asian females is available, yet if life for men in the early days was difficult, then the lives of women must have been doubly difficult. Stories of women going back to work alongside their men almost immediately after childbirth are commonly heard. Evelyn Nakano Glenn sees the Asian females of that period as victims of triple oppression: trapped in the most menial types of work, such as houseworker or seamstress; subjected to institutional racism; and subordinated at home by a patriarchical family system.[11]

Present Data

Summary population data for Asian Americans is based on the U.S. Census reports for 1998, which uses the umbrella term *Asians* to describe the population. In 1990 the total of Asian/Pacific Islanders was over 7,000,000; in 1997 they numbered over 10,000,000. The growth was primarily through immigration—since in 1998, the foreign-born (an estimated 6.4 million) outnumbered the 4.1 million American-born Asians. California remained the state with the most Asians and Pacific Islanders with 3.8 million, followed by New York (952,736), Hawaii (748,748), Texas (523,972), and New Jersey (423,738).

Among counties, Los Angeles had the highest (1.2 million), followed by Honolulu (559,752), Orange County, California (344,330), Santa Clara, California, which includes San Jose (343,387), and Queens County in New York (317,893).

In terms of the proportion of the county population, Honolulu and Kauai were tied for first with 64 percent Asian/Pacific Islanders, followed by Maui (59 percent), Hawaii (58 percent), San Francisco (35 percent), and Santa Clara, (21 percent). As we can see, the majority of Asian Americans and Pacific Islanders continue to reside in California and Hawaii, and the high proportions in Hawaii indicate continued political power. However, as we will indicate in our section on Hawaii, different Asian American groups may be vying for political office based on their ethnic groups, rather than the umbrella identification as Asian.

Both the number (1.5 million) and the percentage (14.0 percent) of Asian Pacific Islanders who were poor in 1997 remained unchanged in 1998. Fifty percent of adults (25 to 29 years) achieved a bachelor's degree in 1997, compared to whites (29 percent), African Americans (14 percent), and Hispanics (11 percent).

The Asian Pacific Islanders had the highest median household income among the nation's race groups in 1997 ($45,249), although their households (3.17) were larger than white households (2.58). As a consequence, estimated household income per household member was lower ($18,569) than whites ($20,093).

Families

Eighty-four percent of Asian and Pacific Islander children under 18 years of age lived with both parents, compared to 77 percent of non-Hispanic whites. Fifty-eight percent of Asian Pacific Islanders aged 15 or over were married, 33 percent had never married, and 4 percent were widowed or divorced. The families were large; over 20 percent had five or more members, compared to 11 percent for non-Hispanic white families. They were a young population, with an estimated median age as of July 1, 1998, of 31.2 years, whereas the median age of the total U.S. population was four years older. Their population growth of 37 percent between 1990 and 1998 was highest of any racial or ethnic group. The Census Bureau estimates that by 2020, the Asian Pacific Islander population is expected to reach 19.7 million, which would be 6.1 percent of the nation's total population. We would expect to find issues of acculturation, ethnic identity, generation and marital practices to be primary topics for discussion. As we have indicated previously, lumping all of the Asian groups together obscures the differences by ethnic group, but unfortunately, data is often reported in this way. We hope to emphasize the differences in the chapters focusing on one or more groups.

PURPOSES OF THIS BOOK

Since the publication of the second edition in 1995 there has been an enormous explosion of scholarly literature about Asian Americans, some of the most significant of which are listed on pages 225–229.

The purpose of our volume is to provide an interdisciplinary account of the Asian American experience, including census material, historical data, and social psychological perspectives. A variety of sociopsychological models are presented to explain different minority-majority group interactions.

The book includes separate chapters on the most numerous Asian American groups and examines their patterns of adaptation, based on the interaction of what they brought with them with the reactions of the host society. Before presenting the groups, we look at immigration legislation (Chapter 2), for legislative acts have been and will continue to be crucial to any understanding of Asians in America.

Chapters 3 and 4 are devoted to the Chinese; Chapters 5 and 6, to the Japanese. These two groups represent the "old" immigrants—the ones who began arriving in the nineteenth century.

Chapter 7 focuses on the Filipinos. (Many contemporary Filipinos prefer the spelling *Philipino*, but we are using the old spelling primarily because the vast majority of our historical references use it.)

Chapter 8 deals with South Asians, particularly Asian Indians who come from the second largest nation in Asia. The Asian Indians are a sizable Asian American minority, but relatively little has been written about them.

Chapter 9 is about the Koreans, one of the fastest-growing Asian groups. Their migration is still under way, but there is a significant literature about them, particularly from the social sciences.

Chapter 10 covers a "hidden" minority, the Pacific Islanders. This chapter looks at the Samoans, the Guamanians, and the native Hawaiians. They do not usually identify themselves as Asian Americans but have been placed in the category by federal authorities, albeit as "Asian American/ Pacific Islanders."

Chapter 11 presents information on immigrants from Southeast Asia— the Vietnamese, Laotians, and Cambodians. They have come largely as refugees rather than traditional immigrants, but their ways of dealing with the new culture have been similar to those of other immigrants.

Chapter 12 presents data on the current status of Asian Americans, reporting on their socioeconomic accomplishments and taking note of the fields in which they are not doing so well. Chapter 13, the final chapter, presents a model for analyzing Asian American adaptation to America.

NOTES

1. Neil Sandberg, *Jewish Life in Los Angeles* (Lanham, MD: University Press of America, 1986).

2. Him Mark Lai, Ginny Lim, and Judy Yung, *Island: Poetry and History of Chinese Immigrants on Angel Island, 1910–1940* (San Francisco: San Francisco Study Center, 1980).

3. Race is difficult to define scientifically, especially the concept of "pure races." The literature speaks of four or five races, popularly known as "white" (Caucasian), "black" (Negroid), "yellow" (Mongoloid), "red" (Amerindian), and sometimes "brown" (Malaysian).

4. Philip Gleason, "American Identity and Americanization," in Stephan Thernstrom et al., eds., *Harvard Encyclopedia of American Ethnic Groups* (Cambridge, MA: Harvard University Press, 1980), pp. 31–58.

5. Ronald T. Takaki, *Iron Cages* (New York: Knopf, 1979).

6. Milton M. Gordon, *Assimilation in American Life: The Role of Race, Religion, and National Origins* (New York: Oxford University Press, 1964).

7. Ibid., p. 80.

8. Robert Blauner, *Racial Oppression in America* (New York: Harper & Row, 1972). See also Harry H. L. Kitano, *Race Relations*, 4th ed. (Englewood Cliffs, NJ: Prentice Hall, 1991), chap. 5.

9. Ronald T. Takaki, *Pau Hana* (Honolulu: University of Hawaii Press, 1983).

10. Roger Daniels, *The Politics of Prejudice* (Berkeley: University of California Press, 1962), pp. 23–24.

11. Evelyn Nakano Glenn, *Issei, Nisei, War Bride* (Philadelphia: Temple University Press, 1986).

Chapter 2

IMMIGRATION LAWS AND THEIR EFFECTS

Discrimination against Asians has been evident from the very early years of their migration to America, although there have been changes in recent years. Nevertheless, "Asian bashing," a relatively modern but appropriate term, most often directed against a specific group, has never fully disappeared. One major issue has been immigration, which has led to restriction and exclusion and raised barriers to Asian "equality," whether immigrant or native born. Words and phrases such as "yellow hordes," "pagans," and "unassimilable" were indicative of majority group feelings against immigrants from across the Pacific, and these prejudices led to anti-Asian legislation. Legalized discrimination took many forms, but immigration and naturalization legislation was especially critical. Thus, a review of that legislation will serve as a background to some of the major problems that Asian immigrants faced.

Many recent historians divide the history of immigration into six periods:

1. The Colonial period, during which neither Great Britain nor the American colonies had effective control of immigration and the overwhelming number of all immigrants came from the British Isles and were Protestant.
2. The era of the American Revolution and beyond (1775–1820), when war, both here and in Europe, inhibited immigration.
3. The era of the "old" immigration (1820–ca. 1880), in which most immigrants came from the British Isles, Germany, and Scandinavia and were primarily

Protestant Christians (large numbers of Irish and Germans were Roman Catholic)

4. The era of the "new" immigration (ca. 1880–1924), when most immigrants came from central, southern, and eastern Europe and were largely Roman Catholic, Greek Orthodox, and Jewish

5. The era of the national origins quota system (1924–1965), in which rigorous regulation reduced the volume of immigration greatly, and most immigrants were from the countries of the "old" immigration or the quota-free new world

6. The era of liberalized restrictions (1965 to the present), in which most immigrants have come from Asia and Latin America, or what is often called the "Third World."[1]

There was no significant immigration legislation before the passage of the Chinese Exclusion Act in 1882. Some eastern states had attempted to stop with restrictive laws what they had considered the flood of undesirable immigration from Ireland and Germany in the 1830s and 1840s, but the U.S. Supreme Court in the *Passenger Cases* of 1849 ruled that such laws were unconstitutional because the commerce clause of the Constitution gave the federal government preemptive control over "domestic and foreign commerce," and immigration, the court ruled, was "foreign commerce."[2] The adoption of the Fourteenth Amendment in 1868 made "all persons born . . . in the United States" citizens (this would later have a tremendous impact on the lives of native-born Asian Americans, although the amendment was concerned solely with blacks). Two years later, in a revision of the naturalization statutes, Congress accordingly made "white persons and persons of African descent" eligible for citizenship. Attempts by Charles Sumner, the radical Republican senator from Massachusetts, and a few others to make naturalization color-blind were overwhelmingly voted down by Congress. Therefore, the definition of who could become American by naturalization barred only Asians.[3]

It should be noted, however, that naturalization procedures were not uniform, and some judges allowed individual Asians—Chinese, Japanese, and Asian Indians—to become citizens. The question was finally settled in two Supreme Court cases, *Ozawa v. United States* in 1922 and *Thind v. United States* in 1923. These cases made it clear that Asians of any hue could not become naturalized. Although since 1870 the Constitution has guaranteed citizenship to persons who are born in the United States, naturalization is governed by statute and, as we shall see, has been modified often.

BEFORE 1924

Direct federal discrimination against Asian immigration began in 1882. In that year Congress passed the first significant restrictive immigration law, the Chinese Exclusion Act, whereby the immigration of Chinese laborers was suspended for ten years. In 1892 the Geary Act extended these exclusion laws for another decade, and in 1902 the exclusion of Chinese immigrants was extended indefinitely.

It is clear that the actions taken against the Chinese were a culmination of a host of anti-Chinese actions, which included lynchings, murders, and race riots. Although there were never more than 125,000 Chinese in the whole United States—almost all of them in the Far West—the fear of massive Chinese immigration and of economic competition, as well as the racism of the majority of whites, was sufficient to offset more moderate voices. *Exclusion,* rather than *restriction,* became the law of the land.

Sizable, but still relatively small, amounts of Japanese immigration began shortly after the Chinese exclusion laws became effective. Similar feelings about their undesirability soon arose; in 1907–1908 there was a diplomatic "Gentlemen's Agreement" between the United States and Japan by which Japan agreed to limit the number of laborers emigrating to the United States.

In 1917, Congress created a "barred zone," whereby natives of China, South and Southeast Asia, the Asian part of Russia, Afghanistan, Iran, part of Arabia, and the Pacific and Southeast Asian Islands not owned by the United States were declared inadmissible. Japan, for diplomatic reasons, was left out of the barred zone. Filipinos and some Samoans were allowed to enter as U.S. nationals, but they could not be naturalized.

Racial, national, and ethnic discrimination was broadened and codified in the Immigration Act of 1924. Japanese were added to the barred list. Europeans were given national quotas. Northern and western Europeans were given relatively large quotas—in 1931, for example, the quota for Great Britain and Northern Ireland was 65,000, Ireland almost 18,000, and Germany nearly 26,000. Eastern and southern European countries received relatively small quotas—in 1931, Poland and Italy got about 6,000 each. Originally Congress spoke of making the admissions representative of the ethnic mix of the current population, but when the majority discovered that this would give relatively large quotas to countries like Italy and Poland, it pushed the determining date of quotas back to the census of 1890. The blatant bias of the act is clear. A person of Chinese ancestry, for example, who was born in England and was a British subject, was still barred as an "alien ineligible for citizenship"; similarly, although Japan and other Asian countries were given token annual quotas of 100, no person of discernible Asian ancestry could enter on those quotas. They were reserved for "white persons" who happened to be born in Asia. (In theory, persons of "African descent" were also eligible to use quota spaces, but there were few, if any, of them.)

Except for Japanese, who were barred by the unilateral abrogation of the Gentlemen's Agreement accomplished by the 1924 act, Asians were not really affected by the 1924 act. They were already effectively excluded. The main brunt of the act was borne by southern and eastern Europeans. The whole anti-immigrant movement was based on a number of factors: fear of foreigners, at first Asians but soon after Europeans with different and sup- posedly inferior cultures and genes; economic fears of being outworked and undercut by people with a lower standard of living; fears, particularly after the Russian Revolution of 1917, of incoming radicals; and a racism that was directed not only against "non-whites" but also held one white ethnic type—variously styled "Anglo-Saxon" or "Nordic"—superior to all the rest. In the 1930s, Adolf Hitler and others would take such notions a step further. Nazi theories of a "master race" resulted in the Holocaust, in which not only millions of Jews but also Poles, Gypsies, and other "inferior types" were put to death. While not going that far, the overwhelming majority of Americans "knew" that it was the "white culture" that had built the country, and the notion that the "yellow races" in particular could ever assimilate was felt to be preposterous.

The sobering generalization concerning this era comes from the work of John Higham, who found that it was not only the crackpots or extremists, although they were certainly involved, but also people of the American mainstream who wished to close America's doors.[4]

THE 1930s

The Great Depression had no legislative effect on the national origins law of 1924, but it did reduce immigration generally, with many immigrants return- ing to their native lands for economic reasons. It seemed as if the exclusion of Asians would remain a permanent part of American policy. Further legisla- tion was enacted to close a loophole concerning the Filipinos, who, after the American conquest of the Philippines in 1898, were legally American nation- als, not aliens, and were therefore free to enter the United States. The loophole was closed by a curious nativist solution. Philippine independence was backed, and a 1934 law promised Philippine independence in 1945. The law gave the islands an annual quota of fifty, as opposed to the unlimited ability to enter that their former status as "nationals" had provided. In addition, two subsequent statutes, in 1935 and 1939, enabled any Filipino living in the United States to return to the Philippines at public expense.[5]

The end of the 1930s and the beginning of the 1940s saw a "refugee problem." Many Jews and others sought to flee the Nazis, but except for a fortunate few, the barriers were not dropped. The thinking that was behind the 1924 act prevailed; the fear of foreigners and the desire to maintain an immigration status quo led to a hands-off policy. Very little assistance was given to the refugees, and, as Vice President Walter Mondale observed in 1979, we could have provided asylum, but we "failed the test of civili- zation."[6]

THE 1940s

The years of World War II saw a few changes in immigration policy; the most important change for Asians was the repeal of Chinese exclusion. Just as the Chinese Exclusion Act in 1882 saw the inauguration of race- and ethnicity-related immigration restrictions, the repeal of Chinese exclusion in 1943 was the start of a legislative process that would end with the removal of race and ethnicity as immigration and naturalization criteria.

The 1943 repeal, however, maintained racist elements. For example, although it set a quota of 105 annually, a Chinese born in Canada would still be charged to the Chinese quota, whereas a white native of Canada could enter as a nonquota immigrant.

The basic reason behind the legislation was China's status as an ally in World War II. President Franklin D. Roosevelt, in signing the legislation, talked about the affection and regard that tied the two countries together and stated that "an unfortunate barrier" had been removed between allies and that the "war effort in the Far East" would be pursued with "a greater vigor" because of it.[7]

The idea that a quota could be granted only to "good governments" does not stand for a principled policy, and there were a few pleas to treat all Asians equally. Owen Lattimore even suggested privately that a repeal of Japanese exclusion, though Japan was then our wartime enemy, would be a message that "we were fighting against Japanese militarism and imperialism, not the Japanese people." However, he realistically saw the difficulty of getting such a proposal passed.[8]

In 1946, Congress extended the privilege of naturalization to Filipinos and "persons of races indigenous to India" and gave a small quota to the latter.[9] President Harry S Truman raised the Filipino quota to 100 by proclamation.[10]

Other Asians, including Japanese and Koreans, were still ineligible for naturalization and thus barred as immigrants. However, in 1946, Congress approved a law that placed Chinese wives of American citizens on a nonquota basis, and in 1950 the law was liberalized to give spouses and minor children of members of the armed forces the same rights.[11] These rights were extended to Japanese and other Asians after 1952.

There was also a continuing liberalization of other immigration policies. In 1948 the first of two Displaced Persons Act was passed, which marked the beginning of a positive policy toward refugees. The United States accepted the International Refugee Organization definition of "displaced persons" as those who were

victims . . . of the nazi or fascist . . . or . . . quisling regimes . . . or Spanish Republicans and other victims of the Falangist regime in Spain . . . [or] persons who were considered refugees before the outbreak of the second world war, for reasons of race, religion, nationality, or political opinion . . . who [have] been deported, or obliged to leave [their] country of nationality or of former habitual residence.[12]

1950–1965

The McCarran-Walter Act of 1952 was the first general immigration act since 1924. In most ways it was a continuation of the national origins model, with several major innovations. It removed all racial and ethnic bars to immigration and naturalization and provided for family unification. Female citizens were permitted to bring alien husbands to America on a nonquota basis. But the act retained enough of the old injustices that one scholar wrote, "Into this omnibus bill, Congress packed all the hypocrisy, the malevolence, the arrogance, the racial resentments of earlier laws and earlier moods."[13]

However, this was probably an overreaction, since race was dropped as a restriction. That was the main reason that many Japanese Americans supported the bill. For the first time, Japan was given a quota of 185 immigrants per year, and Japanese residents, heretofore classified as "aliens ineligible for citizenship," were now able to obtain naturalization. As a consequence, the Japanese American Citizens League lobbied for the legislation and supported an override of President Truman's veto.

Between 1952 and 1964, nearly 63,000 Japanese, more than 5,000 a year, were able to immigrate to the United States. Most of them came as nonquota immigrants, that is, as parents, spouses, children, or siblings of United States citizens. Similarly, more than 30,000 Chinese women, many of whom had been separated from their husbands for decades, entered as nonquota immigrants by 1960.

The Commission on Immigration and Naturalization, appointed by President Truman, issued a report shortly before the end of his administration that was highly critical of the 1952 act. The report made a number of recommendations, including the abolition of the national origins system. It recommended a unified quota system that would allocate visas without regard to national origin, race, creed, or color. Such a system would be based on five principles: the right of asylum, reunion of families, needs in the United States, needs in the "Free World," and general immigration. The report also proposed the annual admission of 100,000 refugees, expellees, escapees, and remaining displaced persons.[14] Many of these recommendations were implemented twelve years later in the Immigration Act of 1965.

The Refugee Relief Act of 1953 authorized the admission of 205,000 nonquota persons for the next two and a half years. Reflecting the Cold War atmosphere, a refugee was then defined as:

> any person in a country or area which is either Communist or Communist-dominated, who because of persecution, fear of persecution, natural calamity

or military operation is out of his usual place of abode and is unable to return thereto, who has not been firmly resettled, and who is in urgent need of assistance for the essentials of life or for transportation.

A new feature in this legislation was the inclusion, for the first time, of refugees of Chinese origin, as long as they were vouched for by the Nationalist Chinese government.[15]

THE 1965 IMMIGRATION ACT

The 1965 Immigration Act abolished the national origins system and substituted hemispheric quotas. Western hemispheric immigration, up to then unlimited, was to be limited to 120,000 annually after 1968, without limitation by country. The eastern hemisphere quota was set at 170,000, with a limit of 20,000 from any one country. President Lyndon B. Johnson, in signing this important piece of legislation, said, "This bill that we will sign today is not a revolutionary bill. It does not affect the lives of millions. It will not reshape the structure of our daily lives, or really add importantly to our wealth or our power."[16]

President Johnson was no doubt accurately conveying the intent of Congress. As David Reimers indicates, the legislators thought that southern and eastern European immigration would grow and did not anticipate the tremendous growth of Asian immigration. In his speech, Johnson stressed the wrong done to immigrants from southern and eastern Europe, and although he did mention "developing continents," there was no other reference to Asian or Third World immigration.

The 1965 act gave high priority to the reunification of families, which has largely become a chain migration. An immigrant family arrives, puts down roots, acquires permanent residence and then citizenship, and brings eligible relatives into the country. Another priority was given to skilled and unskilled workers deemed to be in short supply in the United States. The act also included a large number of qualitative restrictions regarding mental retardation, insanity, addiction, prostitution, and radicalism.

The most visible beneficiaries of the preference provisions of the 1965 law, as amended, have been Asians, especially Chinese, Koreans, Asian Indians, Filipinos, Vietnamese, and other Southeast Asian ethnic groups. In 1940 the Asian American population was about 250,000, with about the same number in Hawaii; in 1960 the figure was 900,000 (including those in Hawaii).

But by 1980 the Asian American population had boomed to nearly 3.5 million and more than doubled in that decade so that by 1990 it had reached almost 7.3 million. Thus the peoples who were first singled out for exclusion became prime beneficiaries of the immigration legislation of the 1960s and

1970s. (The final statute of the liberal era, the Refugee Act of 1980, is discussed in Chapter 11.)

THE TURN AGAINST IMMIGRATION

By the 1980s, however, many Americans were again becoming nervous about "so many foreigners" coming to the United States. And, although the total numbers grew—there had been 2.5 million immigrants in the 1950s, 3.3 million in the 1960s, and 4.5 million in the 1970s—the incidence of foreign-born persons in the population was much lower than in the years between 1860 and 1920. There was also increasing concern—sometimes approaching hysteria—about illegal immigration, largely from Mexico. After years of public and congressional debate, Congress passed the 1986 Immigration Reform and Control Act (IRCA). Despite the hopes of some of its advocates and the fears of some of its opponents, it had little effect on immigrant flows in general and even less on immigration from Asia. Its greatest innovation was its so-called "amnesty program," which, in the decade after its passage, enabled more than 2.7 million illegal immigrants to become naturalized U.S. citizens. Only 128,000 of these—fewer than 5 percent—were Asians. More than two million—almost 75 percent—were from Mexico.[17]

In that same period, 1986–1996, Congress passed sixteen major bills affecting immigration—some of them with such "politically sexy" titles as the Antiterrorism and Effective Death Penalty Act of April 24, 1996—most of which were heralded as "cures" for America's "immigration problems." Some, which denied even legal recent immigrants from participating in certain social service programs, were simply mean-spirited. But, in the final analysis, they were "thunder without lightning"—that is, a lot of noise but with little effect on the number of immigrants who came into the country.

In fact, legal immigration continued to increase. More than 7 million legal immigrants entered 1981–1990, and between 1991 and 1997, almost 7 million entered, suggesting that total immigration for the decade will be more than 9 million. Of these 16 million legal immigrants of the 1980s and 1990, nearly 5 million, about 30 percent, will be from the Asia/Pacific area from Pakistan to the Pacific Islands.[18]

If we look at just the latest period for which full data is available—FY 1998, which ended September 30, 1998—we see that total immigration was reported as 660,477. Almost half of these, 303,440, were already in the United States and merely adjusted their status. 72 percent of all immigrants—475,750 persons—were admitted as family members of persons already here; 11.7 percent—77,517 persons—were admitted on employment-based preferences, which included professionals, skilled workers, and unskilled workers; 8.5 percent—56,280 persons—entered under various refugee and asylum programs; 6.9 percent—45,499 persons—came in under diversity programs; less than 1 percent—about 5,500 persons—were either IRCA legalizations or persons whose deportation or exclusion was canceled, usually by the courts.[19]

Between 1981 and 1998 nearly 15 million legal immigrants came to America. Some 4.75 million of these were Asians, a little over 30 percent of the total. This dramatic change from the conditions of exclusion or near exclusion that existed earlier in this century reflect a basic change in American society. The changes in law, as described in this chapter, have changed Asians from a pariah category to one that includes some of the most numerous and successful of contemporary immigrant groups.

A more detailed account of refugee legislation and its special effect on Asian American groups appears in Chapter 11.

NOTES

1. See Roger Daniels, *Coming to America: A History of Immigration and Ethnicity in American Life* (New York: HarperCollins, 1990). David M. Reimers, *Still the Golden Door: The Third World Comes to America*, 2nd ed. (New York: Columbia University Press, 1992), examines the period after 1965.

2. For brief surveys of constitutional issues and legislation, see Roger Daniels, *Racism and Immigration Restriction* (St. Charles, MO: Forum Press, 1974), and Roger Daniels, "Changes in Immigration Law and Nativism Since 1924," *American Jewish History* 76 (1986): 158–180.

3. Act of July 4, 1870.

4. John Higham, *Strangers in the Land* (New Brunswick, NJ: Rutgers University Press, 1955).

5. Philippine Independence Act, 48 *Stat.* 456 (Mar. 24, 1934); To Provide Means by Which Certain Filipinos Can Emigrate from the United States, 49 *Stat.* 478 (July 10, 1935); and Emigration of Filipinos from the United States, 53 *Stat.* 1133 (July 27, 1939).

6. Mondale speech text, released by the vice president's press secretary, Saturday, July 21, 1979.

7. Samuel I. Rosenman, ed., *The Public Papers and Addresses of Franklin D. Roosevelt*, 1943 volume (New York: Harper, 1950), p. 548.

8. Lattimore letter (Mar. 3, 1942), as cited in Fred W. Riggs, *Pressures on Congress: A Study of the Repeal of Chinese Exclusion* (New York: King's Crown, 1950), p. 49.

9. Act of July 2, 1946, 60 *Stat.* 416.

10. President's Proclamation No. 2696 of July 4, 1946, 11 *Fed. Reg.* 7517 (July 9, 1946).

11. Act of Aug. 9, 1946, 60 *Stat.* 975, and Act of Aug. 14, 1950, 64 *Stat.* 464.

12. Constitution of the International Refugee Organization, annex I, secs. A and B.

13. J. Campbell Bruce, *The Golden Door: The Irony of Our Immigration Policy* (New York: Random House, 1954).

14. President's Commission on Immigration and Naturalization, *Whom We Shall Welcome* (Washington, DC: Government Printing Office, 1953).

15. 67 *Stat.* 401.

16. *Public Papers of the Presidents, Lyndon B. Johnson, 1965,* "Remarks at the Signing of the Immigration Bill, Liberty Island, New York, Oct. 3, 1965" (Washington, DC: Government Printing Office, 1966), pp. 1037–1040.

17. Major Asian American beneficiaries of amnesty, by country, were: Philippines— 26,542; India—20,863; Pakistan—17,215; China—15,352 [includes PRC, Hong Kong, and Taiwan]; and Korea—10,146.

18. Data from U.S. Department of Commerce, Bureau of the Census, *Statistical Abstract of the United States, 1999* (Washington, DC: Government Printing Office, 1999), Tables 8 and 9; U.S. Department of Justice, Immigration and Naturalization Service, *1997 Statistical Yearbook of the Immigration and Naturalization Service* (Washington, DC: Government Printing Office, 1999), Tables A, B, and C.

19. "Diversity programs" were originally a special way for Europeans—mostly Irish—to enter the country. Since 1995, however, up to 55,000 visas annually may be made available to persons applying from countries that had not received 50,000 numerically limited admissions over the preceding five years. This is usually called the *lottery provision.*

Chapter 3

THE CHINESE

The Early Years

No one is sure when the first Chinese came to America. Isolated navigators may have crossed the Pacific before the voyages of Columbus. We know that a few Chinese were in Mexico in the seventeenth century and that some Chinese seamen were in northeastern U.S. ports such as Philadelphia and Boston in the late eighteenth century. But the first trans-Pacific immigrants from China almost certainly came to San Francisco just before the fabled Gold Rush of 1849. By 1860 there were more than 30,000 Chinese in the United States, almost all of them in California. Who were these Asian argonauts, and what drew them 7,000 miles from home?

THE SOJOURNER PATTERN

The second question is easier to answer than the first. The Chinese, along with hundreds of thousands of others, were drawn to California by gold and the economic boom that its discovery set off. Between 1850 and 1860, California's population more than quadrupled to nearly 400,000. Almost all of the Chinese were from one small part of South China, Guangdong, and more than 90 percent of them were adult males. Most of them probably intended to come to the "Gold Mountain"—as the Chinese characters for California can be translated—work for a time, and then return home "rich," which meant, by Chinese standards, with a few hundred dollars. This has caused some scholars to label Chinese as "sojourners" and thus not immigrants, and to proceed to blame many of the troubles the Chinese encountered in America on their refusal to assimilate. This "blaming the victim" for discrimination is an old and ongoing device used by groups in power to excuse their own behavior. The question must be asked: How different were the Chinese from other immigrants to this country?

A recent student of immigration, Thomas Archdeacon, has made it very clear that Chinese sojourners had their counterparts in other ethnic groups.

> The Chinese thought of themselves as sojourners who would return with honor after spending their working years in America. Among members of many European groups . . . the hope became to earn enough money in a brief period to secure the family's farmstead, to provide dowries for female relatives, or to reestablish themselves solidly in the mother country. For these people, migration to the United States became an extension of the international seasonal migrations that were becoming common in Europe.[1]

Archdeacon also shows that many ethnic groups had very heavy male migration (Scandinavians, 61.3 percent; Italians, 74.5 percent; Greeks, 87.8 percent) and a high rate of return migration (Scandinavians, 15.4 percent; Italians, 45.6 percent; Greeks, 53.7 percent).

Thus the sojourner pattern was common to many immigrant groups, European as well as Asian. What made the Chinese experience in America unique were three other factors: (1) their race, (2) the region to which they came, and (3) the fact that in 1882 they became the first group of voluntary immigrants ever to be shut out by the American government. Their continued immigration to America, despite undisguised and brutal discrimination, reflects the often wretched conditions under which they lived at home. China, a once great and powerful empire, was by the mid-nineteenth century in a long period of decline.

THE CHINESE DIASPORA

South China, the home of almost all of the Chinese immigrants to America, had a long tradition of both political rebellion and emigration. South China was the springboard from which most of the worldwide diffusion of Chinese—what can be called the *Chinese diaspora*—began and continued. It was also the main contact point for British, Americans, and other Westerners and the region of their first concessions. Places such as Hong Kong and Macao became ports through which not only foreign goods like opium came in, but also from which Chinese people embarked for new worlds.

The labor migration of Asians outside of Asia—what the British scholar Hugh Tinker has called "a new system of slavery"—began a little earlier in the nineteenth century with the bringing of indentured workers from India to work the sugar fields of Mauritius. The indentured Indians, used largely in the British Empire, were soon followed by Chinese who were taken to places like Cuba and Peru under abominable conditions in what came to be known as the "coolie trade." Later in the nineteenth century and on into the twentieth, Japanese, Filipinos, Koreans, Southeast Asians, and even a few thousand Indonesians were brought under semifree conditions of indenture to labor in the plantation and extractive economies of the Indian Ocean, East and Southern Africa, the Pacific, and the Caribbean.[2] While some of these Asian workers entered willingly into their contracts or indentures, others were kidnapped or "shanghaied," a word that came into the English language in 1871. Still others were tricked into going where they did not want to go. One American consular report from the mid-nineteenth century speaks of Chinese being lured onto ships that took them to work in the deadly guano fields of Peru's Pacific islands or the sugar plantations of Cuba; the Chinese believed that they were being taken to the gold fields of California or Australia. As we shall see, most of the early Asian immigrants to Hawaii, both Chinese and Japanese, were brought in as indentured laborers. Some immigrants to the United States proper, immigrants from both Europe and Asia, came as contract laborers, but such contracts, after the abolition of slavery, were all but impossible to enforce.

The coolie trade did not come to America. Tens of thousands of Chinese, and later other Asians, were too willing to come to the United States to make their "fortunes" for coercion to be necessary. Most of them went into debt to come here. In the 1850s, for example, Chinese in Hong Kong who wanted to come to America could borrow the equivalent of $70—$50 for passage and $20 for expenses—if they would obligate themselves to repay $200. This "credit ticket system" continued for almost a century; its persistence is the best evidence that the Chinese were free immigrants and that most borrowers paid back their loans.[3]

ANTI-CHINESE SENTIMENT

In the first two decades of Chinese immigration—the census of 1870 found some 60,000 Chinese, with almost 50,000 in California—Chinese worked at gold mining, in agriculture, at various urban occupations, and, most spectacularly, as the builders of the western leg of the first transcontinental railroad. After an initial welcome, the Chinese soon became the targets of both legal and extralegal harassment and, beyond that, of sometimes murderous violence. The California Foreign Miners Tax, originally directed at Hispanics, soon had Chinese miners as its chief target. In San Francisco, which became the metropolis of Chinese America, a variety of municipal ordinances put special taxes on their livelihood, fined them for living in overcrowded tenements, and even required arrested Chinese to have their heads shaved.

That most of these regulations, as well as many anti-Chinese statutes passed by the state legislature, were eventually declared unconstitutional by various courts is beside the point. The fact of the matter was, as an early California historian noted, that "the legislation on Oriental labor sprang from the people." The new California constitution, adopted by a popularly elected convention in 1879, was loaded with specifically anti-Chinese provisions, which sought, among other things, to bar the Chinese from employment and ownership of land. As one delegate noted, some sections of this document amounted to "starvation by constitutional provision."[4]

Even worse was the fact that Chinese were often defenseless targets for all kinds of violence, ranging from casual abuse on city streets to mass murder. Until well after the Civil War, California courts refused to accept the testimony of blacks, American Indians, or Chinese; even when Chinese testimony was admitted, testimony against whites was almost always ignored by juries. From Los Angeles to Seattle and as far east as Denver and Rock Springs, Wyoming, Chinese were run out of town or beaten and killed by mobs whose members were almost never brought to justice. The worst atrocities were in Los Angeles in 1871, where between eighteen and twenty-one Chinese were hanged or burned to death; in Rock Springs in 1885, where at least twenty-eight Chinese coal miners were shot to death; and in desolate Hell's Canyon, on the Idaho–Oregon border, in 1887, where thirty-one Chinese gold miners were robbed and murdered. Some of the killers were caught but none was convicted. As a contemporary white rancher noted, "I guess if they had killed thirty-one white men something would have been done about it, but none of the jury knew the Chinamen or cared much about it, so they turned the men loose."[5]

During the 1870s the Chinese population in America increased by about two-thirds, to just over 100,000, with more than 95 percent in the far western states. This decade witnessed the development of the anti-Chinese political movement in California and throughout the West, sparked by working-class agitation led by a recent Irish immigrant, Denis Kearney. The 1870s were a time of economic hardship in the Far West, and the Chinese made convenient scapegoats. Kearney's Workingman's Party demanded a whole range of economic and social reforms, but the one demand that dominated the movement was that "The Chinese Must GO!" As an 1877 party manifesto put it:

> Before the world we declare that the Chinaman must leave our shores. We declare that white men, and women, and boys, and girls, cannot live as the people of the great republic should live and compete with the single Chinese coolie in the labor market. We declare that we cannot hope to drive the Chinaman away by working cheaper than he does. None but an enemy would expect it of us; none but an idiot could hope for success; none but a degraded coward and slave would make the effort. To an American, death is preferable to life on a par with the Chinamen.[6]

The economic radicalism of the Kearneyites never prevailed, although its anti-Chinese sentiments were shared by the overwhelming majority of the population. Some employers of labor insisted that the Chinese presence was necessary for economic growth, and a few Christian missionaries pointed out that their soul-saving endeavors in Asia would be hampered if Chinese here were ill-treated. In addition, the recently negotiated Burlingame Treaty with China (1868), which gave great advantages to American merchants and shippers hungry for the China market, had guaranteed Chinese the right of immigration.

CHINESE EXCLUSION

These obstacles were soon surmounted. In 1875 Congress passed the first piece of national legislation aimed specifically at Asian immigrants. It sought, first of all, to bar contract labor from "China, Japan, or any Oriental country," and secondly, to bar prostitutes. As George Anthony Peffer has shown, this Page Law, although largely ineffective, was aimed chiefly at Chinese women.[7]

In 1880 a new treaty was negotiated with China, giving the United States the right to "regulate, limit, or suspend" Chinese immigration, but not to prohibit it absolutely. After some political maneuvering, including a presidential veto, the Chinese Exclusion Act of 1882 was adopted, which barred the immigration of Chinese laborers for ten years. (The act was renewed in 1892 for another ten-year term and reenacted, without temporal limits, in 1902.)[8]

THE STRUCTURE OF CHINESE AMERICAN SOCIETY

When the Chinese Exclusion Act was passed in 1882, there were perhaps 125,000 Chinese in the United States. From that time until sometime in the 1920s, Chinese population in the United States steadily declined (see Table 3.1).

A major reason for this decline was the heavily imbalanced sex ratio in the Chinese American community. In 1890, for example, only 3,868 Chinese females were recorded by the census; there were 26.8 males for every female. This ratio went down steadily, and by 1940 there were 2.9 Chinese American males to every female. In 1940 citizen Chinese for the first time outnumbered alien Chinese, 40,262 to 37,242. But it is necessary to look more closely at the demographic data to get a true picture of the Chinese American community in the years before World War II. Let us take 1920 for our example (see Table 3.2). It is necessary to examine the age structure of the sexes to complete our picture. Chinese males had a median age of 42 years; the largely citizen females, a median age of just 19 years. The largest

Table 3.1   Chinese in the United States, 1890–1940

Year	Population
1890	107,620
1900	89,863
1910	71,531
1920	61,639
1930	74,954
1940	77,504

Source: U.S. Census data.

single five-year cohort of Chinese males, 5,850, were 50–54 years of age; the largest single five-year cohort of females, 1,418, were under 5 years of age. If we subtract all Chinese, male and female, under 10 years of age in 1920, we find that there were almost ten males to every female—9.84 to be precise.

If one were trying to create a population model that would be likely to resist acculturation, one could do a lot worse than to use the reality of Chinese America. Add to that a heavily male-dominated culture, a history of brutal discrimination, extreme residential segregation, and a high degree of cultural differentiation between Chinese and most other Americans, and one can begin to understand why acculturation took relatively long for Chinese Americans as a community. Individual Chinese, of course, successfully acculturated almost from the beginning of Chinese American history. Perhaps the earliest example was Yung Wing (1828–1912), who was born in southeast China, near Macao. He attended a missionary school in Hong Kong and came to America in 1847. Three years later he entered Yale College and in 1854 became its first Chinese graduate. In the meantime he had become a Christian and, in spite of the law, a naturalized citizen of the United States. He married an American woman and had a long and distinguished career in both China and America.[9]

Table 3.2   Chinese American Population, 1920

Group	Male	Female	Total	Males:Females
All Chinese	53,891	7,748	61,639	7.0:1
Alien	40,573	2,534	43,107	16.0:1
Citizen	13,318	5,214	18,532	2.6:1

Source: U.S. Census data.

CHINESE-AMERICAN INSTITUTIONS

As the small but growing native-born segment of the population evolved, it began to form its own American-oriented organizations. The most notable of these was the Native Sons of the Golden State, an organization that was founded in San Francisco in 1895 and evolved into the Chinese American Citizens Alliance in 1915. The Americanizing thrust of this organization can be seen by the following clause from its first constitution: "It is imperative that no member shall have sectional, clannish, Tong or party prejudices against each other or to use such influence to oppress fellow members. Whoever violates this provision shall be expelled. . . ."[10]

Most Chinese Americans, however, were part of the largely unacculturated "bachelor society" that dominated the Chinatowns of America until World War II. The major institutions of that society were oriented towards China rather than America. Most, if not all, American ethnic groups have had some kind of organizational focus. For many European immigrant groups, much of the focus was provided by ethnic or ethnically oriented churches. Since traditional Chinese religions tended to be familial rather than societal, religion was not a unifying communitywide force, except for the minority who were or became Christians. For most immigrant Chinese, the family association, or clan (that is all those who had a common last name and thus a putative common ancestor), was the primary associational focus. Originally village-oriented and representing real blood relationships, the clan system was adapted by overseas Chinese to fit conditions wherever Chinese settled. Outside of San Francisco, or *dai fou* (big city) as the Chinese called it, one clan tended to dominate the smaller Chinatowns. Thus in Pittsburgh, Yees predominated; in Chicago, Moys; and in Denver, Chins. A Moy in Pittsburgh, for example, whose mother or wife had been a Yee, could affiliate himself with and expect support from the powerful Yee clan there.

An even more complex arrangement, called the *four-clan association,* also arose. Rose Hum Lee has described such a situation in Butte, Montana, whose 710 Chinese residents were in 1880 more than a fifth of the population. There two four-clan associations arose, and almost all Chinese residents were considered members of one group or the other. The associations were used to settle disputes between individuals and functioned as a kind of court; a loser in a local dispute could always make an appeal back to headquarters in San Francisco. The functions of the family associations were similar to those of the benevolent and protective societies of other ethnocultural groups, sometimes called generically *landsmanschaften.* They tendered protection and mutual aid to members. The family associations, however, went far beyond most other such societies, as they were considered extended family groups. Chinese Americans, many of whom had no blood relatives in this country, would speak of all other members of their association as "clan cousins." A wife was considered a member of her husband's clan. If, however, he predeceased her, often she would be financially assisted by her own clan, as her husband's clan might regard her and her children as not being entitled to the clan's scarce resources. Although they were not "incest groups," marriages within clans and clan associations were discouraged. Thus in Butte, according to Lee, where there were special tensions between the two four-clan associations, not one of the ninety-nine members of the Chinese American community born in Butte had married a fellow resident of Butte as late as the mid-1940s![11]

In addition to being a member of a clan, each Chinese, at least in theory, belonged to a district association. Originally based on regional districts of Guangdong Province, the ancestral home of most Chinese immigrants, the associations were eventually governed by an umbrella group, the Chinese Consolidated Benevolent Association, popularly known as the Six Chinese Companies. The Six Companies also resembled *landsmanschaften*, having benevolent and protective functions. They also acted as agents of social control and served as the community's voice to white America. That later capacity was exercised as early as 1853, when Company heads (there were then only four) appeared before a committee of the California legislature. The Companies often hired white lawyers to serve as their spokesmen before national, state, and local governing bodies and courts, and, especially, before the administrative authorities who governed immigration.

In addition, their agents met incoming ships, arranged for the initial housing and employment of migrants, organized medical treatment for the sick, and performed other welfare functions. They also helped to arrange for the shipment of the bones of the dead for burial in China and arbitrated disputes between individual members. In an age when government assumed none of the responsibilities of what is now called the welfare state, ethnic organizations all over the United States performed similar functions.

The Six Companies also came to exert a very high degree of social control over the lives of American Chinese and, in this, were quite unlike most other immigrant community organizations. The association's chief beneficiaries were the merchants who came to dominate it. In China merchants had little prestige and authority; China was governed by a gentry-dominated scholar officialdom whose ideology placed the merchant at the bottom of the social scale. But gentry did not emigrate—the merchants did and quickly turned their economic power into social and political power within the Chinese American community. In addition to trade, merchants derived some of their income from the credit ticket system and from services performed as labor contractors. As the leading lights of the district associations, the merchants used the associations as a mechanism to make sure that individuals not only settled their debts but also paid their share of the Chinese American welfare system. Every Chinese who returned to China was supposed to be checked at the dock to make sure that his debts had been paid. In addition, each returnee was assessed a "tax" to support the welfare functions of the district associations. While, of course, the system was far from 100 percent effective, the fact that it continued to function for decades suggests that it was more than marginally so. Since most Chinese in America thought of themselves as sojourners who would return to China, any system that affected that return was an ideal mechanism for social control.

But parallel to these "establishment" organizations, an "antiestablishment" form of social organization developed, centered around the *tongs,* or secret societies. Tongs had flourished as illegal opposition to the establishment in China since at least the fourteenth century and, as happens in nations where political opposition is illegal, often operated in that gray area between political opposition and crime. The Chinese American tongs were patterned on, and probably had some direct relation with, the Triad Society, and anti-Manchu, antiforeign society based in Guangdong. Unlike the family and district associations, which were universal (all Chinese in America theoretically belonged), the tongs were particularistic. No one knows how many Chinese Americans belonged to tongs. As Chinese were debarred from American political life, the criminal aspect of the tongs predominated here, although it is clear that the tongs played an antiestablishment role within Chinese American society. Eventually, some merchants managed to gain membership and influence in some tongs, and some tong leaders gained respectability among the establishment. After 1900, Dr. Sun Yat-sen's revolutionary movement (which became the Guomindang) found its chief support among American Chinese in the antiestablishment tongs: It was clearly more expedient to support a revolutionary movement through a secret organization. After the Guomindang became the government of China, of course, the Chinese American establishment embraced it publicly.

The tongs were also involved in criminal activities that preyed on, rather than protected, the immigrant community. As Daniel Bell has noted, speaking only of European ethnic groups here, crime has been an "American way of life" for many immigrants and second-generation ethnics. For Chinese criminals, the nature of their crime was dictated largely by the nature of their community. The immigrant working men and petty entrepreneurs wanted recreation that could only be provided within the immigrant community. The most popular entertainment seems to have been gambling, chiefly fan-tan, faro, and lottery; as a testimony to Americanization, poker had become popular by 1900. Opium rather than alcohol seems to have been the favored narcotic, although there is no way of determining what percentage of Chinese used the drug. In addition, Chinese brothels and, to a lesser degree, opium-smoking establishments were frequented by whites. Such establishments were quite numerous in Chinese American communities of any size. Since these activities were illegal, lucrative, and semipublic, it is clear that police and politicians in the white community were involved in sanctioning and profiting from them. Competition for scarce commodities—narcotics and Chinese women—often sparked murderous "tong wars," in which all or almost all of the casualties were Chinese. One such war, between the Hip Sings and the Bing Kungs, began with four assassinations in Butte, Montana, in 1922, and quickly spread to every Chinatown in North America and entailed dozens of killings.[12]

In 1921, as Loren Chan has told us, a tong quarrel that started in San Francisco spread throughout northern California and even to Nevada. On the night of August 27, 1921, a 74-year-old laundry proprietor and nominal member of the Bing Kung tong answered a knock at his door in tiny Mina, Nevada. He was shot to death with a Colt .38 by a 29-year-old Canton-born hit man from San Francisco named Gee Jon, who had come to the United States in either 1907 or 1908. The finger man was Hughie Sing, 19 years old and perhaps U.S. born. Sing had been educated in the Nevada public schools and knew the victim well, having been apprenticed to him for two years. Because the perpetrators were arrested and convicted and because they talked—none of which usually happened in tong killings—we know some of the details.[13]

URBAN CHINESE AMERICA

But most Chinese were not hit men—or "hatchet men" as the sensation-seeking white media liked to call them—and their only connection with tongs was as customers of their illegal establishments. Although agriculture, mining, and railroad building were the chief occupations of Chinese Americans until about the 1880s, after that time urban service occupations—laundries, restaurants, grocery stores—became the pursuits of the majority. Unlike most modern immigrant groups, Chinese were initially found largely in rural and small-town America. In 1880, for example, only about a fifth of all Chinese Americans lived in cities with populations over 100,000. This percentage increased with every census, with close to half of Chinese Americans living in such cities by 1910 and more than seven out of ten by 1940. At first almost all large-city Chinese lived in San Francisco, but by 1940 fewer than one in three did. According to the 1940 census, San Francisco had a Chinese American population of 17,782, with another 3,000 living across the bay in Oakland. There were more than 12,000 Chinese Americans in New York, nearly 5,000 in Los Angeles, and just over 2,000 in Chicago; Seattle, Portland, Sacramento, and Boston each had between 1,000 and 2,000 Chinese.

While it is customary today to write off such ethnic enclaves as ghettos—and the Chinatowns of America certainly had many of the worst characteristics of ghettos—there was, for many of the Chinese immigrants and Chinese Americans of later generations, a positive aspect of these urban neighborhoods. One Chinatown resident remarked in the 1920s:

Most of us can live a warmer, freer and a more human life among our relatives and friends than among strangers. . . . Chinese relations with the population outside Chinatown are likely to be cold, formal, and commercial. It is only in Chinatown that a Chinese immigrant has society, friends and relatives who share his dreams and hopes, his hardships, and adventures. Here he can tell a joke and make everybody laugh with him; here he may hear folktales told which create the illusion that Chinatown is really China.[14]

The shift to larger cities, coupled with a shrinking total population, meant not only disappearance or near disappearance of many smaller Chinatowns (Butte's shrank from 710 in 1880 to 88 in 1940) but also a sharp reduction of the percentage of Chinese found in California and the West in general. Although the Golden State contained an absolute majority of Chinese Americans in every census of the period, save that of 1920, within California the incidence of Chinese in the population contracted drastically. In 1860, Chinese had made up 9.2 percent of California's population; in 1940 they represented about 0.6 percent. In some other western states, particularly Idaho, Montana, and Nevada, Chinese population was once quite high. The Idaho Territorial Census of 1870 reported them as 28.5 percent of the population; in that year they were 9.5 percent of the population of neighboring Montana. A decade later Chinese made up 8.7 percent of the population of Nevada. Each of those figures declined rapidly as Chinese were eliminated from the mining industry and the mining industry itself declined. These Chinese pioneers have largely been written out of the histories of the western states. When Chinese do appear in them it is as exotic curiosities or as victims. Their pioneering role as developers of the economy of the West has simply been ignored.

The heart of Chinese America was San Francisco, whose Chinatown contained between an eighth and a fifth of all Chinese Americans during the years under discussion. But the city was much more important to the Chinese than mere numbers indicated. As one Chinese American recalled about his father's experience early in the twentieth century, San Francisco was always his home base, the "safest place," although his work took him up and down California's valleys and as far away as Alaska, where he packed salmon.[15]

San Francisco was the cultural, economic, and administrative hub of Chinese America, the entrepôt through which Chinese goods and services were distributed, the communications center through which information and people passed back and forth between the old world and the new. And, despite Chinese exclusion, large numbers of persons did continue to go back and forth across the Pacific, legally, illegally, and extralegally. Until 1924, American law did not exclude Chinese per se but rather "Chinese laborers." In addition to diplomats and students, who were not technically immigrants (but many of them did stay here), Chinese merchants, or "treaty merchants" as they are sometimes called, and members of their families were admissible. An 1893 law specifically and insultingly defined a merchant and required that the status of any Chinese merchant had to be sworn to "by the testimony of two credible witnesses other than Chinese." Chinese were held up until 1910 in a grim facility on the San Francisco waterfront called the Shed; after that they were kept in the special detention facility in the bay on Angel Island. A missionary described the Shed around 1900 as a place where

> merchants, laborers are all alike penned up, like a flock of sheep . . . often weeks at their own expense . . . while the investigation of their cases moves its slow length along. . . . A man is imprisoned as a criminal who has committed no crime, but has merely failed to find a white man to prove his right to be here.[16]

Even bona fide upper-class students were often detained. One of the famous Soong sisters, Ailing, was held for more than two weeks when she arrived to attend college even though she was traveling with two white American missionaries and had influential persons intercede for her. As an articulate Chinese diplomat, Wu Ting-fang, put it to New York reporters in 1901: "Why can't you be fair? Would you talk like that if mine was not a weak nation? Would you say it if the Chinese had votes?"[17]

OUTWITTING THE IMMIGRATION LAWS

In addition to the hundreds who came in legally, if with difficulty, there were uncounted others who jumped ship or sneaked across the border; the Puget Sound region, the Mexican border, and Florida seem to have been the most favored places. But perhaps most numerically important of all were the thousands who came in extralegally, that is, by successfully claiming a status they were not entitled to. A combination of circumstances, including incompetent and venal federal employees and the 1906 San Francisco earthquake and fire that destroyed many birth and other records, made it possible for many Chinese men to obtain documents falsely indicating that they were native-born American citizens. If such persons traveled to China and fathered children there, the children were eligible to enter the United States. Those who came in falsely were known in the community as "paper sons." Years later, after a federal amnesty program, begun in the 1950s, was in place, some paper sons were willing to talk. One of them described the process:

> In the beginning my father came in as a laborer. But the 1906 earthquake came along and destroyed all those immigration things. So that was a big chance for a lot of Chinese. They forged themselves certificates saying that they were born in this country, and when the time came they could go back to China and

bring back four or five sons just like that! They might make a little money off it, but the main thing was to bring a son or nephew or a cousin in. Now my father thought he was even smarter than that. When he came the second time he didn't use that native-born certificate he had. He got a certificate saying he was a student. But that didn't make sense at all. He thought he was smart being a student, but then, if you came in as a student, how could you bring a son into this country? If he had used his birth certificate, I could have come in as a native son. Instead we had to go back to the same old thing, "paper son." They had to send me over not as my own father's son, but as the son of another cousin from our village.[18]

Another paper son, Jim Quock, told interviewers in 1979 that:

I came to America because my grandfather was here during the Gold Rush times, the 1860s. Somebody robbed him and he got killed and they never found the body or anything. My grandmother told us that grandpa had a lot of gold, made quite a bit of money, you know. So that's what got in my mind, "Oh, this is a fortune. I'm going over to America to make money." Only fifteen at the time. So the only way I could come is to buy a paper, buy a citizen paper. I paid quite a bit of money, too. I paid $102 gold! That's quite a bit of money at that time in China.[19]

Immigration officials quickly caught on to the paper son and other gambits and subjected Chinese applicants for admission to detailed and quite prolonged interrogations. Ironically, some of the first Chinese to get federal jobs were employed to help discover illegal immigrants. The immigrants, of course, developed elaborate countermeasures. As Jim Quock told it:

They give you a book of about 200 pages to study—all your life, your family, your brother's name, the whole village, almost. They ask you all kinds of questions when you get to the United States, the immigration [station] at Angel Island. . . . I was there for three weeks. They ask you how many steps in your house? Your house had a clock? Questions like that. You got to remember all this. They asked me, "Where do you sleep at your house?" I said, "I sleep with my grandmother and my brother." They say, "Okay which position do you sleep?" All kinds of questions, you got to think. But, I'm pretty smart. I said, "Tonight I sleep over here, tomorrow I sleep over there, it doesn't matter."[20]

Archivists have discovered "crib sheets," obviously written for paper sons, that describe in detail some Chinese village. It is clear that most of the thousands of successful paper sons were intelligent, alert, and more than marginally literate.

U.S. immigration records show almost 95,000 individual entries of Chinese "immigrants" between 1883 and the end of Chinese exclusion in 1943, an average of about 1,500 a year. Many of these were former residents returning, and many individuals came several times. Until 1924, when the immigration law made it impossible, perhaps 150 Chinese women per year were admitted as wives of either citizens or treaty merchants. A 1930 act relaxed this ban, as long as the marriage had taken place before the 1924 law went into effect, and allowed an average of sixty women a year until the Japanese attack on Pearl Harbor. Thus the sexual imbalance of Chinese immigration was reinforced by Chinese custom and American law.

Obviously, large numbers of the "bachelor" immigrants to the United States had wives in China. The 1930 census, for example, showed four times as many married Chinese men here as married Chinese women. These separated families, called "mutilated families" by the sociologist Charles Frederick Marsden, far outnumbered "normal," united families in the Chinese American community until well after the end of World War II. A similar condition prevailed for the same basic reasons in Canada. Peter S. Li's study of the pattern of Chinese marriage in Canada is more thorough than any study done for the United States. Of 22,777 Chinese Canadian families in 1941, Li found only 1,177 "intact conjugal families" (5.2 percent); 1,459 "broken families" (6.4 percent), in which one or both partners were widowed or divorced; and 20,141 "mutilated families" (88.4 percent), with the wife outside of Canada.[21]

The data for the United States are surely similar. Because of this pattern of family life, the acculturation of many Chinese Americans, including many putative native-born citizens, was retarded. Many immigrant "bachelors" of several generations could spend most of a lifetime in American Chinatowns without learning more than a handful of English phrases. Conversely, of course, there were many thousands of second-generation Chinese Americans who broke through at least some of the ethnic barriers and achieved real acculturation.

The contrast is well-illustrated in one of the most annoying Chinese American cultural stereotypes, the Charlie Chan movies, rightly resented by most Chinese Americans today. Yet even stereotypes have their value, and the contrast between the wise, inscrutable Chinese American detective—always played by Caucasian actors—and his wisecracking, shallow number one and number two sons—played by skilled Chinese American actors such as Keye Luke and Victor Sen Yung—is not unrelated to the reality of generational conflict in the Chinese American community in the pre–World War II years. A more sophisticated treatment of the generation gap may be found in the autobiographies of Jade Snow Wong, *Fifth Chinese Daughter* (1950) and *No Chinese Stranger* (1975), and of Pardee Lowe, *Father and Glorious Descendant* (1943).[22]

The Chinese American community was clearly undergoing great change in the years just before the Japanese attack on Pearl Harbor. The rise of the native-born community, although overstated by the enumeration of paper sons, and the dying off of the older generation were pushing the community, as a whole, toward greater acculturation. But World War II, which changed the lives of most Americans, accelerated change within the Chinese and other Asian American communities even more rapidly than for most of the rest of the nation.[23]

SUMMARY

There is no question that the Chinese talked, dressed, and acted differently from the "preferred" norms of the "Anglo" society, but so did members of almost every other immigrant group. More critical was that the Chinese "looked different," which ran into the rampant racism that was a part of the United States at the end of the nineteenth and the beginning of the twentieth century. It is from this background that the adaptation of the Chinese becomes understandable.

Acculturation works most readily for the young, for those who have an opportunity to go through the American school system and for those who expect to participate in the mainstream. It does not work as well for those who are isolated and denied access, who are segregated, who are older, or who expect to return to the home country. A pluralistic adaptation, it is hoped, of some degree of equality seems more appropriate.

Acculturation, integration, and participation in the mainstream are also appropriate for those who come in families. Thus, although parents may never become full participants, it is their expectation that their children will. Being American is also for those who can become citizens and for whom citizenship means access to economic, political, and social opportunities. It means justice and equality; it means a full identity. It does not mean second-class citizenship.

As we have seen, most of the early Chinese did not easily acculturate, integrate, or participate in the American society. The majority were single males. If married, their families were left behind in China. They could not become citizens; prejudice, discrimination, and segregation kept them apart from the mainstream. Jobs were largely limited to the lower part of a dual labor market; social and political opportunities were limited to their own communities. They were "outsiders"; what wealth and leadership qualities they had could only be used from the "outside looking in." They were hemmed in by their own needs and the walls erected by the dominant community. They were identified as Chinese and foreigners; they were not viewed as Americans. It was a pluralistic adaptation, less than equal and primarily involuntary. It was only with changes in their demographic structure and changes in the American society that we begin to see a break away from a segregated existence.

NOTES

1. Thomas Archdeacon, *Becoming American: An Ethnic History* (New York: Free Press, 1983), pp. 138–139. Table V-4, on p. 139, which treats twenty-five groups, shows a high Pearson product-moment correlation of .689.

2. Hugh Tinker, *A New System of Slavery: The Export of Indian Labour Overseas, 1820–1920* (London: Oxford University Press, 1974). For a worldwide survey of indentured labor, see W. Klosterboer, *Involuntary Labour since the Abolition of Slavery: A Survey of Compulsory Labour throughout the World* (The Hague: Mouton, 1960).

3. The best brief description is in Kil Young Zo, "Credit Ticket System for the Chinese Emigration into the United States," *Journal of Nanyang University* 8/9 (1974–1975): 129–138.

4. Elmer C. Sandmeyer, *The Anti-Chinese Movement in California* (Berkeley: University of California Press, 1939); Lucille Eaves, *A History of California Labor Legislation* (Berkeley: University of California Press, 1910), p. 115; *Debates and Proceedings of the Constitutional Convention of the State of California,* vol. 1 (Sacramento, 1881), p. 630.

5. Roger Daniels, ed., *Anti-Chinese Violence in America* (New York: Arno Press, 1978); David H. Stratton, "The Snake River Massacre of Chinese Coal Miners, 1887," in Duane A. Smith, ed., *A Taste of the West* (Boulder: Pruett, 1981), p. 125.

6. Sandmeyer, *Anti-Chinese Movement*, p. 65.

7. George Antony Peffer, *If They Don't Bring Their Women Here: Chinese Female Immigration Before Exclusion* (Urbana: University of Illinois Press, 1999).

8. Charles J. McClain, Jr., *In Search of Equality: The Chinese Struggle against Discrimination in Nineteenth-Century America.* (Berkeley: University of California Press, 1994) and Lucy Salyer, *Laws Harsh as Tigers: Chinese Immigrants and the Shaping of Modern Immigration Law* (Chapel Hill: University of North Carolina Press, 1995) analyze the legal history.

9. Yung Wing, *My Life in China and America* (New York: Holt, 1909); Edmund H. Worthy, Jr., "Yung Wing in America," *Pacific Historical Review* 39 (1965): 265–287.

10. Sue Fawn Chung, "Fighting for Their American Rights: A History of the Chinese American Citizens Alliance," pp. 95–129 in K. Scott Wong & Sucheng Chan, eds., *Claiming America: Constructing Chinese American Identities during the Exclusion Era* (Philadelphia: Temple University Press, 1998).

11. Rose Hum Lee, *The Growth and Decline of Chinese Communities in the Rocky Mountain Region* (New York: Arno Press, 1978).

12. Daniel Bell, *The End of Ideology* (Glencoe, IL: Free Press, 1960); Ching-Chao Wu, "Chinatowns: A Study in Symbiosis and Assimilation" (Ph.D. dissertation, University of Chicago, 1928), pp. 213–214, 232.

13. Loren Chan, "Example for the Nation: Nevada's Execution of Gee Jon," *Nevada Historical Society Quarterly* 18 (1975): 90–106.

14. Wu, "Chinatowns," p. 158. Judy Yung, *Unbound Feet: A Social History of Chinese Women in San Francisco* (Berkeley: University of California Press, 1995) is the best single book on the San Francisco Chinese.

15. Victor G. Nee and Brett de Bary Nee, *Longtime Californ'* (New York: Pantheon, 1973), p. 22.

16. Ira M. Condit, *The Chinaman As We See Him* (Chicago: Revell, 1900), pp. 86–87. For Angel Island, see Roger Daniels, "No Lamps Were Lit for Them: Angel Island and the Historiography of Asian American Immigration," *Journal of American Ethnic History* 17 (Fall 1997): 4–18.

17. As cited by Delber L. McKee, *Chinese Exclusion Versus the Open Door Policy, 1900–1906* (Detroit: Wayne State University Press, 1977), p. 51.

18. Sucheng Chan, ed., *Entry Denied: Exclusion and the Chinese Community in America, 1882–1943* (Philadelphia: Temple University Press, 1991) analyzes the effects of exclusion. Quotation from Nee & Nee, *Longtime Californ'*, p. 63.

19. Diane Mei Lin Mark and Ginger Chih, *A Place Called Chinese America* (Dubuque, IA: Kendall/Hunt, 1982), p. 47.

20. Ibid., p. 48.

21. Peter S. Li, "Immigration Laws and Family Patterns: Some Demographic Changes Among Chinese Families in Canada, 1885–1971," *Canadian Ethnic Studies* 12, no. 1 (1980): 58–73.

22. Jade Snow Wong, *Fifth Chinese Daughter* (New York: Harper & Row, 1950); Idem., *No Chinese Stranger* (New York: Harper & Row, 1975); Pardee Lowe, *Father and Glorious Descendant* (Boston: Little, Brown & Co., 1943).

23. For a detailed look at one aspect of that change, see Renqiu Yu, *To Save China, to Save Ourselves: The Chinese Hand Laundry Alliance of New York* (Philadelphia: Temple University Press, 1992).

Chapter 4

THE CHINESE

After 1943

Although it is quite clear that World War II marked a crucial turning point in the lives of Chinese Americans, it is also clear that significant changes were occurring even before the war began to dominate the thoughts and actions of most Americans at the end of the 1930s. First of all, as we have seen, significant demographic changes had begun in the peaceful 1920s and 1930s. The long population decline that was triggered by the passage of the Chinese Exclusion Act had ended, and a small upturn due to natural increase and ingenuity in evading immigration regulations had set in. Between 1920 and 1940 the census recorded an increase of 25 percent, from 61,000 to 77,000, in the Chinese American population. (This does not take into account the 28,000 Chinese who lived in Hawaii in 1940; residents of Hawaii were counted in national population figures only after statehood in 1959.) Even more significant than the turnaround in sheer numbers was the fact that by 1940 citizen Chinese Americans for the first time outnumbered the alien segment of the community. If we look at the population breakdown for 1940 in Table 4.1, we will see the effect of the paper sons phenomenon.

The fact that there were 75 percent more citizen and presumably native-born Chinese American males than females is probably the best possible numerical index to the number of paper sons in the population, although not all of the difference can be so explained.

Table 4.1 Chinese American Population, 1940

Group	Male	Female	Total	Males:Females
All Chinese	57,389	20,115	77,504	2.9:1
Alien	31,687	5,555	37,242	5.7:1
Citizen	25,702	14,560	40,262	1.8:1

Source: U.S. Census data.

CHANGES IN IMAGE

By the time citizens outnumbered aliens—and we must remember that many of the citizens were small children, meaning that among adults aliens continued to predominate—the image of the Chinese was beginning to change, however slowly. Even before Americans began to see the Chinese people as heroic resisters and victims of Japanese aggression, the picture most Americans had of China and her people was being altered by the daughter of a missionary, Pearl S. Buck (1892–1973). In a whole series of immensely successful novels, beginning with the Pulitzer Prize–winning *The Good Earth* (1931), Buck dealt with all levels of Chinese society, but her focus was on "the character of the Chinese peasant . . . hardworking, strong, persevering . . . kind toward children, respectful toward elders, all in all an admirable [and] warmly lovable character."[1] This idealized image, which was even more unreal in the popular movies made from *The Good Earth* and its sequel, *Dragon Seed*, which dealt with peasant resistance and suffering under Japanese attack, was an important element in making the period after 1937 one that the social scientist Harold Isaacs, in his study *Images of Asia*, called an "Age of Admiration." According to Isaacs, Buck "'created' the Chinese" for a whole generation of Americans, "in the same sense that Dickens created . . . the people who lived in the slums of Victorian England."[2] At a lower level of culture, the cartoonist Milton Caniff created *Terry and the Pirates*, a popular adventure comic strip set in war-torn China, in which American heroes helped the Chinese fight the Japanese.

The Japanese attack on Pearl Harbor made the United States and China allies, and to the growing positive stereotype of the noble Chinese peasant was added the grossly distorted favorable picture of a great democratic leader, Generalissimo Chiang Kai-shek and his Christian, American-educated bride, usually referred to as Madame Chiang Kai-shek. In addition to receiving favorable media treatment, the couple was lauded by American political leaders. One public message from President Franklin D. Roosevelt proclaimed that "all the world knows how you have carried on that fight which is the fight of all mankind."

In China, however, the knowledgeable American ambassador wrote a private memorandum, noting realistically that

> it is unfortunate that Chiang and the Chinese have been "built up" in the United States to a point where Americans have been made to believe that China has been "fighting" the Japanese for five years, and that the Generalissimo, a great leader, has been directing the energetic resistance of China to Japan and is a world hero. Looking the cold facts in the face, one could only dismiss this as "rot."[3]

Although in the long run this false image had unfortunate consequences—it helped make it easy for demagogues in the 1950s to convince many Americans that their country had somehow "lost China"—in the short run it was useful to the Chinese American community. But not all of the improvements in the position of Chinese Americans were based on false images. Other important factors included real changes in the nature of the Chinese American community, changes in the attitudes of the larger society, and the real accomplishments of Chinese Americans. In addition, the favorable wartime climate of opinion was manipulated to bring about significant and lasting changes in American immigration and nationality law, modifications that at first affected only Chinese Americans but also, we can now see, marked a crucial turning point in overall American immigration policy.

DEMOGRAPHIC CHANGES

The demographic changes of the 1940s were quite pronounced. Nearly 20,000 Chinese American babies were born during the decade; for the first time in history the most numerous five-year cohort of Chinese Americans was persons under five years of age. Total population jumped some 40,000, aided, as we shall see, by a relaxation in immigration laws. Large numbers of younger American citizen adults—the children born or brought over in the 1910s and 1920s—assisted by the wartime boom that improved the economic circumstances of almost every group in American society, were able to move outside of the ethnic economy. By the end of the decade about 7 percent of all Chinese workers were in professional jobs, although most employed Chinese were in service, managerial, clerical, and sales positions. The educational achievement of Chinese Americans, once well below the norm, was by 1950 at about the level of the general population: Median years completed were 8.4 for males and 10.3 for the younger and more predominantly native-born females.

Within the larger society the war years had the effect of minimizing, but certainly not eliminating, racism as a stated value in American society. As Philip Gleason has written:

> For a whole generation, the question "What does it mean to be an American?" was answered primarily by reference to "the values America stands for": democracy, freedom, equality, respect for individual dignity and so on. Since these values were abstract and universal, American identity could not be linked exclusively with any single ethnic derivation. Persons of any race, color, religion or background could be, or become, Americans.[4]

While Gleason may be overstating somewhat the pervasiveness of cultural pluralism, it was quite pronounced during the war years, especially among the elite movers and shakers of American society. Nothing more clearly indicates this than the successful campaign for the repeal of Chinese exclusion, a campaign mounted, not by members of the Chinese American community, but rather by members of what can be called the white establishment.

The successful campaign was studied at length years ago as a classic example of "pressures on Congress." The key figure was a New York publisher, Richard J. Walsh, who was also the husband of Pearl Buck. Walsh was the major force behind the Citizens Committee to Repeal Chinese Exclusion and Place Immigration on a Quota Basis. The more than 150 names on the committee's letterhead represented a broad group of the American upper class and intellectuals, from Roger Baldwin of the American Civil Liberties Union on the left to Henry Luce of *Time, Life,* and *Fortune* on the right. Assisted by bipartisan allies in Congress—Democrat Emanuel Celler and Republican Clare Boothe Luce led the way—and by a strong message from President Roosevelt, the fifteen separate laws that had effected Chinese exclusion were repealed in December 1943. The new law was a simple one, in three sections. Section one repealed the old acts. Section two gave a quota to "persons of the Chinese race," later set at 105 per year. The quota retained overt racist features: A Chinese born anywhere in the world would be charged to the Chinese quota rather than to the country of birth or nationality. Section three amended the nationality act to make "Chinese persons or persons of Chinese descent" eligible for naturalization on the same terms as other aliens. Two and a half years later, Congress, feeling that the phrase "Chinese person" was inexact, defined it as "any person who is as much as one-half Chinese blood."[5]

President Roosevelt made it clear in statements urging and then celebrating passage that repeal was essentially a foreign policy matter. He told Congress that the legislation was "important in the cause of winning the war and of establishing a secure peace." FDR admitted that "it would give the Chinese a preferred status" vis-à-vis other Asians but argued that "their great contribution to the cause of decency and freedom entitles them" to it. When he signed the bill, he remarked, "An unfortunate barrier between allies has been removed. The war effort in the Far East can now be carried on with greater vigor and a larger understanding of our common purpose."[6]

Nothing more clearly indicates the lack of concern for Chinese Americans, as opposed to China, than the way that Congress and President Roosevelt ignored bills introduced in Congress that would have allowed the alien wives of Chinese American citizens to enter as nonquota immigrants. Family reunification, later to become a prime factor in our immigration legislation, was not considered important in 1943, at least not for Asian American families. Nevertheless, the repeal of Chinese exclusion was important, both because it reversed the trend of American immigration naturalization law as it related to Asians and because within three years bars would be similarly lowered, as we shall see, for Filipinos and "natives of India," and in nine years for all otherwise eligible Asians.

But for tangible, as opposed to symbolic, importance to the Chinese American community, a little-noted act passed in 1946 was actually more immediately significant. It simply made Chinese alien wives of American citizens, native-born or naturalized, admissible on a nonquota basis. This set off a minor boom in the legal migration of Chinese women and is an example of how, once given a quota, a group, no matter how tiny, could under immigration law and without subterfuge greatly exceed that quota. For the eight years from 1945 to 1952, there was a total of 840 Chinese quota spaces; as Table 4.2 shows, that quota was all but meaningless.

This migration of almost 10,000 females in eight years, almost all of them after the 1946 act and almost all of them adults, had tremendous impact on the structure of Chinese American society, which contained, as late as 1950, only 28,000 women fourteen years of age and older. One must remember that the impact of this relatively large number of adults would serve, in the short run at least, to reinforce Chinese as opposed to Chinese American culture.

Other changes during the war included a significant but little-remarked contribution to the war effort. Almost 16,000 Chinese Americans

Table 4.2   Immigration of Chinese by Sex, 1945–1953

Year	Male	Female	Percent Female	Total
1945	45	64	59	109
1946	71	162	69	233
1947	142	986	87	1,128
1948	257	3,317	92	3,574
1949	242	2,248	90	2,490
1950	110	1,179	92	1,289
1951	126	957	89	1,083
1952	118	1,034	90	1,152
Total	1,111	9,947	90	11,058

Source: Immigration and Naturalization Service, *Annual Reports.*

served in the armed forces between 1940 and 1946. Unlike the Japanese, the Chinese were not placed in segregated units. About 1,600 served, including some as officers, in the more restrictive Navy, which took no Japanese Americans at all. William Der Bing, who became the head of protocol and community affairs for NASA in the 1970s, described some of the obstacles he overcame to become a naval aviator in wartime.

> They were reluctant to give me the application forms. I said, "Either I can get them here or I can get them from my Congressman." The minute I mentioned "Congressman," the next thing I know I had a pile of papers. Even in the Navy there were some real good men, but the majority didn't want a "Chinaman" in their outfit. They made every remark possible to harass you.
> Personally, I was told that "No Chinaman will ever fly in my outfit." I was told that by a doctor—a Navy doctor. He gave me a physical. He said, "I want you to know that I would do anything I can to fail you in your physical." I looked at him and said, "If you do, it would be the most dishonest thing that an officer in this United States Navy would ever do to another member of the United States Navy." I put it just this way.[7]

The bittersweet nature of increasing Chinese American success during the war continued in the immediate postwar years, as the following incidents—trivial in themselves—illustrate. They are the kinds of things that could happen only when successful middle-class Chinese began to move out of the Chinatowns. In San Francisco a former Guomindang officer, Sing Sheng, moved into the middle-class San Francisco suburb of Southwood. After some turmoil about his presence, an informal neighborhood referendum found 174 persons voted against his staying, 28 voted for his continuing, and 14 had no opinion. Yet when the story received widespread publicity, Sheng and his family received invitations to move into scores of communities across the nation. Sheng eventually settled peacefully in Sonoma, in northern California. In the Midwest a fraternity at elite Northwestern University revoked the bid it made to Sherman Wu, the son of a former Nationalist officer, because at least seven Caucasian pledges said that they would not join if Wu was accepted. Again publicity brought a counterreaction: Two other fraternities at Northwestern offered to pledge the young Chinese American, who was understandably hesitant. "If they are sincere enough," the *New York Times* reported him as saying, "I may join one. I don't know yet."

THE COLD WAR

But as World War II eased into the Cold War—and in Asia the crucial event was the victory of the communist forces of Mao Zedong in 1949—the American image of China was again transformed. Harold Isaacs's "Age of Admiration" degenerated into first a brief "Age of Disenchantment" (1944–1949), then quickly into an "Age of Hostility."[8] The latter lasted until 1971–1972, when "Ping-Pong diplomacy" and President Richard Nixon's trip to China, spectacularly covered on television, ushered in a new wave of good feeling toward China. Knowing that in the past attitudes toward China had quickly been translated into worse or better treatment for Chinese in America, many in the Chinese community were nervous about their possible fate after 1949. The nervousness increased when China intervened against American troops in Korea in late 1950. Many feared that Chinese Americans would be placed in concentration camps as Japanese Americans had been just eight years previously.

That, happily, did not happen, and the American view of China *and* Chinese became plural. Just as in World War II, United States policy and ideology had carefully differentiated between "good" and "bad" Germans, in the Cold War era distinctions were made between "good" and "bad" Asians as well. There were now, for most Americans, two Chinas: Mao Zedong's communist, pagan, and threatening China and Chiang Kai-shek's capitalist, Christian, and supportive China. The clearest example of this new attitude can be seen in our insistence during the long negotiations at Panmunjon, which finally brought the fighting in Korea to an end, that Chinese prisoners of war had the right to choose to go back to China or to Chiang's regime on Taiwan. This was a new "right" and one we had denied to the Soviet prisoners of war we had liberated in Europe in 1944–1945. Even more significant for Asian Americans would be the way in which the Cold War would modify our immigration and refugee policies.

The Cold War came to Chinese Americans, too. The Guomindang had enjoyed overwhelming support in America's Chinatowns, before and during the war, as Overseas Chinese here and elsewhere were important mobilizers of support for China in her struggle against Japan. However, slowly but surely, most Chinese Americans—including many who were refugees from communist rule—have come to support or at least be reconciled to the People's Republic, which has, after all, what Chinese call "the mandate of heaven."

One is tempted to say that, just as international developments produced two Chinas, domestic developments produced two Chinese Americas. But that would be a gross oversimplification. As Rose Hum Lee pointed out in the mid-1950s, about half of the Chinese American population was native-born, and this segment of the population, reinforced by elite émigrés from Nationalist China, was becoming increasingly middle class, disassociating itself from the concerns of the American Chinatowns and striving for acculturation, if not assimilation, into American society.

Other positive effects of the Cold War in Asia for Chinese Americans can be seen in changing refugee policy. The 1950 Displaced Persons Act had reserved 4,000 spaces for "European refugees from China," largely White Russians and members of the Shanghai Jewish community, and provided no spaces for Asians. In 1953, for the first time, Asians were designated admissible refugees, and 2,000 visas were reserved for "refugees of Chinese origin." These had to be vouched for by the government on Taiwan, because of the fear in the United States in the 1950s and 1960s about the danger of letting in "red" Chinese. This tiny trickle was the start of a flow, which by the late 1970s became, with the so-called boat people and other Southeast Asian refugees, a major component of American immigration.[9]

Another gain from the Cold War was the permanent addition to the American population of a few thousand "stranded" Chinese. When China "fell" there were perhaps 5,000 Chinese nationals resident in the United States on nonimmigrant visas. A majority of them had come as undergraduate and graduate university students; others were highly trained professionals. They represented very different elements of Chinese society from most of the previous immigrants, who had been largely southern peasants. One student, Donald Tsai, who had come to study at Pomona College in 1941 and went on to do graduate work at MIT, told interviewers:

> Many students came from China on scholarships from the Chinese government, although I myself did not come as a scholarship student. Those were very difficult scholarships to obtain, through competitive examinations, and so on. And the reason why you see so many Chinese people in the United States who are eminent professionals, teachers, and so forth is that many of these were, indeed, the scholarship students. . . . When they arrived, the war occurred and they were either cut off or decided not to return, and they have indeed made out very well. . . . I went to M.I.T. [which] was my father's school also. He studied mining engineering there in 1910. . . . All of the students were planning to go back to China. There was no thought of staying.[10]

Yet as things turned out, a majority of these students did stay, making them the first important segment of the postwar brain drain, which saw more and more technical and professional personnel from less developed countries migrate to the United States and other advanced nations. Some of the students did "return," but to Taiwan rather than China. A very few did choose to go to the People's Republic; the most prominent was physicist Dr. Hsue-shen Ts'ien, who is considered to be the father of the first Chinese satellite.

Although the worst fears of Chinese Americans in the 1950s were not realized—none were sent to concentration camps—they did suffer from domestic aspects of the Cold War. Some of the most traditional and conservative Chinese institutions in America, such as the family associations that united all persons sharing the same last name, ran afoul of J. Edgar Hoover's FBI and other "red-hunting" organizations because of their continuing communications with related clan groups in mainland China. As late as 1969, long after the peak of the Cold War hysteria, Hoover testified before a congressional committee that

Red China has been flooding the country with propaganda and there are over 300,000 Chinese in the United States, some of whom would be susceptible to recruitment either through ethnic ties or hostage situations because of relatives in Communist China. . . . In addition up to 20,000 Chinese immigrants can come into the United States each year and this provides a means to send illegal agents into our Nation.[11]

Another onslaught on the Chinese American community came in late 1955 from the American consul general in Hong Kong, Everett F. Drumwright. He made a report to the State Department about what he called "a fantastic system of passport and visa fraud" and later argued that Chinese communists were using the system to infiltrate agents into the United States. (Ironically, the only spy for China we know of, Larry Wu-tai Chin, who committed suicide after apprehension in 1985, was brought into this country by the CIA.) In march 1956, in an apparent follow-up to Drumwright's charges, agents of the Immigration and Naturalization Service (INS) conducted a series of raids to seize illegal immigrants in the Chinatowns of both the east and west coasts. The major protest of the Chinese American establishment, interestingly enough, stressed economic losses rather than human rights violations. In a complaint couched to appeal to the Eisenhower administration, New York City Chinese leaders claimed that the immigration raids were costing merchants there $100,000 a week in lost sales.

But even some of the "humane" reforms of immigration procedures could be twisted and used as weapons in the Cold War. The government provided an amnesty program, the "confession system," to regularize the status of long-established illegal immigrants, the paper sons of Chinese America. Written into the statute books in 1957 after a trial period as an administrative innovation, the program provided that illegal Chinese immigrants *might* be able to regularize their status if a close relative—spouse, child, or parent—were a citizen of the United States or a permanent resident alien. Because of the climate of fear engendered by the Cold War and because much discretion was placed in the hands of officials of the INS, an agency that Chinese Americans had learned to distrust, most potential beneficiaries probably were not willing to use the program. In some cases the government used information gained under the confession program selectively, hoping to get rid of those who favored the People's Republic of China. Many Chinese Americans also believe that the INS was abetted by informers in the service of the Chinese Nationalist regime. Maurice Chuck, the publisher of a left-wing newspaper, the *San Francisco Journal,* reported an eventually unsuccessful attempt to deport him:

My grandfather used the name of Chuck to come to this country, so naturally my father was under the same name and became a citizen of this country. . . . What happened was [that my father confessed and] they arrested me and tried me and used my father's confession as evidence against me. They didn't use it against my father. . . . They tried to deport me to Taiwan but my activities here in this country were so totally against the Chiang Kai-shek government, it's like sending me to a firing squad.[12]

Obviously there was, and continues to be, illegal immigration, and the Chinese, as the first group to be shut out, were pioneers in developing methods and techniques of entry. No one who has read Maxine Hong Kingston's marvelous book *The Woman Warrior,* with its evocations of "ghost" names and dual lives, can underestimate the impact that illegal status has had on the Chinese American community.[13] But from the 1950s on, illegality was surely less and less important, both statistically and psychologically, as more and more of the Chinese American population was native-born or became naturalized and as more humane American immigration legislation and procedures allowed greater numbers of Chinese to enter the United States legally.

Further psychological strength resulted from the admission of Hawaii as a state in 1959. Hawaii had a majority of persons of color in its population—almost all of them Asian or Pacific peoples. One of its first senators was a Chinese American banker, Hiram Fong, who served in the U.S. Senate until he retired in 1977. The fear of having Asian Americans in Congress had been a major factor in the inordinate delay in the grant of statehood to Hawaii. Statehood bills had passed the House in 1947, 1950, and 1953, but in each instance they were bottled up in the race-conscious Senate. Senator Strom Thurmond of South Carolina, for example, quoted Rudyard Kipling with approval, "East is East and West is West and never the twain shall meet," and stressed the "impassable difference" between the majority of Hawaiians, whose ancestors came from Asia, and the majority of Americans, whose ancestors came from Europe.

By 1960, natural increase and continued, relatively small-scale immigration had changed the Chinese American profile significantly. Including Hawaii, which had 38,000 Chinese Americans, the census recorded a total Chinese American population of 236,000. Though still a male-dominated community—males outnumbered females in every five-year census cohort—that dominance was reduced to 57.4 percent. Just over 60 percent of Chinese Americans were native-born. Three-fifths of all Chinese were located in the four Pacific states of California, Hawaii, Washington, and Oregon; more than 90 percent were found in just thirteen states and the District of Columbia. The age distribution still reflected the bachelor-society pattern established in the nineteenth century. With a median age of 28.3 years for the whole Chinese American population, men were significantly older than women, 30.9 to 25.2 years. Urban centers away from the Pacific coast tended to be more heavily male: The Chinese population in the cities of New York, Chicago, Boston, and Washington, DC was between 58.3 and 62.2 percent male.

Education and income data show a Chinese American community that was increasingly becoming two communities: one educated, relatively affluent, and becoming acculturated to American society; the other largely uneducated, distinctly nonaffluent, and still retaining much of its traditional culture. Some who have written about Chinese Americans have been misled by the median figures, which show for education a number close to the national average—11.1 years—and show females as somewhat better educated than males—11.7 years to 10.7 years. But a close look at the data shows that rather large numbers of Chinese had either a great deal of education or none. In addition, the advantage females had disappears when we look only at the well-educated. At the upper end of the spectrum, just under half of all Chinese Americans were high school graduates, 48.3 percent of the women and 44.1 percent of the men. At the very top of the spectrum, more than a sixth of all Chinese American men and an eighth of Chinese American women were listed as having college degrees. At the very bottom of the educational spectrum, about a seventh of the adult population (14.7 percent for males, 15.2 percent for females) was recorded as having no formal schooling.

Given the number of well- and relatively well-educated adults, the income figures for Chinese Americans were quite low. Chinese American men earned an annual average of $3,471; Chinese women earned only about three-fifths of that amount, $2,067. It is relatively easy to explain the reasons for the depressed earnings of Chinese Americans. Major factors were the long-established patterns of discrimination and their virtual exclusion from some of the best-paid sectors of the economy, particularly those sectors in which effective unionization had occurred. Among Chinese American wage earners, over a third (36.7 percent) were in wholesale and retail trade, more than a quarter provided services (26.2 percent), and hardly any (1.2 percent) were engaged in agriculture, fishing, or forestry. Very few Chinese Americans had good-paying blue-collar jobs: Fourteen percent were in manufacturing—large numbers of them underpaid female garment workers—and just 1.9 percent in construction.

To make these data more meaningful, they should not be compared to national averages and medians, which are depressed by the inclusion of the South, where standards were low. Instead they should be compared with figures for the West, the region in which most Chinese Americans lived. The easiest comparison to make is with California because the state Division of Fair Employment Practices published superb data for 1959–1960.[14] The data clearly show that Chinese Americans were better educated than the white majority, although we must understand that the white data are somewhat depressed by the inclusion of what the census bureau calls "Spanish surname" data (see Table 4.3).

As shown in the national data, Chinese are both less educated and more highly educated than the state norm. Income data do not produce a

Table 4.3 Educational Attainment in California, 1960: Percent of Population, 14 Years of Age or Older

Educational Level	Male	Female
Eighth Grade or Less		
Chinese	40.8	38.7
White	27.2	24.2
Completed at Least One Year of High School		
Chinese	59.2	64.3
White	72.8	75.6
Completed at Least One Year of College		
Chinese	29.2	23.2
White	24.1	19.6

Source: California FEPC, *Californians of Japanese, Chinese, and Filipino Ancestry* (San Francisco, 1965).

similar pattern. The median income was $5,109 for white males and $3,803 for Chinese males. Chinese females earned slightly more than whites, $1,997 as opposed to $1,812, doubtless reflecting larger labor force participation (47 percent of all Chinese women over fourteen and less than 36 percent for white women). If we look at just the income for males 25 years of age or older—the persons who earn the most in American society—the disparities are even more striking, as Table 4.4 shows.

Thus, compared with their white counterparts, Chinese American men were 63 percent more likely to be poor, nearly as likely to be lower middle class, 88 percent less likely to be middle class, and 78 percent less likely to be well-to-do. While it can be argued that the overrepresentation on the lowest rung of the economic ladder reflects the larger number of poorly educated Chinese, their underrepresentation in the two higher brackets fails to reflect their educational achievement. On the other hand, the data show clearly that, however they might be disadvantaged vis-à-vis whites, the California Chinese (and Japanese, see Chapters 5 and 6) were achieving

Table 4.4 Annual Income in California of Men 25 Years of Age and Older, 1959

Annual Income	White	Chinese
$1–$3,999	29.4%	48.0%
$4,000–$6,999	38.9%	34.8%
$7,000–$9,999	19.6%	10.4%
$10,000+	12.1%	6.8%

Source: California FEPC, *Californians of Japanese, Chinese, and Filipino Ancestry* (San Francisco, 1965).

middle-class status and income much more rapidly than California Filipinos and other nonwhites, only about 1 percent of whom had incomes of $10,000 or greater.

What the data show is that although increasing numbers of Chinese Americans were finding niches in the larger, as opposed to the ethnic, economy, there were still significant barriers, both real and psychological, to their advancement within that economy. One of the readily discernible patterns was that although well-trained Chinese Americans could find suitable employment with relative ease, it was still very difficult for them to gain promotion to supervisory and higher administrative positions. Many were clearly overqualified for the jobs they held, and it was clear that many employers were reluctant to place Chinese Americans in jobs that gave them the power to hire and fire whites. As a corollary to this, it was almost equally clear that some Chinese Americans were reluctant to be placed in such positions. Both phenomena were clearly carry-overs from the more racist past. No rational observer should attempt to deny that substantial progress toward equality has been made since the years before World War II; at the same time there should be no attempt to deny that discrimination and deprivation have continued. Yet in the years after 1960 the continued existence of discrimination was denied time and again. In addition, the relative success of Chinese and other Asian American groups was used as a kind of rhetorical club to belabor groups whose measurable progress was less outstanding.

Since 1960 the most striking characteristics of the Chinese American population have been its rapid growth and the degree to which much of the Chinese American population would begin to be viewed as a "model minority." In 1960 no one could have predicted that the Chinese American population would increase more than fourfold in the next twenty-five years (see Table 4.5).

These dramatic increases had two primary sources: the Immigration Act of 1965 and the admission of refugees from Southeast Asia, particularly after the fall of Saigon in 1975. (A sizable number of these refugees were of Chinese ethnicity, although most were born in Southeast Asia and had never seen China.) A secondary cause of population growth was the natural

Table 4.5   Chinese American Population, 1960–1990

Year	Number	Increase per Year (Percent)
1960	237,292	5.8
1970	436,062	8.4
1980	812,178	8.6
1990	1,645,472	10.2

Source: U.S. Census and Population Reference Bureau.

increase of the population, whose median age was slightly below that of the general American population. It should be noted that in 1980 the fertility of Chinese American women was significantly below that of whites and most other identifiable groups in the population. Chinese women had 1,020 children per 1,000 women; white women had 1,358. In comparison, Vietnamese, black, and Hispanic women had 1,785, 1,806, and 1,817, respectively (it was clear that these rates were more reflective of class than of ethnicity).

Under the Immigration Act of 1965, the quota system was scrapped, and a complex system of preferences was set up that favored persons with close kin in the United States or who had professional and entrepreneurial skills. The refugees were not as carefully selected—and were to a great degree self-selecting. Since the Chinese in Vietnam and elsewhere in Southeast Asia tended to be entrepreneurial rather than agricultural, large numbers of the Chinese refugees were psychologically prepared to adapt to the economic aspects of American life.

Nothing better symbolizes some of the changes of attitude toward Chinese immigrants than the Chinese Student Protection Act of October 1992. Enacted in the wake of the massacre of the students who demonstrated for democracy in Beijing's Tiananmen Square in June 1989 and the subsequent mass executions and imprisonments, the law has enabled Chinese students—21,000 in 1994 alone—who were in the United States and did not want to return to become permanent residents.

THE "MODEL MINORITY"

By the early 1980s, the American media were noticing the great success of many Asian Americans. In 1982, *Newsweek* headlined a favorable story: "Asian-Americans: A 'Model Minority.'"[15] The catch phrase, "Model Minority," has an interesting history. Coined in 1966 by sociologist William Petersen, who at first applied it only to Japanese Americans, it has become the new stereotype. Like all stereotypes, it has some relationship to reality but is no more indicative of the variety of Chinese American experience than the former "coolie laborer" stereotype was. It is ironic, as Peter I. Rose has put it, that the image of Asians has gone from "pariahs to paragons," and certainly among the current generation of Chinese Americans there are many paragons.[16] For example, in 1983 the grand winner of the Westinghouse Science Talent Search was Paul Ning, a 16-year-old Taiwan-born student at the Bronx High School of Science. But even more significant than his achievement was the fact that of forty finalists in Westinghouse's national contest that year, no fewer than twelve—30 percent—were Asian Americans, nine of them immigrants. Nor was spectacular success limited to the young. Two of the first 100 persons on *Forbes*'s 1983 list of the "richest" Americans were Chinese: An Wang, the 63-year-old proprietor of Wang

Laboratories, the fifth on the list, was said to be worth $1.6 billion, and Kyupin Philip Hwang, the 46-year-old head of TeleVideo Systems, logged in at $575 million.[17] Such achievements, plus a very good press, clearly made the Chinese American community more self-confident than it had been, say, in the 1950s. The fact that after 1972 American relations with the People's Republic of China were all but regularized and quite friendly was also a factor leading to greater community self-esteem.

Chinese Americans were also attaining places of prominence in American culture, higher education, and politics. Following the trail blazed by Jade Snow Wong and Maxine Hong Kingston, a whole host of other Chinese American writers, including Frank Chin, Amy Tan, and David Hwang, achieved both critical and popular success. A young Chinese American sculptor, Maya Lin, designed the haunting Vietnam War Memorial in Washington, DC, the most stunning memorial executed in America in this century. The Chinese American scholar Tien Chang-Lin assumed the position of chancellor of the flagship Berkeley campus of the University of California and the Los Angeles councilman Michael Woo became the first Chinese American to contend for a major political position in the Los Angeles mayoral election in June 1993. Woo, a liberal, lost to a conservative Caucasian, but garnered almost half the votes.

This very self-confidence enabled some community leaders to demand better treatment and redress for wrongs. Early in the 1960s, Chinese American leaders on each coast called for federal assistance for the needy in their communities. Irving S. K. Chin, chairman of the Chinatown Advisory Committee to the Borough President of Manhattan (the mere existence of such a body speaks volumes about social change), told a U.S. Senate committee that Chinese were a "silent minority," who had not previously protested very much because of their problems with English, "a lack of familiarity with the American governmental system," "fear of government," lack of political influence, and a philosophical and cultural reluctance to engage in political activity. Ling-chi Wang, a San Francisco community activist and later chairman of the Asian American Studies Department of the University of California, Berkeley, spoke to the same committee about the "silent" Chinese of San Francisco. Wang advocated "manpower" training programs, which he said were "long overdue," "much needed," and "relevant." Wang also cited evidence showing that in San Francisco's inner-city Chinatown unemployment was almost double the citywide average, that two-thirds of the housing stock was substandard, and that tuberculosis rates were six times the national average. He argued that the major social problems for Chinese Americans were discrimination, educational handicaps, lack of marketable skills, language barriers, citizenship requirements, and culturally biased and irrelevant tests.[18]

How is it possible to square these complaints of poverty and deprivation with reports about "model minorities" and superior educational achievement? It is possible because there is more than one Chinese America. Chinese Americans often speak of the differences between ABCs and FOBs, that is, between American-born Chinese, and the Fresh-off-the-boat (or plane) immigrant Chinese. The former tend to be college-educated, have middle-class occupations, and live outside of the inner-city Chinatowns. Many of the FOBs are poorly educated and deficient in English, live in Chinatowns, and ply the low-wage service trades or sweatshop manufacturing plants typical of inner cities. (Although large numbers of recent Chinese immigrants are poor, many are both middle-class and well-educated and have brought a good deal of capital with them.) The bifurcated nature of the Chinese American community is indicated quite clearly by some census data. In 1970, to cite just one example, although about a quarter of Chinese American adults were college graduates, another quarter had never completed elementary school.

In the 1980s and 1990s sharp educational and other differences also became apparent among new Chinese immigrants, whether from China, Hong Kong, Taiwan, or Southeast Asia. On the one hand, large numbers were relatively poor—such as the thousands of immigrant workers, largely women, who found jobs in the Chinese-dominated sector of New York City's garment industry. Like their Eastern European Jewish predecessors at the beginning of the twentieth century, they worked long hours for relatively low pay under abominable working conditions for Jewish immigrant entrepreneurs. These contemporary Chinese workers also are exploited by bosses who are largely immigrants of their own ethnicity.[19]

On the other hand, there were the Chinese immigrant entrepreneurs in California's Silicon Valley, the vital center of America's computer industry. Anna Lee Saxenian, a researcher at the University of California, Berkeley's Public Policy Institute, reported that in 1988 the 2,775 firms there started by Chinese [and Asian Indian] entrepreneurs in the previous eight years accounted for nearly $17 billion in sales and over 58,000 jobs.[20]

> These new entrepreneurs, most of whom arrived in the United States after 1970, have created an extensive network of activities that facilitate information exchange, job search assistance, and access to managerial expertise and capital. The region's most successful Chinese and Indian managers rely heavily on such ethnic resources while simultaneously integrating into the mainstream technology economy. Nor are these networks merely local. These entrepreneurs are building far-reaching business and professional ties with regions in Asia, and they are uniquely positioned to do so: Their language skills and technical and cultural know-how allow them to function effectively in the business culture of their home countries as well as in Silicon Valley. Their long-distance networks are enhancing opportunities for entrepreneurship, investment, and trade both in California and in newly emerging regions in Asia.

Although some scholars write as if prejudice and discrimination against Asians were a thing of the past, others have understood the ambivalent nature

of the status of Asian Americans in post-1965 America. Bryan Man examined
the achievement patterns of Chinese and white men in California and Hawaii
in 1960 and 1970. He concluded that race, country of birth, migration experience, and the social structure of American society all had continuing effects.
"While some Chinese equal or surpass whites in occupational achievements,"
he wrote, "it is quite clear that many Chinese achieve less than their white
counterparts, all things being equal. This fact, then, calls upon us to seriously
question the notion that the Chinese are a 'model minority.'"[21]

In the mid-1980s and early 1990s the national media linked a number
of criminal events with Chinese American society. Crime and violence by
inner-city youth gangs on both coasts—including the mass execution of thirteen Chinese by youths recently immigrated from Hong Kong during the
robbery of an after-hours gambling establishment in Seattle—traumatized
many in the Chinese community. The grounding of the freighter *Golden
Venture* in plain view of New York City with 288 illegal Chinese immigrants
aboard on June 6, 1993, exposed large-scale smuggling operations that
alarmed some of the public, already apprehensive about incoming Hispanic
"feet people." Apparently, each of the Chinese on the *Golden Venture* had
agreed to pay $30,000 to the smugglers, who were connected to criminal
groups in Asia and America. If all paid the trip would gross almost $9 mil-
lion. Most of the immigrants had at least made a down payment: One had
paid $6,000 before boarding.

A year later the *New York Times* reported that 224 of the 288 passengers
were still locked up, ten were dead, five had escaped INS custody, and
forty-nine had been released. Twenty-five of the latter had been granted
asylum as refugees: Chen Benxu, for example, was granted asylum based
on his opposition to China's one-child policy, and Wang Libin, a former student, because of his involvement in China's democracy movement. Another
ten had been able to post bond, while fourteen were released as juveniles.
Those who were still being held were costing the U.S. government about
$30,000 a year each, the same sum that each one was supposed to pay to
come to America.

Similarly, there was a several-month-long campaign of leaks to the
press accusing Dr. Wen Ho Lee, a naturalized American citizen born in Taiwan, of being a spy for the People's Republic of China. Lee, a scientist employed at the government's Los Alamos National Laboratory, was first
publicly fired in March 1999 and finally indicted in late 1999 on fifty-nine
separate counts of "mishandling classified information." The *Washington
Post*, which had printed the various leaks from the FBI and other security
agencies without naming its sources, eventually took a "neutral" position in
an editorial:

> Mr. Lee is, of course, innocent until proven guilty—a presumption that he has
> been largely denied in the public arena throughout much of the investigation.
> But the seriousness of the allegations against him should give pause to those
> convinced in advance of Mr. Lee's innocence, just as surely as the shifting na-

ture of the allegations against him should give pause to those convinced he is a nuclear spy. Given the poor handling of this investigation to date, it is well worth reserving judgment until the government proves the very grave accusations it has now leveled.

What the *Post* editorial failed to ask was the question that many students of Asian American affairs asked: "Would this kind of campaign have been conducted against a Caucasian scientist?"

In September 2000, after nine months in solitary confinement as a dangerous threat to "national security," the federal prosecutors dropped all but one charge against Dr. Lee and, as part of a plea bargain, released him with time served. President Bill Clinton publicly criticized the long incarceration but was "sure" that anti-Asian prejudice was not a factor in the admitted miscarriage of justice.[22]

Chinese Americans reacted to these and similar incidents in various ways. Some tried to ignore them; others pointed out, accurately, that Chinese American criminal activities, although significant, involved only a small percentage of the community. Still others, such as Oakland attorney Alan S. Yee, called for a united front of all Asian Americans:

> Even though the Asian-American community has traditional divisions . . . we find that, from the outside, we're all perceived as the same, and, despite an image as "model minorities," we see the search for scapegoat still there.

We would point out, however, that despite this and other calls for pan-ethnic unity, the various ethnic communities that comprise Asian America are more divided than united.[23]

But Yee's premise needs to be considered. Were Chinese Americans in the last decade of the twentieth century a model minority or scapegoats? The more than 1.5 million Chinese Americans comprise a diverse community whose differences are probably increasing more than they are decreasing. Chinese Americans, although clearly overrepresented in many areas of achievement in American life, are also overrepresented among America's poor. And even for those who have "made it," there are often the nagging reminders of a racist past. Diana Fong put it well on the op ed page of the *New York Times:*

> We're still not fully integrated into the mainstream because of our yellow skin . . . we still cannot escape the distinction of race.[24]

NOTES

1. Dorothy Jones, *The Portrayal of China and India on the American Screen, 1896–1955* (Cambridge, MA: MIT Press, 1955), p. 36.
2. Harold R. Isaacs, *Images of Asia: American Views of China and India* (New York: Harper, 1972), pp. 71, 155. (Originally published as *Scratches on Our Minds.*)
3. Ibid., p. 187.

4. Philip Gleason, "Americans All: World War II and the Shaping of American Identity," *The Review of Politics* 43 (1981): 483–518, at p. 484.

5. Fred W. Riggs, *Pressures on Congress: A Study of the Repeal of Chinese Exclusion* (New York: King's Crown, 1950).

6. Samuel I. Rosenman, ed., *The Public Papers and Addresses of Franklin D. Roosevelt*, 1943 vol. (New York: Harper, 1950), pp. 429–430, 548.

7. Quoted in Diane Mei Lin Mark and Ginger Chih, *A Place Called Chinese America* (Dubuque, IA: Kendall/Hunt, 1982), p. 96.

8. Isaccs, *Images of Asia*, pp. 123–124.

9. Roger Daniels, "American Refugee Policy in Historical Perspective," in J. C. Jackman & Carla Borden, eds., *The Muses Flee Hitler: Cultural Transfer and Adaptation, 1930–1945* (Washington, DC: Smithsonian Institution, 1983), pp. 61–77.

10. Mark and Chih, *Chinese America*, pp. 104–105.

11. Quoted in Stanford M. Lyman, "Red Guard on Grant Avenue: The Rise of Youthful Rebellion in Chinatown," in Lyman, *The Asian in North America* (Santa Barbara, CA: Clio Press, 1977), p. 198.

12. Mark and Chih, *Chinese America*, p. 104.

13. Maxine Hong Kingston, *The Woman Warrior* (New York: Knopf, 1976).

14. California Department of Industrial Relations, Division of Fair Employment Practices, *Californians of Japanese, Chinese, Filipino Ancestry* (San Francisco, 1965).

15. *Newsweek,* Dec. 6, 1982, pp. 39 ff.

16. William Petersen, "Success Story, Japanese American Style," *New York Times Magazine,* Jan. 6, 1966, pp. 20 ff.; Peter I. Rose, "Asian Americans: From Pariahs to Paragons," in Nathan Glazer, ed., *Clamor at the Gates: The New American Immigration* (San Francisco: ICS Press, 1985), pp. 181–212.

17. "Confucian Work Ethic: Asian-born Students Head for the Head of the Class," *Time,* Mar. 25, 1983. *Forbes* list as cited by the Cincinnati *Enquirer,* Sept. 30, 1983.

18. Testimony in Integrated Education Associates, *Chinese-Americans: School and Community Problems* (Chicago, 1972), pp. 12–17, 18–28.

19. Xiaolan Bao, "'Holding Up More Than Half the Sky': A History of Women Garment Workers in New York's Chinatown, 1948–1991," unpublished Ph.D. dissertation, New York University, 1991.

20. Scott Thurm, "Asian Immigrants Help to Reshape Silicon Valley as Entrepreneurs," *Wall Street Journal,* June 24, 1999.

21. Bryan Dai Yung Man, "Chinese Occupational Achievement Patterns: The Case of a Model Minority" (Ph.D. dissertation, UCLA, 1978). The quotation is from *Dissertation Abstracts International* 39 (1978): 3172A.

22. The *New York Times* for September 14–16, 2000 contains some important documents about the case.

23. Material about the 1980s and 1990s comes from a variety of sources, including personal observation. Especially useful were two newspaper articles: David Smollar, "Violence, Slurs—U.S. Asians Feel Trade Backlash," *Los Angeles Times,* Sept. 14, 1983, and Robert Lindsay, "The New Asian Immigrants," *New York Times Magazine,* Sept. 10, 1983, pp. 22ff. Story on *Golden Venture* from Ashley Dunn, "After the Golden Venture, the Ordeal Continues," *New York Times,* June 5, 1994. "Estimated Undocumented Immigrants . . . 1996," *Statistical Abstract of the United States, 1999.* (Washington, DC: Government Printing Office, 1999), Table 10, and *Washington Post,* December 16, 1999, p. A38.

24. Diana Fong, "America's 'Invisible' Chinese," *New York Times,* May 1, 1982.

Chapter 5

THE JAPANESE

The Early Years

BACKGROUND

Although there had been a number of Japanese visitors, students, merchants, and officials in the United States from the middle of the nineteenth century—and at least one short-lived small Japanese colony at Gold Hill, California, near Sacramento—significant immigration began only toward the end of the century.[1] The first large group of Japanese migrants to travel east across the Pacific went to the then-independent kingdom of Hawaii as indentured laborers; after the United States annexed Hawaii in 1898 many of them re-emigrated to the American West Coast. There, by the late 1880s, a steady and growing immigration, largely of young men, had begun to create a Japanese American community. In 1900 the census identified almost 25,000 Japanese on the West Coast; by 1920 there were more than 110,000, almost two-thirds of them in California. Although at first this migration seemed to parallel that of the Chinese—which was halted, as we have seen, just before that of the Japanese began—the differences between them are as striking as the similarities.

The similarities, noted by contemporary observers, were that each immigration was predominantly male and that each group worked at physically difficult, low-prestige, and low-paying jobs. The Chinese were employed in mining, agriculture, and railroad building; the Japanese in agriculture and railroad maintenance. Both groups were composed of peasants. However, whereas the Chinese were almost all from one small district in South China, the Japanese were drawn from rural areas in several parts of Japan and the Ryukyu Islands (Okinawa). In addition, the countries from which they came were in quite different stages of development. China was weak and growing weaker; it had not yet, to any significant degree, begun to take steps toward modernization. Japan had begun the transition toward modernity after the Meiji Revolution (1869) and by the turn of the century was an emerging modern power; increasing numbers of Japanese had been exposed to at least the basics of compulsory education. In the United States, the Chinese presence in agriculture, once quite significant, diminished after the 1880s; however, the Japanese, after initially working at many urban occupations, became more heavily involved as agricultural proprietors and tenants than any other twentieth-century immigrant group. And, perhaps the most important difference of all, the Japanese had behind them a government that inspired and demanded growing respect, whereas the protests of the weak Chinese government about bad treatment were all but ignored. What the Japanese government most dreaded in its negotiations about the rights of Japanese nationals in this country was the enactment of a Japanese exclusion act on the model of the 1882 law barring Chinese. As Hilary Conroy pointed out, the Japanese government, not noted for its concern about human rights, kept an "ever jealous watch against discriminatory treatment abroad" to emigrants from Japan; this concern was chiefly motivated by the desire to protect Japan's "prestige as a nation."[2]

THE STRUCTURE OF JAPANESE AMERICAN SOCIETY

As we shall see, the influence of the Japanese government was not, in the final analysis, able to offset the combination of American racism and unscrupulous politicians. But—and this was crucially important for the development of the Japanese American community—the pressures of the Japanese government did delay effective exclusion for about two decades, until the barring of the immigration of "aliens ineligible to citizenship" in 1924. In the meantime, the nature of Japanese migration would change from a male-dominated to a female-dominated flow. Thus, by the time immigration was cut off, a firm demographic foundation had been established for a native-born, citizen generation of Japanese, the Nisei,[3] who by 1940 would greatly outnumber their parents, as shown in Tables 5.1 and 5.2.[4]

Consequently, the demographic experience of Japanese Americans was quite different from that of Chinese Americans. For the latter, as we have seen, the bachelor society established before passage of the 1882 Exclusion Act prevailed for decades, and the overall population underwent a decline for nearly half a century. Only in the 1950s did the Chinese American population reach the levels it had attained in the 1880s. For Japanese Americans there was only a slight dip in the 1930s, and by 1940 nearly two-thirds

Table 5.1 Sex Ratio of Japanese in the Contiguous United States, 1900–1940

Year	California			Other States			Total		
	Male	Female	Percent Female	Male	Female	Percent Female	Male	Female	Percent Female
1900	9,598	553	5.4	13,716	405	2.9	23,314	958	3.9
1910	35,116	6,240	15.1	27,954	2,847	9.2	63,070	9,087	12.6
1920	45,414	26,538	36.9	27,239	11,765	30.1	72,653	38,303	34.5
1930	56,440	41,016	42.1	25,331	16,047	38.9	81,771	57,063	41.1
1940	52,550	41,167	43.9	19,417	13,813	41.6	71,967	54,980	43.3

Source: U.S. Census data.

Table 5.2   Japanese Citizenship Status in the Contiguous United States, 1920–1940

Year	Total	Aliens	Natives	Percent Native
1920	111,010	81,338	29,672	26.7
1930	138,834	70,477	68,357	49.2
1940	126,947	47,305	79,642	62.7

Source: U.S. Census data.

were native-born citizens. Thus in many ways, by 1940 the acculturation process of the Japanese American community was farther advanced than that of the Chinese Americans, even though significant migration of the latter had begun about half a century earlier.

THE ANTI-JAPANESE MOVEMENT

Because the West Coast had "learned" to discriminate against Asians in the 1860s and 1870s, the anti-Japanese movement arose while the Japanese population was still quite small. There was an abortive anti-Japanese movement in the 1890s, but the effective movement against immigrants from Japan dates from newspaper agitation in 1905. It became notorious and a matter of diplomatic concern in 1906 as a result of the so-called San Francisco School Board incident, which involved an attempt to force Japanese pupils in San Francisco to attend the long-established segregated school for Chinese.[5] The incident set a pattern that would prevail for nearly twenty years: state, local, or regional discrimination offset in part by federal intervention. President Theodore Roosevelt mediated the San Francisco segregation matter himself; he called San Francisco officials to come to the White House and jaw-boned them to back down. Roosevelt, in return, promised to negotiate with Japan to halt further immigration.

The result of Roosevelt's negotiations was the Gentlemen's Agreement of 1907–1908—actually a series of notes exchanged between the American and Japanese governments—which hinged on restriction by the Japanese rather than by the American government. Tokyo simply promised not to issue any more passports good for the United States to "laborers." Not fully understanding what would happen—diplomats and legislators have often been ignorant about the facts of life for ordinary people—both governments agreed that Japanese residents in the United States who were established and self-supporting could bring over their wives and other family members.

Thus, although the Gentlemen's Agreement was presented to the public as tantamount to exclusion, it allowed a predominantly female migration for the next sixteen years, which, as we have seen, nearly balanced the

Japanese American sex ratio and led to a continuing increase of the Japanese American population. This caused westerners to believe that they had been betrayed by unscrupulous leaders in Washington. Although under American law only the federal government could regulate immigration, state and local governments could, and did, discriminate against Japanese by statute and ordinance. The famous Alien Land Acts of 1913 and 1920 in California and similar statutes in other western states were based on the federal naturalization statutes that made Japanese and other Asians "aliens ineligible to citizenship." Other restrictions were based simply on race (racial segregation would not be declared unconstitutional until 1954). School segregation, despite the 1906 hullabaloo in San Francisco, was not widely practiced,[6] but state law did prohibit the marriage of Asians and whites, restrictive covenants were written into many deeds making it illegal to sell the property to a nonwhite, movies usually made Asians sit in the balcony or on one side of the theater, and some municipal swimming pools and even beaches were barred to Asians.

The federal government long resisted overt anti-Japanese legislation: In 1917, for example, a restrictive "barred zone" act kept out all Asians except Filipinos, who, as American nationals, could not be kept out, and Japanese. Finally, in 1924, in a deliberately insulting move, Congress denied immigration quotas to any foreigners who were "aliens ineligible to citizenship," which affected only Japanese, although they were not specifically mentioned. This abrogation of the Gentlemen's Agreement was one of the seemingly irreconcilable issues between Japan and the United States in the years before the Japanese attack on Pearl Harbor.

JAPANESE IMMIGRANT ORGANIZATIONS

In the meantime the Japanese American population grew, some prospered, and many of the Nisei, or second-generation children, became increasingly acculturated. The Issei, or immigrant generation, were also exposed to the American world but, in common with most immigrant groups, developed their own organizations. Some of these were influenced by the government of Japan. From the 1890s until the attack on Pearl Harbor—but particularly in the period up to 1924—Tokyo tried very hard to apply various measures of social control to the Japanese immigrants to the United States, largely because it was convinced that Japan's prestige as a nation would be affected by the behavior of its residents abroad.

Crucial to this control were Japanese consular officials and the immigrant organizations they created and nurtured. Evidence of such attempts at control exists as early as 1891. But it was after the Gentlemen's Agreement, which placed certain control responsibilities on the Japanese government, that such control became most important. In 1909 the consulate general in

San Francisco formed the Japanese Association of America, the premier institution of the Issei. Theoretically, all Japanese in the United States had to belong to the association; annual membership, through a local or regional association, cost from $1 to $3 a year. To encourage membership, the Japanese government through its consulates gave the associations an official role and made them the intermediaries through which individual Japanese residents had to pass if they wished to retain official connection with the Japanese government. Both Japanese law and the Gentlemen's Agreement required the Japanese consular service to issue certain documents to resident Japanese. The responsibility for these certificates was delegated to the associations, which in turn could collect fees for their issue.

Such certificates required by the Gentlemen's Agreement were related largely to travel abroad, with the right to return and the ability to bring into the country wives, children, parents, and even other relatives. Thus, any Japanese who wished to keep or establish family ties across the Pacific was forced to do so through the appropriate Japanese association. In addition, Japanese law required men of military age who had not fulfilled their military obligations to register yearly, and other certificates were required to register marriages, divorces, births, inheritances, and other vital statistics.

There has been much debate over the true nature of the Japanese associations. Exclusionists, like V. S. McClatchy of the *Bee* newspaper McClatchys, and congressional demagogues, like Representative Martin Dies of Texas, insisted that the associations were part of some kind of sinister Japanese plot to take over America. Apologists for the Japanese, such as Stanford historian Yamato Ichihashi, claimed that the associations were merely self-help groups analogous to those that flourished among other immigrant groups. Neither was accurate. The associations were semiofficial organs of the Japanese government, but their function was essentially bureaucratic, not sinister. In addition to controlling certificates, the associations encouraged Japanese residents to acculturate and, above all, to send their children to school and have them excel there.

Of all the certificates the associations came to control, the most crucial was the one that gave the right to bring a wife to the United States. From the point of the Japanese government, which tried to abide by the terms of the Gentlemen's Agreement, the major problem was how to determine the socioeconomic status of each Issei male who wished a passport for his wife. Eventually a guideline was established: Anyone who could show liquid assets of $800 or more would be eligible. This was a sizable nest egg. Interviews with surviving Issei indicate that these regulations were often evaded. One successful ruse involved the pooling of $800 by a group of "bachelors" in what they called "show money" and transferring it from one account to another; in time, the same $800 would provide passports for a number of wives or other relatives.[7]

At the time of the Gentlemen's Agreement and the founding of the Japanese associations, there were perhaps 60,000 Japanese in the entire United States, with about two-thirds of them living in California. In the next fifteen years there was a net immigration of some 25,000 Japanese women. These women, some of whom were "picture brides"—married by proxy to immigrant men they would not see until they arrived in the United States—began to have children at what seemed to many Caucasian observers an incredible rate. By the early 1930s, the citizen children of these and other immigrant marriages would outnumber their parents.

JAPANESE AMERICAN ENTERPRISES

Thus despite a whole series of discriminatory actions and a generally hostile atmosphere, the first generation of Japanese Americans provided a firm demographic base for the future of the community. Part of the reason that it was able to do this was that it created for itself an important economic niche in the agricultural economy of the Far West in general and California in particular.

Although a few Issei immigrants, such as George Shima (1863–1926), the famed "Potato Baron," came to this country with some capital, most began as laborers, and some remained so all of their lives. Many others, however, soon became proprietors and, from British Columbia to San Diego, began to carve out special niches for themselves. Some, like Shima, ran large-scale, diversified operations, but most were small proprietors concentrating on labor-intensive specialty crops, chiefly fruits, vegetables, and flowers. They also developed essentially ethnic marketing organizations in such centers as Los Angeles and Seattle. By 1919, in California alone, where agriculture occupied about half the Japanese population, Issei farmers controlled over 450,000 acres of farmland, about 1 percent of the state's acreage. But the intensive, high-yield agriculture they practiced brought in more than $67 million, more than 10 percent of the total value of California's crops.

Those who lived in cities worked primarily at service trades and in small businesses, many of which catered either to the ethnic community or as the marketing adjuncts of Japanese American agriculture. Initially, San Francisco and Seattle were the major *nihonmachis,* or Japantowns, but by 1910, Los Angeles began to prevail. By 1940, Los Angeles was clearly the metropolis of Japanese America, with nearly 37,000 persons; Seattle had the second largest Japanese American population, numbering almost 7,000, with another 4,700 in its outlying regions. Although San Francisco ranked third in numbers, with some 5,000, it remained culturally quite important. Its *nihonmachi* was one of the liveliest; it was the headquarters for the major organizations of each generation—the Japanese associations and the Japanese American Citizens League—and it served as a center for the more than

6,000 Japanese in the Bay Area. Only four other cities in the United States had ethnic Japanese communities of 1,000 or more: Sacramento and Stockton in California; Portland, Oregon; and New York City.

THE PREWAR JAPANESE AMERICAN COMMUNITY

By the 1930s the Japanese American community on the West Coast had achieved, economically at least, lower-middle-class status. But there were enough problems faced by the growing Nisei generation that a grant of $40,000 was awarded by the Board of Trustees of the Carnegie Corporation to study the "educational and occupational opportunities offered to American citizens of Oriental races." A book, aptly titled *The Second Generation Japanese Problem*, provided data garnered from interviews with the Nisei during the late 1920s and early 1930s. There was widespread despair and disillusionment. For example, one subject responded:

> If, in order to avoid troublesome contact with American workers, we man a whole industry . . . with Japanese . . . the cries of "yellow peril" . . . are raised . . . if we limit ourselves to . . . only the Japanese community . . . we are accused of being unassimilable and clannish.[8]

The major issue was race. Americans in the early third of the century simply could not accept Japanese Americans or other Asians as equals. One Japanese American wrote, "So, many of my friends are giving up the fight. 'Why get an education?' they say. 'Why try to do anything at all?' Probably we were meant to be just a servile class."[9]

This was also the period of the Great Depression, a time when job opportunities were limited for all Americans. A few Nisei emigrated to Japan; most stayed in Hawaii and on the West Coast. They developed their own local organizations; there were Japanese American social clubs, athletic leagues, and church groups, where individual Nisei could participate with ethnic peers. There was a high degree of acculturation; most of the groups were modeled on American rather than Japanese or Issei models (i.e., Boy and Girl Scouts, the YMCA and YWCA), but there was very little integration with the dominant community. It was the era of structural separation. Even though Nisei topics of interest were thoroughly American, discussion was limited to members of their own ethnicity. The separation was forced rather than voluntary; even if Nisei desired to enter mainstream groups, opportunities were limited.[10]

But the community was still controlled by the Issei. Most Nisei were economically dependent upon their parents, and there were complaints that the younger generation was becoming American too fast. A relatively large number of Nisei were college and university students, and they were beginning to take on middle-class characteristics. Unlike their parents, they could, as citizens, enter the learned professions—law, medicine, and denistry, in particular—and they set up their own generational organization, the Japanese American Citizens League (JACL).

The JACL, like many other second-generation organizations, regardless of ethnicity, was hyperpatriotic. Its creed, written in 1940, clearly expressed the hopes, if not the experience, of the second generation:

> I am proud that I am an American citizen of Japanese ancestry, for my very background makes me appreciate more fully the wonderful advantages of this nation. I believe in her institutions, ideas and traditions; I glory in her heritage; I boast of her history; I trust in her future. She has granted me liberties and opportunities such as no individual enjoys in this world today. She has given me an education befitting kings. She has entrusted me with the responsibilities of the franchise. She has permitted me to build a home, to earn a livelihood, to worship, think, speak and act as I please—as a free man equal to every other man.
>
> Although some individuals may discriminate against me, I shall never become bitter or lose faith, for I know that such persons are not representative of the majority of the American people. True I shall do all in my power to discourage such practices, but I shall do it in the American way—above board, in the open, though courts of law, by education, by proving myself to be worthy of equal treatment and consideration. I am firm in my belief that American sportsmanship and attitude of fair play will judge citizenship and patriotism on the basis of action and achievement, and not on the basis of physical characteristics. Because I believe in America, and I trust she believes in me, and because I have received innumerable benefits from her, I pledge myself to do honor to her at all times and all places; to defend her against all enemies, foreign and domestic; to actively assume my duties and obligations as a citizen, cheerfully and without any reservations whatsoever, in the hope that I may become a better American in a greater America.

It should also be noted that the JACL deliberately tried to distance itself from the previous generation. By requiring that all members be citizens, it barred persons born in Japan from membership and, unlike most ethnic organizations, which maintained ties with the country of origin, tried to separate itself completely from Japan and Japanese culture. In the short run at least, the effort of JACL members to separate themselves from their parents and their parents' homeland was a failure. When war came between the United States and Japan, all persons of Japanese ethnicity on the West Coast—regardless of citizenship, age, or sex—were herded unceremoniously into concentration camps, euphemistically called "relocation centers."

EXILE AND INCARCERATION

This wartime exile and incarceration—often called the relocation of the Japanese Americans—was and remains the central event of Japanese American history. It makes that history unique, setting off the Japanese American experience from that of not just other ethnic groups from Asia but from all other immigrant ethnic groups. Because the event has been studied widely, we will provide only a summary here.[11]

At the outbreak of hostilities, the federal authorities responsible for internal security, according to plan, rounded up a few thousand enemy aliens—Japanese, Germans, and Italians—and interned them. Each internee eventually had a hearing as an individual, and as a result of these hearings, some were released. Most of the interned Japanese were community leaders. In addition, the bank accounts and other assets of Japanese nationals were frozen, which meant that the whole community was economically disadvantaged. Almost from the very moment that bombs fell on Pearl Harbor, the federal government began to discriminate against Japanese American citizens. Travel out of the country was barred for German and Italian nationals and all persons of Japanese ancestry. By late December 1941, the armed forces stopped accepting Japanese Americans either as volunteers or as draftees, even though the Selective Service Act barred racial discrimination. There was a great deal of agitation from the old anti-Japanese forces, from a number of influential persons in the media (including the widely respected columnist Walter Lippmann) and from many senators and representatives. Finally, after a formal recommendation from Secretary of War Henry L. Stimson, President Roosevelt, on February 19, 1942, issued Executive Order 9066, which, as a matter of "military necessity," authorized the army to exclude "any or all persons" from as yet unspecified "military areas." That military area turned out to be the entire state of California, most of Washington and Oregon, and part of Arizona. The persons moved were all Japanese.

As a result, the entire Japanese American population of the affected area—men, women, and children, alien and citizen alike—were herded, under military auspices, first to "assembly centers," usually close to where they lived, and eventually to one of ten "relocation centers," run by a newly created civilian agency, the War Relocation Authority.

There has been much controversy regarding the nature of the relocation centers. On more than one occasion during the war, President Roosevelt, who authorized their creation, referred to them bluntly as "concentration camps," as did U.S. Supreme Court Justice Owen J. Roberts. However, the uncovering of the incredible dimensions of the Nazi Holocaust in Europe made the term "concentration camp" synonymous with "death camp" or "extermination camp." Thus, many who were involved in the relatively humane incarceration of the Japanese Americans, such as Dillon S. Myer, the Department of Agriculture bureaucrat who ran the War Relocation Authority so "well" that a grateful government made him commissioner of Indian affairs, vehemently rejected the notion that the places where Japanese Americans were kept should be called concentration camps.[12]

But, whatever one calls them, the camps created to house the Japanese American population were places where persons were confined with neither charge nor trial, simply on the basis of their ancestry and their place of residence. Age, sex, and citizenship meant nothing. The camps were surrounded by barbed wire and were patrolled by armed soldiers, who in several instances shot and killed persons whom they were guarding. Unlike the camps of the Nazis, those of the Soviet Gulag Archipelago, or those in the killing fields of Cambodia, the American camps cannot be called "death camps." Many more persons were born in them than died there. Yet, they were, indeed, "concentration camps," as the term has been used since it was introduced by the British during the Boer War at the turn of the century.

It is important to note that not all Japanese Americans were incarcerated. The Japanese Americans who lived east of the proscribed area—or were able to move there before the Army ordered them "frozen" in the early spring of 1942—were left in nervous liberty. There were about 10,000 such persons. In addition, the more than 150,000 Japanese Americans who lived in Hawaii—then a territory—were largely left alone. Martial law was established in Hawaii, but even though Hawaii had actually been a theater of war and its Japanese Americans represented about one-third of the islands' total population, the military authorities there did not deem it necessary to intern them. It was even pointed out to Washington that their continued labor was vital to the successful conduct of the war. This—and not the foolish vaporings of media strategists, politicians, and chair-borne generals—was true "military necessity."

THE STRUGGLE FOR REDRESS

That the mass incarceration of the West Coast Japanese not only was morally wrong but actually retarded rather than advanced the American war effort has long been recognized by scholars. As early as 1948 the United States government admitted that there was some injustice in the procedure by enacting the Japanese American Claims Act, which allowed some of the victims of the relocation and incarceration to collect damages for property lost—but not for wrongful imprisonment. In 1976, partially in recognition of the bicentennial of American independence, President Gerald R. Ford repealed FDR's executive order by proclamation and declared that:

> We know now what we should have known then—not only was the evacuation wrong, but Japanese-Americans were and are loyal Americans. . . . I call upon the American people to affirm with me this American Promise—that we have learned from the tragedy of that long-ago experience forever to treasure liberty and justice for each individual American, and resolve that this kind of action shall never be repeated.[13]

Finally, in 1980, the Congress created the Commission on Wartime Relocation and Internment of Civilians (CWRIC) to investigate the whole process and make whatever recommendations seemed appropriate. In early 1983, after a long and detailed investigation, the CWRIC found that a "grave injustice" had been done to the Japanese American people. How and why had that injustice been done?

During the war, the whole procedure was given the color of law by the American judicial system, which has traditionally bowed to the executive and legislative branches during wars and national emergencies. Three cases, known collectively as the Japanese American cases, were decided by the Supreme Court in 1943 and 1944. In effect, the court endorsed what the government had done, but it did rule in December 1944, when the war was clearly won, that Japanese Americans who were American citizens and still being held behind barbed wire were free to go anywhere—including the West Coast—that other citizens could go unless there were individual charges against them. It should be noted that the high court was not unanimous in sanctioning the relocation: In 1944 three of the nine justices argued that the whole relocation procedure, as it was applied to American citizens, violated the Constitution. The judge who most vigorously attacked the majority was Justice Frank Murphy, who, in dissenting from what he called a "legalization of racism," argued that:

> All residents of this nation are kin in some way by blood and culture to a foreign land. Yet they are primarily and necessarily a part of this new and distinct civilization of the United States. They must accordingly be treated at all times as the heirs of the American experiment and as entitled to all the rights and freedoms guaranteed by the Constitution.[14]

In 1982 former Supreme Court Justice Arthur J. Goldberg, then a member of the CWRIC, remarked that Justice Murphy's 1944 dissent would surely be a majority, if not a unanimous, opinion were the case to be heard by a contemporary court. But in 1944, Murphy was virtually alone. Although many Americans regretted what one official called the "unavoidable injustices" involved in the relocation, the overwhelming majority supported putting their fellow citizens of Japanese ancestry in concentration camps and, if wartime public opinion polls are to be believed, would have supported much harsher measures. Large numbers—an absolute majority in some polls—wanted all Japanese Americans sent "back" to Japan after the war, even though most of them—native-born citizens—had never been there!

During World War II, the lives of almost all Japanese Americans were turned upside down. By the closing days of the war more than half of those who had been in the wartime camps had left them for work and residence east of the coastal mountain ranges, for college, or for military service. In 1942 and 1943, some Japanese Americans had been allowed to volunteer for military service, and in 1944 the draft was reinstituted for Japanese American young men, even those still behind barbed wire! The wartime military service of 25,000 Japanese Americans, including a hundred or so members of the Women's Army Corps, was largely either in segregated combat units in Europe—the famed 100th Battalion and the 442nd Regimental Combat Team—or in particularly dangerous military intelligence work with front-line units in the Pacific. The well-orchestrated publicity that the former group received, including a postwar White House ceremony at which President Harry S Truman awarded the survivors the Presidential Unit Citation for bravery, was an important element in the relatively rapid rehabilitation of the reputation of the Japanese Americans. As we will show in the next chapter, within two decades this one-time pariah group was being hailed as a "model minority."

But for thousands of Japanese Americans, this rehabilitation came too late. Their lives had been ruined, their property lost or badly damaged by neglect, vandalism, and theft, their self-esteem shattered. Some 5,000 persons of both generations, hopelessly embittered by the treachery of American democracy that had promised so much and delivered so little, chose to emigrate or repatriate to Japan after the war. Others, particularly older people, were never able to resume their shattered lives. Several hundred Japanese Americans, insisting that their incarceration was a violation of American principles, resisted the draft and were tried, convicted, and sent to federal penitentiaries. The image of a resilient, spunky Japanese American population rolling up its sleeves and successfully pursuing upward social and economic mobility after the war has been a popular one that the public and conservative ideologues like S. I. Hayakawa, Thomas Sowell, and William Petersen liked to dwell on and exploit. After all, as William Dean Howells pointed out a century ago, what the American public really wants is a tragedy with a happy ending. For many, if not most Japanese Americans, there has been a relatively happy ending, although as with most happy endings, there were many unreckoned costs.

But for tens of thousands of Japanese Americans the relocation was a tragedy without a subsequent triumph. Beginning in the mid-1970s some community activists began to campaign for some kind of compensation or "redress" for their wartime incarceration. As noted, Congress established the CWRIC in 1980 to investigate if any such redress was proper. During its subsequent public hearings all across the nation, hundreds of survivors of America's concentration camps appeared and told their stories, often for the first time. Only then was it possible to imagine how deep the scars of the wartime experience were and how much pain they were still capable of inflicting.

In 1983 the CWRIC officially recommended that the federal government formally apologize and that each survivor be granted a tax-free, one-time payment of $20,000. Five years later the Civil Liberties Act of 1988 was passed, putting into effect the CWRIC's recommendations. The last payments were made shortly before the fiftieth anniversary of the incarceration. By then nearly half of the victims were dead. What happened to Japanese Americans is, happily, a unique experience in modern America. Americans have suffered in other wars, but only in this instance was their suffering inflicted by their own government. Despite its "happy" ending—redress—the Japanese American experience should trouble all Americans, for it demonstrates how fragile their constitutional protections can be in a time of crisis.[15]

NOTES

1. John E. Van Sant, *Pacific Pioneers: Japanese Journeys to America and Hawaii, 1850–80* (Urbana: University of Illinois Press, 2000).

2. Hilary Conroy, *The Japanese Frontier in Hawaii, 1869–1898* (Berkeley: University of California Press, 1953), p. 140.

3. Japanese immigrants in the New World have used forms of the words for numbers to distinguish between generations. Thus, the first generation are called "issei" (ichi = one); the second generation, "nisei"; the third, "sansei"; the fourth, "yonsei"; and the fifth, "gosei." Nisei who were sent to Japan for education are called "kibei."

4. Because there are minor discrepancies in the 1920 census data, the figures in these two tables, taken from different places in the fourteenth census, do not agree. For example, at different places native-born Japanese are enumerated at 29,506 and 29,672.

5. Donald T. Hata, Jr., *"Undesirables": Early Immigrants and the Anti-Japanese Movement in San Francisco, 1892–1893* (New York: Arno Press, 1978); Roger Daniels, *The Politics of Prejudice: The Anti-Japanese Movement in California and the Struggle for Japanese Exclusion* (Berkeley: University of California Press, 1962).

6. Irving G. Hendrick, *Public Policy Toward the Education of Non-White Minority Group Children in California, 1949–1970* (Riverside: University of California Press, 1975); Charles M. Wollenberg, *All Deliberate Speed: Segregation and Exclusion in California Schools, 1855–1979* (Berkeley and Los Angeles: University of California Press, 1977).

7. Roger Daniels, "The Japanese," in John Higham, ed., *Ethnic Leadership in America* (Baltimore: Johns Hopkins University Press, 1978), pp. 36–63; Yuji Ichioka, "Japanese Associations and the Japanese Government: A Special Relationship, 1909–1926," *Pacific Historical Review* 45 (1977): 409–437.

8. Edward K. Strong, *The Second Generation Japanese Problem* (Stanford, Calif.: Stanford University Press, 1934), p. 2.

9. Ibid., p. 12.

10. David K. Yoo, *Growing Up Nisei: Race, Generation, and Culture among Japanese Americans of California, 1924–1949* (Urbana: University of Illinois Press, 1999).

11. Roger Daniels, *Prisoners Without Trial: Japanese Americans and World War II* (New York: Hill & Wang, 1993).

12. Richard Drinnon, *Keeper of Concentration Camps* (Berkeley: University of California Press, 1986). Drinnon sees Myer as the prototype of the dull, faceless, spineless bureaucrat who is promoted because of his willingness to serve. The term "the banality of evil" comes to mind.

13. President's Proclamation No. 4417 of Feb. 19, 1976, "An American Promise," *Fed. Reg.* 35 (Feb. 20, 1976).

14. *Korematsu v. U.S.,* 323 U.S. 214 (Dec. 18, 1944).

15. Mitchell T. Maki, Harry H.L. Kitano, & S. Megan Berthold, *Achieving the Impossible Dream: How Japanese Americans Obtained Redress* (Urbana: University of Illinois Press, 1999) tells and analyzes the redress story. The official report, Commission on Wartime Relocation and Internment of Civilians, *Personal Justice Denied* (Washington, DC: GPO, 2 vols., 1982 & 1983; reprint edition, University of Washington Press, 1997), is worth reading.

Chapter 6

JAPANESE AMERICANS

After 1946

The world and the nation had changed after World War II and so had the Japanese Americans. The United States had become one of the leading world powers along with the Soviet Union, so that there was an antagonism between capitalism and communism. The term "Cold War" was used to describe the tensions between the two powers.

The Japanese Americans were busy trying to reestablish themselves after the concentration camp experience. They entered a more open society; jobs were easier to obtain and the primary targets of racism were now African Americans—many of whom had migrated to places like California and taken over housing left vacant by the evacuees—and Mexicans, who had filled jobs in the agricultural sector. As a consequence, Japanese Americans were no longer the pariahs; in addition, the Japanese nation was now an important ally to contain the spread of communism. It is important to note that when Japan and the United States are on friendly terms, the perception and treatment of Japanese Americans becomes favorable.

The purpose of this chapter is to provide a picture of the Japanese Americans through a presentation of generations and their effects on the ethnic community and family. It will also include a more thorough analysis of how redress came about.

U.S.-JAPANESE RELATIONS

U.S.-Japanese relations have affected and continue to affect the treatment and status of Japanese Americans. Although Japanese Americans have continuously stressed their American upbringing, it is still difficult for many Americans to differentiate between the Japanese, born and raised in Japan, and Japanese Americans, born and raised in the United States. It is still common for Nisei and Sansei to hear such remarks as "You speak English so well" and "You people make such wonderful cars." And when asked of one's origin, the answer of San Francisco is insufficient—the follow-up remark is "But where are you really from?" It is clear that the questioner would only be satisfied with an answer such as Tokyo.

It is therefore not surprising that the perceptions and treatment of Japanese Americans have been closely tied to relations between Japan and America. This was true in the early part of the century and has not changed. But there has been a change in the message. In the early 1900s, the basic message was that of inferiority—that Japan was an inferior nation with an inferior culture—the producer of shoddy goods and a second-class imitator. In the 1940s it was as an enemy nation—cunning, warlike, with a fanatical disregard for life. The next several decades saw Japan as an ally and a base for containing China and the Soviet Union—a democratic nation serving to control the spread of communism. The current picture is that of a fierce economic competitor, with the current term, "Japan bashing," indicating part of the American response.

Japanese Americans have lived through different eras. The most traumatic was the wartime incarceration; despite later monetary redress and a presidential apology, bitter memories persist a half century later. A number of violent episodes (discussed in Chapter 13) and the rise of other hate crimes are reminders that the prejudice that was a strong part of the early Japanese American experience unfortunately remains alive and all too well a century later.

THE ISSEI

The early Issei are a passing generation. Their migration took place prior to 1924; the majority were already young adults, so that today few remain. Survivors are in their late eighties and nineties; some have even passed the century mark. An analysis of the obituary column in the *Pacific Citizen* of May 21, 1993 indicates the following: Of the eight deaths of persons who were born in Japan (Issei), seven were over 90 years of age, with the average age at death being 90.8 years; of the twelve deaths of persons born in the

United States (Nisei), four were in their eighties, five were in their seventies and three were in their sixties, and the average age at death was 74.4 years.[1]

What was once a young and vigorous group is now in its twilight years: The issues of aging are of the highest concern. Health needs, housing, social and family supports, long-term care, safety, and transportation are current concerns. Questions involving such matters as the placing of dependent elderly in institutions and the role of the family are new to the Japanese American community. The image of the Japanese family and community taking care of their own may limit assistance from mainstream organizations. It should be emphasized that most of the surviving Issei have limited English-speaking ability and may prefer ethnic foods and a cultural ambience, whereas older Nisei have different cultural characteristics.

The early Issei community served in what D. S. Massey labeled the "migration network."[2] Since the early immigrants arrived with little knowledge of the language and culture and were greeted with indifference and outright hostility, the Issei community was vitally important. The network included personal and family ties, village and *ken* (province) relationships, and the commonality of Japanese ancestry. The community provided a support system that enabled the immigrants to handle some of the emotional, social, and economic costs of migration. It was also able to provide assistance in terms of such basic needs as transportation, housing, and jobs, as well as social and recreational needs. Discrimination and segregation reinforced the ethnic enclaves, so that ethnic organizations, rather than organizations developed by the larger society, served the community. In general, the Issei community, even with internal divisions based on personalities, ideology, and the like, was a relative cohesive entity that provided organizations and services to meet most of the needs of its population.

After the Evacuation

The wartime evacuation, coupled with advancing age, hastened the Issei generation's loss of power. Leadership in the camps was deliberately kept out of the hands of Issei; release from the camps marked the closing stages of the traditional Issei community. In post-war America, housing was much more scattered, and job opportunities developed by the Issei were no longer important services to the Nisei. Jobs in the larger community, although not totally open to Nisei, were much more attractive than working for Issei businesses.

The major Issei organization, the Japanese Associations, were prominent until the late 1950s. Changes were inevitable—the Issei were aging, their quest for citizenship had been achieved, and the importance of supporting their type of organizations had diminished. Needs and priorities were different; Nisei, instead of following in the steps of their parents, preferred to join their own ethnic organizations and groups in the larger community.

Goals

Although the goal of becoming a full-fledged American, including citizenship and active participation in the mainstream, may have appealed to some, most Issei felt that cultural differences and discrimination made such a goal unrealistic. Rather, if there was to be a move toward the mainstream, it would be made by their children, the Nisei. The phrase *kodomo no tame ni* (for the sake of the children) connotes sacrificing one's own life for the next generation.[3] The opportunity to obtain citizenship in the 1950s came much too late in their lives to have a significant effect on becoming American, although many Issei studied diligently and became quite knowledgeable about the presidents, Congress, and other American institutions. Parents would often ask their children obscure questions about this or that aspect of the Constitution; however, the depth of their feelings about America rarely ran as deep as their feelings about the country of their birth.

But it would be too simple to imply that they ignored American models. Rather, the Issei developed a parallel community, especially in areas where their need for services would otherwise remain unmet because of discrimination. When hospitals erected racist barriers, the Japanese developed their own hospitals; when faced with other restrictions, they developed their own organizations. There were Issei doctors, businessmen, realtors, and the like, so that the Issei did not have to depend on mainstream organizations and services to satisfy their major needs.

Hence, most Issei did not aim at acculturation, integration, and assimilation; thus the majority were outside of the mainstream. However, the Issei developed their own relatively independent, self-sufficient communities, which retained traditional cultural modes. The lack of social problem behavior—crime, delinquency, mental illness, poverty, and dependence on welfare—are measures of the success of their structurally pluralistic model. Seen in the context of the racist, hostile, and punitive America that they faced throughout most of their lives, their adaptation was remarkable.

As the rapidly diminishing number of Issei survivors look back on their lives, they find much satisfaction in the lives of their children, many of whom have been outwardly more successful than they, and thus, in their view, worthy of their own sacrifices. They have also overcome the many racist barriers erected against them; citizenship, land ownership, and choices in housing are no longer barred to them. Even relations between Japan and America, with their ups and downs, are seen as more positive, and Issei admit that when they were in the World War II camps, they could not have anticipated these changes, even in their wildest dreams. The one regret for some is that many of these changes came about much too late in their lives.

THE NISEI

The period during and after World War II can be viewed as the Nisei era. Before the war, most Nisei were too young to assume leadership, and those of employable age were hemmed in by racial discrimination. As one consequence, many were forced to work in ethnic jobs and in the ethnic community. Urban ethnic jobs meant gardening, working in ethnic shops and stores and in small business, relying on ethnic clientele. The stereotype of college-educated Nisei working in fruit stands was common; despair about the lack of opportunity, even for those with college degrees, was widespread. In rural areas, farming and farm employment provided opportunities.[4]

The World War II incarceration led to a change in the lives of the Nisei. Because so many of the Issei leaders were rounded up by the FBI and imprisoned, Nisei were thrust into leadership positions, often prematurely. In the segregated camps, ethnicity was no longer a mark of the outsider; Nisei competed with other Nisei for jobs behind the barbed wire fences, although the positions of authority were held by whites from the outside. Nisei could be foremen, truck drivers, teachers, firemen, and policemen ("internal security")—jobs which they could not hold on the outside—high schoolers could be student body leaders, athletic heroes, and play the leads in school plays.[5]

Those who were able to gain leave from the camps discovered a new world east of the Mississippi. Life in New York, Minneapolis, Chicago, and Cleveland had its share of hardships, but the barriers of racism that locked the Nisei out were not as high as in California. There were other pariah groups—blacks, Jews, and poor whites served as surrogate targets. Factory jobs were available, as well as positions more appropriate to their level of education and training. Some chose to spend their whole lives in these new environments in the Midwest and the East.

Nisei who volunteered for the army experienced new life experiences. Many went abroad for the first time and served as conquerors. After the war Nisei would not be content to limit themselves to pre–World War II occupations in the ethnic community.

Dramatic changes occurred in Hawaii. The children of the early recruits to plantation life had already broken away through opportunities in education; returning World War II veterans added to the impetus towards becoming a part of the Hawaiian mainstream. By 1954, Nisei veterans began to challenge the Republican majority in the legislature. Along with some Caucasian friends who had supported them during the hard times, they developed a powerful Democratic party group that eventually gained control of the legislature as well as influential elective positions. Senator Daniel K. Inouye was one of the early leaders; others who served in the United States Congress included the late Spark Matsunaga and Patsy Mink. Another Japanese American, George Ariyoshi, served as Hawaii's governor in the 1980s.

The Nisei and Sansei continue to hold important positions in the state economy. Hawaii is no doubt the one state where Japanese ancestry is not viewed as a handicap in terms of social and occupational opportunities.

Camp Norms

One of the more intriguing and perhaps unanswerable questions deals with the effects of the concentration camp experience. Does life under incarceration prepare one for life on the outside after release? Life in the camps entailed dependence on the government for food, shelter, and clothing; breakup of family life; diminution of the power of the Issei; cynicism concerning concepts such as freedom and democracy; and the innumerable restrictions of camp life.

Much of what was learned in camps was different from the norms that guided pre-camp life, and would have proved inappropriate for life in a competitive society. Hard work, long hours, loyalty, and responsibility were difficult to maintain under camp conditions. One common response was "waste time," a phrase that covered a variety of situations, such as lack of dedication to the job and little extra effort. There was a tendency to "borrow" government property—lumber, coal, and other government supplies—among residents who had never "borrowed" before. There was a dependence on the government for the basic necessities of life: food, shelter, clothing, and jobs. The one saving grace of the period was that camp life was relatively short-lived, so that most of the dysfunctional norms were short lived and not internalized.

However, many of the norms and values that were a part of the Issei culture continued to be carried on by the Nisei. Concepts such as *amae* (the need to be loved), *enryo* (deferential behavior), and *shi-ka-ta-ga-nai* (acceptance, literally "it can't be helped"), remained familiar. Indirect, Japanese-style communication—as opposed to direct American-style communication—was also maintained.

A Different America

For the majority of the Nisei, in common with their Issei parents, release from the camps, which were closed in 1946, meant reestablishing themselves, no matter where they were. It meant extra work, overtime, multiple family workers, and multiple jobs per worker. Gardening was one temporary but popular occupation, even for those who did not possess the necessary skills or talents. The G.I. Bill was important; education and hard work were finally beginning to bear fruit.

Although the Nisei had changed, reflecting both the camp experience and life away from the West Coast, important changes had also occurred in the dominant community. There was an increased liberalization of attitudes, behaviors, and laws concerning Asians. After 1952, immigration and naturalization laws were no longer exclusionary; legal discrimination in housing gradually disappeared; antimiscegenation legislation was overturned in California in 1948 and nationally by the Supreme Court in 1967. Occupations such as public school teaching began to open in the 1950s, and the stereotype of Nisei college graduates working at fruit stands became a distant memory. College degrees, always a part of Nisei expectations, began to lead to realistic career choices.[6]

Barriers in the social and recreational areas were more resistant to change. Although there was no longer segregation in swimming pools and other public facilities, most prestigious private organizations, such as country clubs, fraternities, and sororities, remained off limits. De facto housing discrimination began to be breached in the 1960s, which meant that Japanese Americans began to be much more geographically dispersed.

Pluralistic Nisei athletic and social organizations reemerged. The basketball leagues and social groups of the 1940s to 1960s were strikingly similar to those that had flourished from the 1930s to the evacuation. But there were also important differences. Whereas there was almost no chance to participate in the wider community prior to World War II, now individual Nisei could go out of the ethnic community. Social functions, such as Nisei conventions in the 1930s, were usually held at modest ethnic facilities, often at a local church, whereas post-war gatherings, especially in more recent times, have been at first-class venues. This change has sometimes brought complaints from old-timers who hark back to the old days, and complain about the high costs of recent conventions.

Nisei now discuss retirement, health issues, and how to understand the new generations. They generally keep a low profile, though some, such as Norman Mineta and Robert Matsui, gained prominence in politics, representing California in the U.S. House of Representatives. In June 2000, Mineta, then aged 68, was named Secretary of Commerce by President Clinton, the first Asian American to achieve cabinet rank. That they were elected and reelected from areas where the Japanese American population is well under 5 percent remains a source of wonder. Noriyuki "Pat" Morita has gained prominence through his roles in the *Karate Kid* movies.

The greatest Nisei contributions have been in everyday activities, often associated with the middle class and the Japanese culture, such as working hard, saving, raising children, low rates of crime and delinquency, and demonstrating good citizenship. The surviving Issei are surprised that the aging Nisei have become very much like them. Whereas at one time the

Nisei were castigated for irresponsible behavior—for becoming American too fast and being too materialistic—the Nisei now seem to reflect Issei values. And in common with perceptions of most generations when looking at the next group, the Nisei have reservations and doubts about the character and value systems of the Sansei.

In summary, the Nisei have lived through a wide variety of images. They were a "problem minority" in the 1930s, "quiet Americans" in the 1960s, a "model minority" in the 1970s, and now a mature group, ready for retirement.

THE SANSEI

The Sansei, or third generation era, begins in the 1970s, although by that time the generational references were beginning to lose their meaning. The relatively clear-cut generational differences that once characterized the Japanese American community have been eroded by new immigrants, the mixture of fourth- and fifth-generation Japanese Americans, and the influx of Japanese businessmen (most here for a temporary stay), students, and the ubiquitous Japanese tourists. A broader term, Nikkei (Japanese people), has become more popular, since it refers to Japanese Americans as a whole, rather than to specific generations.

The Sansei, the Yonsei, and the Gosei, or fourth and fifth generations, are the most "American" of any Japanese group; many of them have never faced overt discrimination, and some have never had close ethnic ties or ethnic friends. They flock to colleges and universities, eager for good jobs, especially in medicine, engineering, and law. Like many of their mainstream peers, they question the lifestyle and values of their parents but are the primary beneficiaries of the material success of the previous generation. Family life may now often include as many as four generations: Issei great-grandparents, Nisei grandparents, Sansei parents, and Yonsei children, although the number of Issei survivors diminishes with each passing year. Most of the old Japanese ways are also passing with the Issei; new input, new technology, and "modern American values" appear more comfortable for each new generation.

Questions raised by many Sansei that are difficult for many Nisei to answer relate to their behavior during the wartime evacuation. Why was there so little organized protest? What about litigation? Why did they go so meekly? For generations who grew up during the turbulent campus protests of the 1960s and 1970s, these questions are natural. And for the Nisei, the answers are also time related. They grew up in an era when dissent and overt protests by minority groups were rare. Further, the unequal power relationships, the wartime atmosphere, and the inexperienced leadership precluded any organized action. But because these issues were seldom discussed in the homes—many Sansei students complain that verbal exchange, especially about personal matters, has not been a part of their family style—questions of this nature come as a surprise. Japanese American homes appear harmonious to outsiders, especially since areas of potential conflict are often carefully avoided.

Although there are more opportunities to interact with the mainstream community, many Sansei still prefer ethnic organizations. For example, although more fraternities and sororities now accept Asians, all-Asian fraternities and sororities also continue to flourish. The atmosphere and the activities are identical, except that one group features all Asian faces.

One of the more surprising survivals in the tide toward the mainstream is the continued existence of the Japanese athletic leagues. In the past the Nisei athletic teams (the most popular sport was basketball) served a definite need—social and recreational opportunities were limited—but by the time of the Sansei, ample opportunities were available outside of the ethnic community. Acculturation and integration have occurred, but in some places, such as Los Angeles, Sansei basketball and volleyball leagues continue. It is interesting to note that ethnic norms often come into play; for example, players who "hot dog," shoot a lot and go for individual glory, are often controlled by their more team-oriented peers, who do not pass to them.[7]

Other ethnic activities also continue. The Nisei Week celebration in Los Angeles (which could probably be more accurately retitled as Nisei participation diminishes) has its counterparts in Hawaii, San Francisco, and other cities. One mainstream tradition, queen contests, are an integral part of these festivities—who will be the Nisei Week Queen, or Miss Cherry Blossom? But this bit of Americana raises some interesting questions. The contestants by now are Sansei and Yonsei, but with the rise of interracial marriage, the question is, must they be "full-blooded" Japanese? What about those who are of mixed parentage? And from a feminist perspective should there be such contests at all?

The new generations reflect the growing openness of American society. The ethnic community and family offer supportive frameworks, but opportunities, especially in terms of employment, are primarily in the dominant community. Gone are the Japanese gardeners, the "mom and pop" grocery stores, and other service occupations; perhaps other newer immigrant groups have taken them over. Sansei, like most other Americans, usually do not follow the trades of their parents, especially if they are low-status positions. And since the major occupations of many Nisei parents are in the professions, they have to earn their positions, rather than inherit them.

Sansei are more apt to reflect the ambience of their surrounding communities, rather than a strictly ethnic one. A Japanese American growing up in St. Louis will be more Missourian than Japanese, just as Sansei from Los

Angeles, Honolulu, and New York will reflect the culture of these cities. The testimonies of individual Sansei make this point clearly.

One Sansei grew up in Gardena, a suburb of Los Angeles, which is often referred to as the Japanese American city. With a population made up of about a quarter Japanese, Gardena has Japanese councilmen, a Japanese cable TV station, and numerous ethnic stores. She tells a story of growing up that reflects a strong ethnic culture. This Sansei grew up in a bilingual, bicultural background and was surrounded by Japanese Americans throughout her high school years. She dated only other Sansei, and she was part of the "in group" in high school—scholarship society, class officer, cheerleader. Culture shock for her was enrolling at UCLA, where there were so many non-Japanese.[8]

Conversely, another Sansei grew up in the only Japanese American family in a suburb of San Diego. Her only contact with other Japanese was through the ethnic church; her primary contacts, especially her close friends, were Caucasians. For her, culture shock was the large number of Asian Americans at UCLA.[9] It is interesting to note that she now has a Sansei boyfriend, although her behavior and her expectations appear much more "American" than "Japanese American."

A survey of students attending colleges and universities in the Los Angeles area shows a number of interesting findings.[10] Although the bulk of respondents represented the Sansei generation, there were even responses from fifth- and sixth-generation Japanese Americans. Respondents still believed in such values as hard work, good education, family and community solidarity, and perseverance—values passed down from their Issei and Nisei heritage. Most of them represented a Yuppie outlook, but it should be noted that they also held part-time jobs while attending school. The majority came from materially affluent backgrounds and enjoyed good relationships with their parents. They felt most comfortable with other Asians and belonged to Asian organizations such as the Community Youth Council, the Nisei Athletic Union, the Orange County Sports Association, and the Crescent Bay Optimists. In spite of these continuing ethnic ties, they overwhelmingly believed in interracial dating and marriage. Therefore, there appears to be a continuity between the Japanese generations on certain values, but the belief in interracial marriage adds to the possible acceleration of assimilation as the future of the Sansei and subsequent generations.

But there remains one common factor that still shapes Japanese American experiences. It is that of visibility: No matter how acculturated or talented a Sansei may be, the physical features identify him or her as an ethnic. Show business provides an example of this dilemma. For Japanese and other Asian Americans, acting positions remain primarily as stereotypes. Roles for Japanese actors include the gardener, cook, the camera-carrying tourist, the enemy soldier—always with an accent. Female roles are a sexy geisha or a compliant, submissive, "confused about America" character.

The desired body type and physical image in America remains that of a Caucasian: It may take time and the continued introduction of new immigrants before the image of an American includes other models.

There are signs that the variable of visibility may be changing. As mentioned, both Norman Mineta of San Jose and Robert Matsui of Sacramento have been elected and reelected to the U.S. Congress in areas where the number of Asian American voters is negligible. Sansei are entering occupations and fields that were once considered closed, such as advertising, the performing arts, journalism, and broadcasting. They are also taking over the leadership positions in such ethnic organizations as the Japanese American Citizens League (JACL).

Nisei leaders sometimes appear just as reluctant as the old Issei used to be in giving up positions of power and authority; the accusation that the new generation wants things too quickly and easily, without "paying their dues," has a familiar ring. For example, an interview by a Sansei reporter with Dan Aoki, a World War II veteran and reputed "hatchet man" of the Governor Burns Democratic political machine of Hawaii, gives a flavor of one Nisei's attitude toward the Sansei.[11] Aoki complains that the Sansei take everything for granted. He grew up when children of immigrants were "poisoned" by the idea that *haoles* (whites) were superior and when the highest position for Nisei college students was bank teller or clerk. The World War II experiences transformed naive plantation kids, including himself, into belligerent ex-soldiers, fighting for their rightful place in Hawaiian society. His message was that the younger generations did not understand the struggles of the older and that things that came too easily were never fully appreciated. Many Sansei hear the same story from their Nisei parents, just as Nisei remember hearing a similar story from their Issei parents.

The most appropriate generalization concerning the Sansei deals with their heterogeneity. There are those who shop along Rodeo Drive in Beverly Hills, concerned primarily with brand names, status, and upward mobility; there are activists and militants who have little use for material possessions; some serve in the armed forces; others participate in almost every endeavor open to Americans everywhere. But the majority choose the so-called safer professions, where visibility is not as important as the quality of their education and credentials.

Most Sansei have acculturated; there is a high degree of integration in terms of housing, education, and occupations. A great deal of marital assimilation is taking place (see Chapter 13). But there is also the retention of pluralistic structures, especially in areas with large Japanese (and other Asian) populations, such as Honolulu and Los Angeles. The major difference between the old ethnic community and the newer ones is that of voluntarism. In the old days, segregation was forced; in the current era, there are choices.

Perhaps this difference is an apt commentary on the changes that Japanese Americans have lived through.

RECENT EVENTS

Two events in the early 1990s, both occurring in the South where Japanese Americans are few in number, are related to the Japanese experience. One deals with JAP Road in Beaumont and Vidor, Texas. Efforts to have the sign changed by Tanamachi Nakata have met with growing resistance on the part of the local communities. She has received hate mail and comments concerning the deaths of Americans at Pearl Harbor. As the president of the Houston Chapter of the JACL, Betty Waki, pointed out, it is hard for people in California to recognize how isolated parts of the country are in relation to Japanese Americans.[12]

The second incident took place in Baton Rouge, Louisiana, and involved Yoshihiro Hattori, a 16-year-old exchange student from Japan. A supermarket butcher, Rodney Peairs, mistaking the lad for a robber, shot and killed him. A jury found Peairs not guilty and spectators applauded the verdict. The trial received extensive coverage in Japan, and for Japanese Americans, it became a sobering reminder that although there is change, there are also areas where time seems to stand still.[13]

THE PASSAGE OF REDRESS

The most significant positive action for Japanese Americans in their short history in the United States was the passage of the Civil Rights Act of 1988. The Act granted redress for the actions of the United States government during World War II and included a presidential apology and a cash payment of $20,000. What was viewed as impossible became a reality in 1988; it should be recalled that the 1942 wartime incarceration was also viewed as impossible, so that Japanese Americans faced two "impossibles" that became realities.

THE KITANO–MAKI PROPER ALIGNMENT MODEL[14]

The Kitano–Maki proper alignment model (Table 6.1) was developed in order to answer three questions.

1. What were the variables that led to the incarceration during World War II (1942–1946)?

Table 6.1   Kitano–Maki Proper Alignment Model: Achieving the Impossible Dream

Years	History		Legislative Branch		Judicial Branch	Executive Branch
	Community	U.S. Society	Senate	House		
1987–88	+	N+	+	+	N+	+
1983–86	+	N+	N	N	N+	–
1979–82	N+	N+	N	N	N	N–
1970–78	N+	N	N+	N+	N	N+
1945–69	N	N	N	N	N	N
Pre-WWII/Exclusion/ Incarceration	–	–	–	–	–	–

2. Why did it take from 1946 to 1988 for the passage of redress?
3. What were the variables that led to the passage of redress in 1988?

The model indicates that a proper alignment of variables was necessary for the passage of the Civil Rights Act of 1988. The variables are signified by either a plus (+), a minus (–), or neutral (N), with a plus (N+) or minus (N–). The proper alignment is achieved when there are all pluses (+), all neutral pluses (N+), or all minuses (–). The variables in our model are the ethnic community, the overall U.S. society, including the media and public opinion, and the legislative, judicial, and executive branches of government.

For example, the era prior to World War II and leading to the evacuation shows that all of the variables were lined up in a negative fashion. The ethnic community was divided by age and generation—the younger Nisei were U.S. citizens by birth, while the older Issei were aliens. In the mix were the Kibei, U.S. citizens by birth, but receiving much of their early socialization and education in Japan. There were differences by age, citizenship, acculturation, ethnic identity, and identification with Japan, so that the ethnic group did not present a cohesive front against the evacuation. The general public, led by the Hearst papers, was constantly bombarded with images of Japanese spies, Japanese treachery, and the "yellow peril." The ethnic group had little access to the media, the mainstream, or to Congress. They were the primary target of racist attacks, which ranked them as inferior, with animal-like qualities, so that when President Roosevelt signed Executive Order 9066 (EO9066) on February 19, 1942, it was a popular action supported by the mass media, the general public, the Congress, and the courts. There was no organized opposition, even from the ethnic community, so that there was a proper alignment of the variables (––––––) for incarcerating the Japanese Americans, both citizens and aliens.

SCIENTIFIC RACISM

Social science explanations of race and culture in the early 1900s were racist and supported white supremacy. Social Darwinism claimed racial groups could be ranked on an evolutionary scale with Europeans the most advanced, followed by Asians and Blacks. Racial categories are influenced by evolution through inheritance and natural selection.[15] Racial prejudice and discrimination were mechanisms that served to keep racial groups apart and protected the "superior races" from contamination from their "inferiors." The image of Japan, as well as all Asians, was that of an inferior race, and analogies to animals, such as apes, monkeys, and spiders, were common. Since the immigrant Japanese and the American-born Nisei were considered racially Japanese, they were also viewed as inferior and were the targets of discrimination, including antimiscegenation laws, housing restrictions, and lack of equal opportunity.

Dower refers to a meeting of distinguished social scientists, psychiatrists, and Japan specialists who met under the auspices of the Institute of Pacific Relations in New York in December 1944 that attempted to understand the Japanese character structure. One generalization was that Japanese character structure and behavior was similar to that of the American adolescent. Talcott Parsons observed that Japanese found security by fitting into culturally defined patterns of group life, while Margaret Mead found that the conformity in American adolescents was a characteristic of all Japanese life. Terms such as primitive and mental and emotional instability were attributed to the Japanese enemy. The character structure of the Japanese was akin to the American gangster. There were also references to severe toilet training, small body size, and inferiority leading to aggressive behavior. One comment was that if the Japanese were three inches taller, Pearl Harbor would not have happened.[16]

Perhaps the most important generalization was that Japan was one nation with one will and one purpose. The perception was supported by Japanese propaganda which emphasized that it was a united nation with racial solidarity and the common purpose of defeating the enemy. This was translated into racial solidarity with one united purpose: to demonstrate their superiority over the West, with the society willing to die to achieve that purpose. Japanese Americans, presumably of the same race, were believed to be similarly motivated.

SUMMARY

The variables leading to the decision to incarcerate Japanese Americans were properly aligned in 1942. The division of the ethnic community, the mass media in favor of incarceration, and the history of anti-Japanese feelings—including the inability of many Americans to differentiate between Japan and Japanese Americans (which continues to the present day)—were aligned for incarceration. The Congress found anti-Japanese actions to be politically popular; the legal system had little problem, especially since much of the ethnic leadership were non-citizens, and President Roosevelt had other major concerns, such as winning a war, and could not be bothered with such a small, powerless minority. The concentration camp era was from 1942–1946.

Discussion about redress did not surface in the Japanese American community until 1970. The post–concentration camp period from 1945–1946 to 1970 was spent by most mainland Japanese Americans in reestablishing their economic and social lives. Actions toward redress were neutral (N). The newer generations were getting further education and developing their human capital, while the gradual opening up of the American society meant economic mobility, better housing, and a move toward the mainstream.

During the period from after World War II to 1970, there was a move of all of the variables in the model away from the minuses of 1942. The ethnic community was gaining in political sophistication, including the election of Senators Daniel K. Inouye and Spark M. Matsunaga from Hawaii, and Congressmen Norman Y. Mineta and Robert T. Matsui from California. Immigration restrictions became less racist, Issei gained naturalization privileges, antimiscegenation laws were overturned, and housing became more open. By 1988, there was a proper alignment of pluses (+ and N+) for the passage of the Civil Rights Act.

NOTES

1. *Pacific Citizen,* May 21, 1993, p. 8.

2. D. S. Massey, "Economic Development and International Migration in Comparative Perspective." *Population and Development Review* 14 (1988): 383–413.

3. Dennis Ogawa, *Kodomo No Tame Ni* (Honolulu: University of Hawaii Press, 1978).

4. Edward K. Strong, Jr., *The Second Generation Japanese Problem* (Stanford: Stanford University Press, 1934).

5. Harry H. L. Kitano, *Generations and Identity: The Japanese American* (Needham Heights, MA: Ginn Press, 1993).

6. Ibid.

7. According to a Sansei Ph.D. candidate in history at UCLA, there is a "jock" mentality among some Sansei: World affairs and politics are unimportant; their primary interest is how many points they scored and whether their teams are winning in the local athletic leagues. Then there are many others intensely involved in community change, in searching for an identity, and their role in American society. The wide spread is similar to the diversity seen in the larger Los Angeles community.

8. Joy Taguma, "What Gardena Means to Me" (term paper, UCLA, 1985).

9. Karen Amano, "Interracial Marriage: A Comparative Analysis of the Views of Asian Americans" (independent study, UCLA, 1985).

10. Linda Takahashi, "Studying the Sansei Generation" (independent study, UCLA, 1985).

11. Roland Kotani, "Dan Aoki, 1918–1986," *Hawaii Herald,* July 4, 1986, p. 1.

12. Gwen Muranaka, "A Tough Battle in Texas Towns," *Pacific Citizen,* May 21, 1993, p.1.

13. William Booth, "Jury Acquits Man Who Shot Japanese Youth," *Los Angeles Times,* May 24, 1993, A-4.

14. Mitchell Maki, Harry H. L. Kitano, & Megan Berthold, *Achieving the Impossible Dream: Japanese Americans Obtain Redress* (Urbana: University of Illinois Press, 1999).

15. Michael Banton, *Racial and Ethnic Competition* (Cambridge: Cambridge University Press, 1983).

16. John Dower, *War Without Mercy* (New York: Pantheon Books, 1986).

Chapter 7

THE FILIPINOS

The history of Filipinos in the United States is, in one way, different from that of all other Asian ethnic groups in the United States: Their history was, initially, a direct and unforeseen result of American imperialism. Because of this, Filipino Americans enjoyed, for a time, a unique status among Asian immigrants. They were not "aliens" but enjoyed a "privileged" status as American nationals. In other ways, the early history of twentieth-century Filipino immigrants bears a resemblance to that of other Asian migrations.

BACKGROUND

The earliest Filipinos were students; then, largely in the 1920s and early 1930s, came farm laborers; finally, after 1965, came what some writers have called the "third wave" of Filipino immigrants—educated, upwardly mobile professionals and would-be entrepreneurs, similar to those coming from India. We now know that long before the American conquest of the Philippines in 1898 there were handfuls of Filipinos settled in the United States, almost all of them having come via Mexico as a result of Spanish imperialism. As early as the eighteenth century there was a tiny group of such immigrants in and around New Orleans, and there may well have been other Filipinos in what later became the United States.[1] But there was no connection between these pioneers and twentieth-century Filipino migrants.

The Spanish-American War of 1898, a series of disconnected skirmishes on land and sea over a period of ninety days, was called by one contemporary a "splendid little war." At the cost of 389 combat dead, the United States humbled once-mighty Spain, drove her from the New World, and, in the process, gained a protectorate over Cuba and took possession of Puerto Rico, Guam, and the Philippine Islands. In addition, in the wave of martial patriotism that flooded the United States, Congress agreed to annex Hawaii, which it had refused to do earlier.

But the relatively bloodless Spanish-American War was followed by the bloodier and much longer Philippine-American War, which the American government called the Filipino Insurrection. This was an early and unsuccessful example of a third-world anticolonial war, what some would call a war of national liberation. A segment of the Filipino people, who, under the leadership of Emilio Aguinaldo (1869–1964), had been resisting Spanish rule, proclaimed themselves independent after the United States defeated Spain, but the Americans refused to recognize their government and insisted that the Filipinos were not ready to rule themselves.

To establish American sovereignty firmly, an army of 100,000 was shipped to the islands, and, in the guerrilla war that followed, both the Americans and their opponents resorted to the kinds of atrocities that irregular warfare usually breeds. The Filipino "insurrection" was officially ended in 1902, although some fighting continued in the southern Philippines for several years. Altogether 4,243 American soldiers were killed "pacifying" the islands and many times that number of Filipinos, both guerrillas and civilians. After the fighting was over, the first American civilian governor of the Philippines, William Howard Taft, began nearly half a century of avowedly benevolent despotism by proclaiming his concern for the welfare of the people of the Philippines, whom he described as our "little brown brothers." United States leaders soon realized that the Philippines could not be defended in case of war, so the Filipinos were promised independence by 1945. World War II unavoidably delayed that timetable, but the United States did grant the Philippines independence in 1946. (The United States maintained military bases there, chiefly naval facilities on Manila Bay and the northern Luzon air complex at Clark Field, until 1992.)

The more than 7,000 Philippine Islands lie off the shores of Southeast Asia and today have a population of some 78 million persons. The islands were visited by the Portuguese explorer Fernando Magellan in his circumnavigation of the globe in 1521. Later in the sixteenth century, Spain took possession of the Philippines. Most of the Filipinos, Malaysian people ethnically, had been converted to Roman Catholicism long before the Philippine-American War, although a considerable population in the southern Philippines, particularly on Mindanao, had been converted to Islam. Although there are many languages spoken in the Philippines—all of them of the Malayo-Polynesian group and enough alike that most are mutually understandable—just three indigenous languages are spoken by about 85 percent of the population: Visayan, a language of the central Philippines, is spoken by about 44 percent; Tagalog (now Filipino and since 1946 the official language), a language of central Luzon, is spoken by about 25 percent; and Ilocano, a language of northern Luzon, is spoken by about 16 percent. In addition, both Spain and the United States imposed their own languages; thus the educated elites have spoken Spanish or English. Virtually all of those who have immigrated to the United States have been Roman Catholics, and a majority have been Ilocano speakers.

THE *PENSIONADOS*

The first Filipino immigrants to the United States were students, the *pensionados*, who were chosen, financed, and sponsored by the U.S. government. This program, which lasted from 1903 to 1910, provided several hundred students with practical training. In 1907, for example, 183 students were reported at forty-seven American educational institutions, largely in the Midwest. The two largest enrollments were at the University of Illinois (13 percent) and Purdue (11 percent). Education attracted forty-four students; civil engineering, thirty-two; agriculture, twenty-three; mechanical engineering, nineteen; and medicine, seventeen.[2] Thousands of Filipino young men, usually underfinanced, continued to come to the United States to study. One early scholar of the Filipino American experience, Benicio T. Catapusan, himself a student who earned a Ph.D. in sociology at the University of Southern California in 1940, estimated that between 1910 and 1938 some 14,000 Filipinos had enrolled in American educational institutions. Most, for one reason or another, were never able to complete their studies, but the bulk of those who did—from institutions such as the University of California, Columbia, Cornell, Harvard, Northwestern, Stanford, the University of Washington, and Yale—returned to the Philippines to occupy important positions in government and business.[3] The majority of those who stayed in the United States usually plied the manual labor occupations that employed most Filipino Americans in those years.

One of the survivors of that experience told an interviewer in Portland, Oregon:

> When I finished high school in the Philippines I intended to study agriculture at Oregon State University. I went and looked at the campus. Then the depression came. It was hard for me to find a job. I found a job in the fraternity house, waiting tables for room and board. I was not able to continue my studies. When the depression was over, I thought I was too old. I said I would rather work. At that time we were not able—even with how educated we were—the only jobs to do were odd jobs: cooks, janitors, waiters, busboys, and farm work, but there were no white collar jobs.[4]

A surprising number of Filipino intellectuals lived and worked in America, the most notable of whom was Carlos Bulosan (1911–1956), who spent the last twenty-six years of his life here. Bulosan and others came to the United States filled with democratic ideals they had learned in American-run schools and with an unrealistic vision of what their life in the United States would be like. Thus their reaction was often bitter. As Bulosan wrote to a friend:

> Do you know what a Filipino feels in America? . . . He is the loneliest thing on earth. There is much to be appreciated . . . beauty, wealth, power, grandeur. But is he part of these luxuries? He looks, poor man, through the fingers of his eyes. He is enchained, damnably to his race, his heritage. He is betrayed, my friend.[5]

THE SECOND WAVE

But as with most other immigrants, it was economic rather than intellectual aspiration that motivated most Filipinos who came. The *Manilla Times* described it very well in 1929:

> The migrating Filipino sees no opportunity for him in the Philippines. Advertise in a Manila paper and offer a job (at below a living wage) and you will get a thousand applicants. Make the same offer in any provincial town, and the response will be twice as great, comparatively. Is it any wonder, then, that the lure of pay four to ten times as great, in Hawaii or the United States, draws the Filipino like a magnet? Plus the certainty he feels that he will get a job?[6]

The first important magnet was Hawaii, where, after the Gentlemen's Agreement of 1907–1908 made it impossible to continue to recruit male Japanese laborers, the Hawaiian Sugar Planter's Association (HSPA) began to recruit workers in the Philippines. Between 1909 and 1934, according to the careful work of Mary Dorita Clifford, the HSPA arranged for 119,470 Filipinos to come to work in their sugar fields and mills. Of these, 86.6 percent were men, 7.5 percent women, and 5.9 percent children. Most of those who came were under three-year contracts. Upon expiration of the contracts, some continued to work in Hawaii, others went back to the Philippines, and still others went on to the West Coast of the United States.[7] Table 7.1 shows the number and incidence of Filipinos in Hawaii's population.

The migration of Filipino laborers to the American mainland, either from Hawaii or directly from the Philippines, was primarily a product of the post–World War I years (see Table 7.2).

Filipino laborers occupied exactly the same niche in California agriculture as their Asian predecessors had, except that by the end of the 1930s, significant numbers of them were working for Asian American agricultural entrepreneurs, most of whom were of Japanese ethnicity. As both the

Table 7.1   Filipinos in Hawaii, 1910–1990

Year	Number	Percent of Population
1910	2,361	1.23
1920	21,031	8.22
1930	63,052	17.17
1940	52,569	12.42
1950	61,062	12.22
1960	69,070	10.91
1970	95,354	12.41
1980	109,203	13.08
1990	168,682	14.87

Source: U.S. Census.

Hawaiian and California data show, the pre–World War II Filipino migration was overwhelmingly male (94 percent in 1930).

Unlike earlier Asian immigrants, Filipinos actively sought white female companionship, and this overt sexuality enraged much white opinion. California newspapers focused on commercial dance halls, some of which catered exclusively to Filipino men, where, at 10 cents a dance of only momentary duration, an agricultural worker could spend a week's wages in an hour or two. Headlines in the *Los Angeles Times* tell the story:

> Taxi Dance Girls Start Filipinos on Wrong Foot
>
> Lonely Islanders' Quest for Woman Companionship Brings Problems of Grave National Moment
>
> Mercenary Women Influence Brown Man's Ego
>
> Minds Made Ripe for Work of Red Organizers[8]

Although the focus of nativist attention was on these transitory commercial sexual relationships—and several of the anti-Filipino riots began in

Table 7.2   Filipino American Population, 1910–1950

Year	Continental United States	California	Percent in California	Males in California	Females in California
1910	406	5	1.2	—	—
1920	5,603	2,674	47.7	—	—
1930	45,208	30,470	67.4	28,625	1,845
1940	45,876	31,408	68.5	—	—
1950	61,645	40,424	65.8	30,819	9,605

Source: U.S. Census.

and around dance halls—a significant number of more lasting interracial relationships took place. Some involved marriage, and Californians discovered, to their horror, that the existing miscegenation statutes forbade
marriages only between white persons and Negroes, mulattoes, and Mongolians. Although California Attorney General U. S. Webb, a racist of long
standing, conveniently ruled that Filipinos were Mongolians, he was reversed by the courts. So in 1933, California amended the statute to include
"members of the Malay race," and within four years, Filipino-white marriages were also forbidden in Oregon, Nevada, and Washington.[9]

We know very little about these interracial marriages in general, but
Barbara Posadas in a sensitive study has examined a number of Filipino-
white marriages in and around Chicago in the pre–World War II years. Almost all of these were marriages between Filipino men and the daughters of
eastern European immigrants; they were the foundation of a small but stable Filipino American community in Chicago, some of whose breadwinners
were Pullman porters.[10] There were clearly more such marriages in the Far
West, but no one has published findings about them.

In addition to agriculture and menial service jobs, such as dishwash-
ing, Filipino workers also played a significant role in Alaska's fish canner-
ies. Most cannery workers were recruited in Seattle, which became the
major non-California center of Filipino American population. One cannery
worker wrote in his diary for June 1924:

> Worked in the ship unloading salmon cans, at $.75 an hour. It was my first
> time in America to work. Worked exactly ten hours. Donning the overall for
> the first time in my life, handling the wheelbarrow, and carrying salmon
> boxes, was a thrill and an unforgettable experience. . . . Was laughing at the
> easy job and easy money. $7.50 for working 10 hours. In the Philippines it
> takes a month for a policeman to earn that. Such is the better prospect of life in
> this beautiful country.[11]

This worker and others soon discovered that if wages were higher, so were
living costs. They also learned that canning runs last only for the summer
months. Their involvement in the Alaska canning industry—by 1930 they
outnumbered all other ethnic groups combined by about two to one—
brought many Filipino Americans into contact with the trade union movement. More than any other Asian American group of this era, they became
involved in both union activities and radical politics. This, however, did not
stop the American Federation of Labor (AFL) from agitating for their exclusion. Starting in 1928, national AFL conventions passed a series of resolutions such as the following:

> Whereas, the desire for cheap labor has acted like a cancer . . . destroying
> American ideals and preventing the development of a nation based on racial
> unity; and
> Whereas, . . . this desire has exploited the Negro, the Chinese, the Japanese,
> the Hindus, as in turn each has been regulated and excluded; and

> Whereas, the Malays of the Philippines were in 1924 omitted from the general policy excluding all who cannot become citizens; and
>
> Whereas, there are a sufficient number of Filipinos ready and willing to come to the United States to create a race problem equal to that already here ... we urge exclusion of Filipinos also.[12]

Although labor took the lead in opposing Filipino immigration, even before the Great Depression of the 1930s stemmed the migration, a broadly based anti-Filipino movement developed in California and elsewhere on the Pacific coast. Beginning in 1929 there were anti-Filipino riots in Watsonville and other small central California cities. Civic organizations, such as the Los Angeles and northern Monterey County chambers of commerce, deplored their presence. In 1930, one California judge declared from the bench that Filipino were but ten years removed from the breechcloth. Another, after the depression had set in, insisted that "it is a dreadful thing when these Filipinos, scarcely more than savages, come to San Francisco, work for practically nothing and obtain the society of white girls. Because the Filipinos work for nothing, decent white boys cannot get jobs."[13]

In many ways the anti-Filipino agitation resembled that of previous anti-Asian movements. C. M. Goethe, a Sacramento businessman associated with the nativist Joint Immigration Committee, ignoring the absence of women in the Filipino migration, argued that 10 million American blacks were descended from "an original slave nucleus of 750,000" and insisted that "Filipinos do not hesitate to have nine children," which means "729 great-grandchildren as against the white parents' twenty-seven."[14] But, as suggested earlier, the fact that the Philippines was an American possession and Filipinos were American nationals made the majority of Congress unwilling to exclude them along with all other Asians, as a bill first introduced in 1928 proposed to do. After six years of discussion and debate and one presidential veto, Filipino immigration was tied to independence for the Philippines. The Tydings-McDuffie Act of 1934 successfully combined the two issues. The Philippines were promised independence in 1945, and, effective almost immediately, Filipinos were given an annual quota of fifty immigrants, half of the previous minimum. This was at least a small defeat for exclusionists such as Senator Hiram W. Johnson, who had wanted total exclusion.[15] Nonetheless, Filipinos remained "aliens ineligible for citizenship." To demonstrate further that Filipinos were unwanted, Congress in 1935 passed resolutions providing free passage on army transports for Filipinos desiring to return home. Although the resolution spoke of "humanitarian" considerations, its Senate sponsorship by Hiram Johnson indicated the true motives of most of its supporters. As it turned out, only 2,190 Filipinos took advantage of the offer.

For the rest of the 1930s, Filipinos, like other noncitizens, saw their relative economic status undermined. A fairly large number, 7,869 in 1930, were employed in the American merchant marine. In 1936, Congress enacted legislation mandating that 90 percent of each ship's crew be American citizens, which eliminated most Filipino jobs. Ironically, Filipinos were still allowed to serve in the U.S. Navy, where they were restricted to menial employment as mess stewards. Although the U.S. Civil Service Commission allowed Filipinos, as nationals, to take examinations for federal jobs, this was of little use to Filipino Americans who were uneducated (in Chicago there was a small group employed in the post office). Most states had laws that required that practitioners of all kinds of activities—from doctors to plumbers to barbers and hairdressers—be licensed and often insisted that all licensees be citizens. During the worst of the depression, Filipinos were barred from federal relief, until in 1937, Federal Relief Administrator Harry L. Hopkins made them eligible, but on a nonpreferential basis.

Between 1934 and the end of World War II, no significant migration from the Philippines occurred, and the heavily male Filipino population aged and declined. The onset of wartime prosperity and the removal of Japanese Americans from West Coast agriculture created economic opportunities for Filipino Americans, and the overglamorized media portrayals of all Filipinos as loyal friends of America and enemies of Japan made them, along with Chinese Americans, at least "assistant heroes" in the great Pacific war. In 1946, as a reward for this loyalty, Congress made Filipinos eligible for citizenship, and President Truman boosted the quota for the Philippines to a "normal" 100 annually.

THE THIRD WAVE

However, as was true with other groups of immigrants from Asia, non-quota immigrants—usually close relatives of U.S. citizens—far outnumbered quota immigrants. For the thirteen years of the McCarran-Walter Act, 1953–1965, when a quota of 100 was in effect and would have yielded a total of 1,300 immigrants, the Immigration and Naturalization Service recorded 32,201 Filipino immigrants. In addition, even larger numbers of nonimmigrants—tourists, businesspeople, students—were admitted, and many of these became permanent additions to the American population. In 1963, for example, 3,618 Filipino immigrant entrants were outnumbered by the arrival of 13,860 nonimmigrants. Thus in the twenty years after World War II, many more Filipinos entered the United States than in the previous half century. The scrapping of the quota system in 1965 transformed immigration from the Philippines, and in all of the years since then, the Philippines has been one of the chief suppliers of immigrants to the United States. Table 7.3 illustrates that growth and includes Filipinos on the mainland and in Hawaii.

Not only has the post-1965 immigration changed dramatically the size of the Filipino American population, but it has radically changed its composition as well. Perhaps two-thirds of the immigrants since 1965 have been of the professional classes, particularly health professionals. Filipino American nurses are the most conspicuous single group of employed Filipinos, and in part because of them, a greater percentage of Filipino American women were in the labor force in 1980 than were any other group of Asian American women. Filipino Americans had about as much education as white Americans and slightly less than East Asian Americans. But they were strikingly better educated than Filipinos who stayed in the Philippines. In 1980 just over a quarter of all Filipinos aged 25 to 29 in the islands were high school graduates; of those in the United States who were recent immigrants, the figure was almost 85 percent. The median income of Filipino American full-time workers in 1979 was $13,690, well below that of most other Asian American groups and about halfway between the wages of white American workers on the one hand and black and Hispanic workers on the other. But partly because of the greater employment of Filipino American women, only 6.2 percent of their households were in poverty, a rate below every other group (including whites) except Japanese Americans. Another reason was that recently arrived Filipino American households were larger than those of other ethnic groups. In 1980 such households contained, on average, 5.4 persons, 60 percent of whom were *not* nuclear family members. By comparison, all Filipino American households averaged only 3.6 persons, only a sixth of whom were not, as the census put it, "householder, spouse or children." Such larger household units are and have been typical of recent immigrants. Filipino Americans are highly concentrated in California and Hawaii, where in 1990 almost two-thirds of them (64 percent) lived. Of Asian American groups, only Japanese Americans were more concentrated in those two states, with 71 percent of them living there.

In common with most immigrant groups, it is the diversity of the Filipinos that is most striking. There are the first-generation old-timers, primarily males who emigrated in the 1920s. These survivors can often be found living in dingy hotel rooms in California valley towns—Stockton is one favorite—or in urban centers such as Los Angeles, San Francisco, and Honolulu. Many had lived their lives as itinerant fruit pickers; Filipino

Table 7.3   Filipinos in the United States, 1960–1990

Year	Total	Male	Female	Percent Female
1960	181,614	114,179	67,435	37.1
1970	336,731	183,175	153,556	45.6
1980	774,652	374,191	400,461	51.7
1990	1,419,711	656,765	762,946	53.7

Source: U.S. Census.

labor gangs were known for their efficiency in the fields and their strong work ethic. There was little acculturation and integration among them, except for the few who "out-married" and started family life.

The American-born second generation shared many of the problems that children of other Asian immigrants faced: a lack of social acceptance, low income, negative self-image. In contrast to some of the other Asian groups, there was little encouragement to obtain higher education. Even those who wanted to go to college frequently found the financial burdens an obstacle. Further, they knew little about the roots of their culture and yet could not gain full acceptance into the mainstream. Questions of an identity and some understanding of their role in America became major preoccupations during the civil rights struggles of the 1970s. It is also interesting to note that when Asian Americans were deemed ineligible for affirmative action consideration by the University of California system in the 1980s, protests were mounted, and the Filipinos were then included in such programs.

World War II veterans made up another important element in the community. Many had arrived in their adult years, most with impressive-sounding diplomas that did not qualify them for much in the new country. They had served with the Filipino Scouts during World War II or as mess stewards in the U.S. Navy; they had lived under armed forces discipline and shared a mixture of high patriotism and a naive view of life in America. Although life in the United States was marginal—poor housing, low-status jobs, and minimal income—it was deemed better than what they could have expected in the Philippines. Acculturation and participation in the American mainstream were minimal. Many continued to retain close ties with the Philippines and to live within their own cultural network.

The newly arrived make up the bulk of the current Filipino population. As with the other fast-growing Asian groups, their numbers are the result of the 1965 immigration legislation. Reasons behind their immigration are familiar—unstable economic and political conditions in the home country, family reunification, and the expectation of better economic and educational opportunities in the new country. Many come with advanced training—medical degrees are common—and some are able to continue their careers. Many others, however, find difficulty in obtaining jobs commensurate with their past background. Filipino lawyers may find work as clerks; teachers, as secretaries; dentists, as dental aides; and engineers, as mechanics. Still, a low-paying job in America often pays more than a higher-status job in the home country.[16]

Alfredo Munoz's study of the adaptation of the Filipinos contrasted the different lifestyles and the subsequent transformation in the new country.[17] Whereas a more leisurely pace would be appropriate in the Philippines, immigrants learn that the American style calls for work with a vengeance. Moonlighting becomes a new way of life; the goal of making money and retiring in the Philippines has become popular.

The new immigrants face a variety of problems, including education, finances, unemployment, child guidance, and the elderly. Culture shock, racism, credentials, and licensing are other issues.[18] Perhaps the major problem of the Filipinos has been their lack of cohesion. There are island differences, different languages, ideological rifts, and subgroup cultures that separate the community. It appears difficult to form a unified Filipino organization because of the strength of local groups and their competing loyalties. Filipino organizations tend to multiply rather than to unify.[19]

Tania Azores studied Filipino high school seniors in the 1980s and found that a very high percentage had aspirations for a college education.[20] However, many of them lacked the grades. Azores suggested three possible reasons for this dilemma:

1. Filipino students have unrealistic expectations.
2. High aspirations may not be linked to personal commitment.
3. Students may feel that there are characteristics other than grades that define a good student.

Her findings contradict a commonly held belief that many Filipino Americans do not aspire toward higher education.

Pyong Gap Min compared Filipinos and Koreans in terms of their orientation toward small business.[21] Koreans turned to small business because of language difficulties and other disadvantages in the labor market, whereas Filipinos, who were less disadvantaged in language and were more familiar with American practices, were able to bypass the small-business model. Koreans also had the availability of family and other kinship networks for the intensive labor often required in small business; there were also such factors as the industrialization of South Korea and import-export ties. In contrast, the English-speaking Filipinos, especially those with degrees in medicine and nursing, can find employment relatively easily outside the ethnic community.

Nevertheless, when looking at the group as a whole, Filipinos suffer from economic inequality. Researchers analyzed the status of Filipino Americans in California.[22] Using the 1980 census, they found that Filipinos remained in a subordinated position in relation to other Asians and the white majority, whether "sailors or professionals, educated or less educated, skilled or unskilled." They were often clustered in the secondary labor market, where the pay is low and mobility is limited.

MEDICAL PROFESSIONALS

A very large percentage of the women who have been the dominant group among post-1965 immigrants from the Philippines have been nurses and, to a lesser degree, occupational therapists trained in the Philippines. In the

United States they are most likely to work in relatively low-paying entry-level jobs in public hospitals. Although English is the second language of the Philippines, many immigrants have had on-the-job difficulties because of language deficiencies, and in 1998 American immigration authorities began to require that these professionals pass English-language examinations such as the TOEFL (Test of English as a Foreign Language), the TWE (Test of Written English), and the TSE (Test of Spoken English) to get the "green card" necessary for legal employment or, in the case of nurses already established in the United States, to have their green cards renewed.

Dexter B. Rosario, a Los Angeles-based immigration lawyer, has established an English-language review school in Manila to prep nurses for these examinations. The tuition is expensive by Philippine standards; in addition, they must pay a total of $225 to take the tests. Once certified in English, these women can begin at $16.75 an hour in Los Angeles, with lots of overtime. Rosario claims:

> A lot of nurses own big homes in Los Angeles, earning more than their husbands do, living very comfortably. There are the middle-aged nurses, with a lot of experience and continuing education, with therefore higher rates. $45 an hour is ordinary for them. . . . [23]

Filipino doctors, many of them with some U.S. training, have been among the beneficiaries of the 1994 American law that allows foreign-born, noncitizen physicians to stay in the United States after their student visas expire if they agree to practice in areas without enough medical staff. In 1998 some 22,000—almost a fifth—of the 104,000 medical residents training in U.S. hospitals come from other countries. Most come here on visas that require them to leave at the end of their training, presumably to apply their medical knowledge back home. The 1994 law gives each applying state twenty such immigration waivers annually and thirty-eight states have taken advantage of it. Minnesota, for example, has used forty-eight waivers since 1994 and in 1999 used all twenty of its waivers for the first time. One of the twenty was Dr. Rommel Aquino, a Philippine-born family-practice physician, to Duluth, Minnesota's Bay Area Health Center.

Aquino is just one of perhaps 150,000 foreign-born doctors practicing in the United States in 1998. They represented about a quarter of the 600,000 physicians in America. The Philippines, along with India and Pakistan, furnished the largest contingents of foreign doctors. Many of these doctors work in places that most American-born physicians shun, and, on average, earn significantly less than American-born doctors but much more than they could earn in their home countries. In addition, their families live in a more secure and more advantageous environment.[24]

EFFECTS ON THE PHILIPPINES

A few Filipino Americans have arrived as political exiles in recent decades, largely exiles from the dictatorship of Ferdinand E. Marcos, who ruled the Philippines from 1965 to 1986. Most prominent of these exiles were Benigno S. Aquino and his wife, Corazon. Benigno returned to the Philippines to lead the opposition to Marcos but was assassinated, with apparent government complicity, upon his arrival at the Manila airport on August 21, 1983. His wife then took up the reform cause and daringly challenged the dictator. Although she was counted out in an election, she was so clearly the winner that Marcos and his wife, Imelda, were forced to flee into exile outside Honolulu.

Despite some political reforms and a popular government under "Cory" Aquino and her successor, the same lack of economic opportunity for educated persons that led hundreds of thousands of Filipinos to emigrate in past years continues to prevail. Only a minority of these immigrants—50,000 to 60,000 a year during the 1990s—could get to the United States, while another 10,000 went to Canada. Most of the rest go to Asian countries where wages and working conditions are far from ideal. But these overseas workers provide, by their remittances home, some $6 billion annually to the Philippines, about 3 percent of the nation's gross domestic product.

POLITICAL PROGRESS

In 1994, for the first time, a Filipino American won a major political office. Benjamin J. Cayetano (b. 1939) got married just after high school and moved to Los Angeles. Commenting later about his early life in Hawaii, he noted that he had "never met a Caucasian who wasn't a boss." In California he earned a B.A. at UCLA and a law degree at Loyola University in 1971. Returning to Hawaii, he moved steadily up the political ladder, serving two terms in the Hawaiian House of Representatives, two terms in the state senate, and two terms as lieutenant governor, before winning the governor's chair in 1994. He was reelected in 1998. A winner of eight consecutive elections in a multiracial state, he explained his formula for political success:

> The only way to overcome the racial issue is to find common ground. . . . My campaigns have always been mixed—issue-oriented and performance-based. . . . My advice for candidates is to run a broad-based campaign for all the people. I've seen Filipino candidates run for office spending time only in the Filipino community and the result is predictable—defeat.[25]

THE FUTURE OF FILIPINO AMERICANS

By the year 2000 Filipinos, who had been very little in the mainstream press, had become the most numerous Asian American group. As long as American immigration laws remain roughly the same and the economic and social conditions in the Philippines stay as they are or deteriorate, similarly high levels of Filipino immigration may be expected.

Surely the growing numbers of American-born children of the middle class and professional immigrants will play a larger role in twenty-first century America than their predecessors played in the twentieth. The nature of that role is yet to be determined.

NOTES

1. Marina E. Espina, *Readings on Filipinos in Louisiana* (privately printed, ca. 1982).

2. Barbara M. Posadas, *The Filipino Americans* (Westport, CT: Greenwood Press, 1999), is the best account.

3. Benecio T. Catapusan, "The Social Adjustment of Filipinos in the United States" (Ph.D. dissertation, University of Southern California, 1940).

4. Quoted in Tricia Knoll, *Becoming Americans* (Portland, OR: Coast to Coast Books, 1982), p. 100.

5. Carlos Bulosan, "Selected Letters of Carlos Bulosan," *Amerasia Journal* 6 (1979): 143. For a more recent work on Bulosan, see Susan Evangelista, *Carlos Bulosan and His Poetry: A Biography and Anthology* (Seattle: University of Washington Press, 1985).

6. Quoted in Bruno Lasker, *Filipino Immigration to the Continental United States and Hawaii* (Chicago: University of Chicago Press, 1931), p. 233.

7. Mary Dorita Clifford, "The Hawaiian Sugar Planter Association and Filipino Exclusion," in J. M. Saniel, ed., *The Filipino Exclusion Movement, 1927–1935* (Quezon City: University of the Philippines, 1967), pp. 11–29.

8. *Los Angeles Times,* Feb. 2, 1930, p. 1.

9. Melendy, *Asians in America: Filipinos, Koreans and East Indians* (Boston: Twayne, 1977), p. 53.

10. Barbara M. Posadas, "Crossed Boundaries in Interracial Chicago: Filipino American Families since 1925," *Amerasia Journal* 8 (1981): 31–52. See also Barbara M. Posadas, "The Hierarchy of Color: Filipino Immigrants, the Pullman Company and the Brotherhood of Sleeping Car Porters," *Labor History* 23 (1982): 349–373.

11. Diary, Victorio A. Velasco Collection, University of Washington Archives, Seattle.

12. American Federation of Labor, *Proceedings* (Washington, DC, 1928).

13. *San Francisco Chronicle,* Jan. 22, 1936. See also Howard A. DeWitt, "The Watsonville Anti-Filipino Riot of 1930: A Case Study of the Great Depression and Ethnic Conflict in California," *Southern California Quarterly* 61 (1979): 291–302.

14. C. M. Goethe, "Filipino Immigration Viewed as a Peril," *Current History* (January 1934): 354.

15. For details, see Robert A. Divine, *American Immigration Policy, 1924–1952* (New Haven, CT: Yale University Press, 1957), pp. 68–76.

16. Fred Cordova, "The Filipino American: There's Always an Identity Crisis," in Stanley Sue and Nathaniel Wagner, eds., *Asian Americans* (Palo Alto, CA: Science and Behavior Books, 1973), pp. 136–139.

17. Alfredo N. Munoz, *The Filipinos in the United States* (Los Angeles: Mountainview Publishers, 1971).

18. Royal F. Morales, *Makibaba* (Los Angeles: Mountainview Publishers, 1974).

19. H. Brett Melendy, "Filipinos," in Stephan Thernstrom et al., eds., *The Harvard Encyclopedia of American Ethnic Groups* (Cambridge, MA: Harvard University Press, 1980), pp. 354–362.

20. Tania Azores, "Educational Attainment and Upward Mobility: Prospects for Filipino Americans," *Amerasia Journal* 13, 1 (1986): 39–52.

21. Pyong Gap Min, "Filipino and Korean Immigrants in Small Business: A Comparative Analysis," *Amerasia Journal* 13, 1 (1986): 53–71.

22. Amado Cabezas, Larry H. Shinagawa, and Gary Kawaguchi, "New Inquiries into the Socioeconomic Status of Filipino Americans in California," *Amerasia Journal* 13, 1 (1986): 1–21.

23. "Many Filipino Nurses Lack English Proficiency," *Business World* (Philippines), December 29, 1999.

24. Melanie Evans, "Foreign doctor waiver program popular: Minnesota, Wisconsin having success with plan allowing physicians serving in underserved areas to stay," Duluth *News-Tribune*, October 7, 1999; Jonathan Bor, "Tide turning for doctors from abroad," Baltimore *Sun*, August 4, 1998.

25. Posadas, *Filipino Americans*, pp. 154–55. For an example of successful Asian American multiethnic politics on the local level in California, see Leland Saito, *Race and Politics: Asian Americans, Latinos, and Whites in a Los Angeles Suburb.* (Urbana: University of Illinois Press, 1998).

Chapter 8

SOUTH ASIANS

Asian Indians, Pakistanis, and Bangladeshis

This history of peoples from South Asia in the United States may most readily be divided into two parts. A relatively small number came during the period when most of South Asia was a part of the British Empire. Up until independence in 1947 perhaps 10,000 or so came, mostly in the years around 1900. Many more have come since then, and by 2000 there were well over a million South Asians in the United States, most of them from India, with a considerably smaller number from Pakistan, and much smaller numbers from Bangladesh and other nations of the region.[1]

BACKGROUND

Although there were a few Indian seamen reported in New England in the late eighteenth century and tiny communities of Indian merchants were established in the eastern United States from the mid-nineteenth century on, statistically significant migration of Indians began just after 1900. Like most other Asian immigrants at that time, they came on trans-Pacific ships, usually via Hong Kong, as there was no direct passenger service between India and the West Coast. Although the first sizable group of Indian immigrants—a few hundred—came to the Pacific Northwest after landing at Vancouver, British Columbia, California became the goal of most of the early Indian immigrants.

India is a huge country with dozens of distinct and diverse ethnic groups, but, as was the case with immigrants from China, most early Indian immigrants came from just one region, the Punjab, a prosperous fertile region of North India. The Punjab, unlike most of the areas from which other Asians immigrated, is not a coastal region. Because of the advanced railroad network—one of the few positive achievements of the British rule in India—Punjabi immigrants could get to seaports quickly, cheaply, and safely.

The overwhelming majority of these Indians were Sikhs, although some Hindus and a few Muslims immigrated as well. Sikhism, which developed in the Punjab early in the sixteenth century, was an attempt to reconcile Muslim and Hindu in a region that was then and still is multiethnic. By the eighteenth century, the Sikhs had become implacable enemies of the Muslims and had become a largely military caste in which all members took the name Singh (Lion). At that time the still-current practices that give the Sikhs high visibility were adopted: wearing turbans, wearing a dagger and an iron bracelet at all times, and never cutting the hair or beard. Modern Sikh life is dominated by the Akali Dal (Army of God) movement, which demands the creation of a Sikh state in the Punjab.

ON THE WEST COAST

The early Sikh migrants to California, perhaps 5,000 strong, were first employed in lumbering and railroad work but soon turned to agriculture, initially as laborers and later as proprietors and tenants. In two areas of the state, the Imperial Valley in the south and the Sacramento Valley in the north, they became a numerically significant minority. They experienced the same kinds of legal and extralegal discriminations as did other Asians. The alien land laws, for example, were used against them. While a few racist Californians saw the East Indians, as they were usually called, as superior to other Asians, others saw them as "the least desirable race of immigrants thus far admitted to the United States." Immigration records showed some 5,800 East Indian immigrants entering between 1901 and 1911, only 109 of them female.

Despite the very small number of women, large numbers of the Asian Indian migrants appear to have been married. One Immigration Commission survey—the only one we have for this period—questioned 474 laborers working on the West Coast. Slightly more than half said that they were married, but in every instance reported that the wife was "abroad." This was a pattern common to all Asian working men on this continent, a condition sociologists have called "mutilated marriage." Large numbers of these men planned to be sojourners, that is, work here for a time, save some money, and send it home to buy land. According to H. A. Millis, the first scholar to study East Indians in America, $2,000 was the goal of many. Since agricultural laborers could expect to save, at best, between $15 and $25 a month, and since, even assuming continuous employment, it would take seven to eleven years to amass such a sum, most sojourners were bound to be frustrated. Yet savings did occur, and money was remitted to India. The Marysville, California, post office, for example, in an area in which many Indians worked, reported that in one eight-month period ending in mid-1908, $34,000 in postal remittances were sent to India. How many immigrants sent money home? No one knows. The Immigration Commission interviewed seventy-nine millhands in Washington and California in early 1909. Thirty-one of them—about 40 percent—said that in the previous year they had sent a total of $4,320 to India, an average of nearly $140 for each of those who sent but only about $55 for the whole group.[2]

MANGOO RAM (1886–1980)

Many immigrants who were not Sikhs were, like the Sikhs, Punjabis. It is very difficult to imagine what life was like for these toilers, rural proletarians in California's factories in the field, but thanks to Mark Juergensmeyer, we do know a great deal about one of them, a man named Mangoo Ram, who was born a Hindu on January 14, 1886, in the Punjab. His father had left the traditional Chamar caste occupation of tanning hides and had become a hide merchant. First taught in his village, Mangoo Ram later attended a number of district schools. As the only scheduled caste student in most of his schools, he had to sit in the back of the classroom or sometimes in a separate room listening through an open door. When he attended high school, he had to stay outside of the building and listen through an open window.

Mangoo Ram left school in 1905, married, and worked for his father for three years. In 1909 in the Punjab, as Juergensmeyer puts it, "America was in the air." Scores of upper-caste farmers from Mangoo Ram's part of the Punjab had gone there. It was arranged for him to go, too. There was a tight network. The labor contractor for whom Mangoo Ram first worked in the orchards of central California was the brother of a local landlord in the Punjab. Part of Mangoo Ram's passage was paid by the contractor, who took it, plus interest, out of the young man's wages. This was quite similar to the credit-ticket system pioneered by the Chinese in the mid-nineteenth century. In California, Mangoo Ram picked fruit in orchards up and down the central valley and worked in a sugar mill.

Mangoo Ram's life was very much like other sojourners until 1913, when he became someone special. In that year he joined the revolutionary Gadar movement in San Francisco, and from then until his death in 1980 at age 94 he was a figure in Indian history. For his activities during World War I as what we would now call a freedom fighter—the British called him a terrorist—he was sentenced to death. He escaped from prison and, after a sojourn in the Philippines, made his way back to the Punjab only in 1925. There he helped form the Ad Dharm movement of untouchables in 1926.

Unlike most early Indian immigrants, Mangoo Ram was not an anonymous individual. As Juergensmeyer indicates, his sixteen years abroad helped transform him, as, of course, did his education. While abroad he was treated as an individual, not as a Chamar. The hostility to all East Indians in America tended to blur differences within the immigrant community; in addition, as Ram himself puts it, within the Gadar movement "we were treated as equals."[3]

THE GADAR MOVEMENT

The tragic and quixotic story of the Gadar movement, often referred to by American historians as the Hindu Conspiracy, must be considered briefly here. While Gadar was special and violent in its aims and involved only a small minority of the Indian immigrants in America, almost all of them were, in one way or another, involved in or at least sympathetic to the Indian freedom movement. Gadar—the name may be translated as "revolution" or "mutiny"—was nothing less than an attempt to overthrow the Raj from a base in San Francisco. It was founded in San Francisco in 1911 by Har Dayal, a brilliant young Indian scholar who had resigned a British government scholarship at Oxford University to undertake revolutionary activity in the United States. He was a radical who had been an officer of the syndicalist Industrial Workers of the World. Gadar was primarily an organization of young intellectuals and students. These Indian students—by 1913 there were thirty-seven at the University of California at Berkeley alone—formed the backbone of the freedom organization here, although later this role was taken over by merchants and established farmers and ranchers.

With the outbreak of World War I, the Gadarites, who used both romantic and socialist rhetoric, citing Mazzini and Marx, began to receive financial support from the German government. Almost from the beginning, the movement had been penetrated by British moles and agents provocateurs; in the final analysis, the conspiracy here had no chance even to strike a blow, much less topple the Raj. The San Francisco Gadarites managed to charter two vessels in California and tried to get them loaded with arms purchased in Mexico, intending to sail to India to start an armed revolt, another mutiny. In addition, perhaps as many as 400 Asian Indians left North America and, by various routes, returned to India to foment revolution. Almost all were apprehended; many were executed. One vessel, without arms aboard, got as far as Java.

There were also less radical groups of Asian Indians working for free-dom here in those years. One such peaceful organization, formed in New York in 1918, was the India Home Rule League. For the next three decades—until Indian independence was achieved—one or more patriotic organizations existed in the Indo-American community. It must be recognized that in those days the United States was not thought of as a bastion of suppressive regimes throughout the world and that only the United States had an established revolutionary tradition. Many Asian revolutionaries of that era, including Sun Yat-sen and two of the leading Asian members of the Communist International, Japan's Sen Katayama and India's M. N. Roy, spent some time in the United States as either agitators or settlers.[4]

THE STRUGGLE FOR CITIZENSHIP

World War I all but stopped Indian immigration, and in 1917 the U.S. Congress, as part of an immigration act whose most heralded feature was a largely ineffective literacy test, excluded almost all Asians and all East Indians by means of a so-called barred zone, expressed in degrees of latitude and longitude. That exclusion was not total; skilled professionals, ministers, religious teachers, students, and travelers for pleasure were largely exempt from its provisions. In any event, from 1914 to 1946 there was no sizable immigration of East Indians.

As we have seen, the U.S. naturalization statutes had made Asians "aliens ineligible for citizenship." In the *Ozawa* case of 1922, the Supreme Court had ruled unanimously that "white persons" in the 1870 statute meant persons of the Caucasian race. In 1923 a case brought by Bhagat Singh Thind came before the Court. Thind, a Sikh who had been granted citizenship by a federal court in Oregon, was denied citizenship by the Supreme Court even though, as a Caucasian, he passed the test set up by *Ozawa*. The Court, speaking through Justice George Sutherland, now held that the word "white" in the 1870 statute meant "white" in the "understanding of the common man." Whatever we may think of the result, it is clear that in *Thind* the Court was adhering to the intent of Congress.

The *Thind* decision meant that Indian farmers were still subject to the provisions of alien land laws in California and other western states. As one Indian immigrant, who nevertheless became a very successful California rancher, remembered it years later:

> It was made quite evident that people from Asia—the Japanese, Chinese and Hindus—were not wanted. . . . A friend of mine, a property owner in the Imperial County, helped me by holding my lease contracts in his name. . . . I had also leased some property in my wife's name since she was an American citizen. However some landowners didn't like to take a chance on leasing land even to an Asiatic's wife for fear of violating the Alien Land Act.[5]

Thus for a variety of reasons, the Asian Indian population of California—and of the nation as a whole—declined precipitously from its pre–World War I high of perhaps 10,000. The census, notoriously inaccurate for minority populations generally, could find only 1,873 persons born in India in California in 1930 and 1,476 in 1940. Since hardly any of the agricultural laborers and entrepreneurs who dominated this small population had come with wives, the majority of those who stayed were "bachelors." Yet, as Bruce La Brack and Karen Leonard have demonstrated, a significant number of these California agriculturalists did get married, and these small communities demonstrate patterns of acculturation worth noting.

La Brack and Leonard have tracked and reconstituted almost 400 Asian Indian families in California before 1946, mostly in the Imperial and Sacramento valleys. Of these marriages only nine—fewer than 2.5 percent—seem to have been with Asian Indian women. The overwhelming majority, some 80 percent, were with Hispanic women, most of whom were from Mexican and Mexican American migratory worker families. Frequently, the Hispanic marriage partners had picked cotton or had done other work on the men's farms. Such a bride often moved into an established male household consisting of her husband and several Punjabi immigrants. Surviving wives often speak of the men's "single-minded concentration" on putting their resources into farming. Often immigrant—and perhaps bigamous—husbands were simultaneously sending remittances to a family in India. There was a tendency for sisters to marry partners, so many households contained related women.

Not surprisingly, these marriages were conflict ridden. In Imperial County, for example, at least a fifth of them ended in formal divorce, with husbands and wives filing in roughly equal proportions. The men's petitions stress neglect of duty, refusal to cook and clean for the husband's friends, verbal disobedience, too much visiting of mothers and sisters, shopping in town, using makeup, and dancing with other men. The women complained that their husbands drank, beat them, committed adultery, and demanded unreasonable services. Leonard also investigated 220 marriages of children resulting from Asian Indian–Mexican marriages; only eleven of them involved two "Mexican-Hindu" partners.[6]

It is necessary to contrast these Asian Indian–Mexican American marriages with the kinds of marriage patterns that tended to develop in other contemporaneous American immigrant communities. Very large numbers of these latter immigrants lived in ethnic enclaves; although men greatly outnumbered women in these enclaves, there were usually enough women that a majority—often a very large majority—of marriages were intraethnic. Among most other immigrants from Asia, but particularly among those from Japan, enough women were able to immigrate, and a pattern of intraethnic marriage prevailed in those communities as well. The only other group of Asian immigrants of this era for whom a pattern of extraethnic marriage has been reported is the Filipinos. As noted in Chapter 7, Barbara Posadas described with great sensitivity the marriages of Chicago Filipino immigrants with first- and second-generation daughters of eastern European immigrants.[7]

IN THE EAST AND THE MIDWEST

Smaller Asian Indian communities were developing in New York and other eastern and midwestern cities. Most of the few hundred members of these communities were merchants and middle-class professionals; ethnically most were Hindu, with a sprinkling of Sikhs and Muslims. Almost all were involved, in one way or another, in the struggle for freedom in India. They founded a surprisingly large number of organizations, which were generally peaceful and legal. The most spectacularly successful was the India League of America, whose leading figure was J. J. Singh, a Sikh merchant with a talent for public relations and lobbying. Singh was able to exploit two very different streams of sympathy for India that existed in the minds of many Americans and were wholly unrelated to immigration. One stream was religious and cultural; the other, political.

Although it is traditional to begin discussions of American perceptions of Hinduism with the Swami Vivekananda's dramatic appearance at the World Parliament of Religions held in conjunction with the Chicago World's Fair of 1893, Carl Jackson has shown that the roots of sympathy can be traced back, however tenuously, to the seventeenth century. And it is important to note that sympathy was a two-way current. If Emerson, and through him Thoreau, were influenced by Eastern thought—however misperceived—Thoreau, in particular, was a strong influence on Gandhi, who in turn provided much of the inspiration for Dr. Martin Luther King's philosophy of nonviolent change.[8]

Vivekananda and a small group of successors, the most important of whom was the Swami Yoganananda, who first came in 1920, established small but influential Western outposts of Hindu religious thought in America through organizations like the former's Vedanta Society and the latter's Self-Realization Fellowship. Unlike the contemporary Hare Krishna movement, membership in these societies did not involve public begging or other "outlandish" behavior. Most of their members, who probably numbered in the low thousands, were drawn from middle- and upper-middle-class Protestants. In addition, many secular movers and shakers from India also visited the United States, although a much-discussed visit by Gandhi never materialized. Of particular importance were the several visits by the Bengali poet and Nobel laureate Rabindranath Tagore, who first came here in 1916. On a later visit he had some celebrated difficulties with American immigration officials, who treated him as if he were attempting to come in as a la-

borer. Tagore was an important influence on many moderate Indian reform-
ers here, as marked by the establishment of Tagore Societies on both coasts.[9]

The political sympathy was largely an outgrowth of the American tradition of anticolonialism and was often abetted by strong anti-British feelings on the part of American ethnocultural groups, particularly Irish and
German Americans. During the years between the two world wars, many
American "progressives" adopted an isolationist stance and used anticolonial rhetoric as one argument against an Anglo-American alliance. But some
internationalists were anticolonialists, too. As William Roger Louis has
demonstrated, few issues so divided Franklin D. Roosevelt and Winston
Churchill as the future of India.[10]

Singh and other pro-Indian lobbyists utilized both these streams of
sympathy. The Sikh import merchant had been born into an elite family in
Rawalpindi in 1897 and came to the United States in 1926. In a perhaps
overadmiring profile of him in *The New Yorker* in 1951, Robert Shaplen
wrote:

> Sirdar Jagjit Singh, the president of the India League of America, a privately
> sponsored organization that seeks to interpret India to, and to further Indian
> causes in, this country, is, at fifty-three, a handsome six-foot Sikh who by
> means of persistent salesmanship, urbane manners, and undeviating enthusi-
> asm, has established himself as the principal link between numberless Ameri-
> cans and the vast mysterious Eastern subcontinent where he was born.[11]

By the time Shaplen wrote, Singh had already engineered his greatest
triumph, the passage through Congress of the Act of July 2, 1946, which
gave the right of naturalization and a small immigration quota to "persons
of races indigenous to India." This act followed by less than three years the
repeal of Chinese exclusion (see Chapter 4) and was accompanied by a similar dispensation for Filipinos, but not for other Asians, who remained until
1952 "aliens ineligible for citizenship."

THE 1946 ACT

Had not the 1946 act—and the even more important 1952 and 1965 acts—
drastically changed the patterns of immigration from Asia, the "circuitous
assimilation" of Asian Indian immigrants and their children would probably have continued. But the renewed postwar immigration rejuvenated established communities. La Brack has carefully documented these changes
for the northern Sacramento Valley. There, a population of 400 aging Punjabi Sikhs in 1950 swelled, by immigration of persons of both sexes and by
natural increase, to more than 6,200 by 1981.[12]

Obviously, the 1946 law did not, as some of its opponents had predicted, result in a "flood" of immigrants from India. The immigration data

show that fewer than 7,000 "East Indians" entered the United States in the seventeen years between 1948 and 1965. Almost 6,000 were nonquota immigrants, mostly close relatives of persons who were or became American citizens. Since the Asian Indian population base was so small in the United States, the rights of naturalization and immigration did not have the numerical impact as did the granting of similar rights to Japanese Americans in 1952. With its much larger population base, that community attracted, as we have seen, more than 40,000 new immigrants between 1952 and 1960.

The most spectacular individual Asian Indian beneficiary of the 1946 act was Dalip Singh Saund. Born in 1899 just outside Amritsar, the holy Sikh city in the Punjab, into a family headed by an illiterate but well-to-do contractor, Saund graduated with a degree in mathematics from Punjab University. Shocked by the Amritsar massacre (1919) in which British troops fired repeatedly into a crowd of peaceful protesters, killing hundreds and wounding thousands, and attracted by what he had read about America, Saund resisted his parents' wishes that he enter government service and came to the United States, via England, in 1920. He entered the University of California, living, rent free, in a "clubhouse" just off the Berkeley campus that had been established and maintained for Indian students by the Sikh Temple of Stockton, California. Saund eventually earned three degrees: an M.A. and a Ph.D. in mathematics and, more practically, an M.S. in agricultural science, specializing in food preservation. He was offered professorships by two Indian universities, but he decided to make America his home.

Despite his education, Saund soon concluded that "the only way that Indians in California could make a living" was to join with compatriots who were successful in farming. So he settled in California's Imperial Valley, working first as a foreman on a cotton ranch operated by Indian friends— surely the only agricultural straw boss ever with a Ph.D. in math!—and then became a rancher and a businessman. He was determined to acculturate— he had begun shaving and stopped wearing a turban shortly after he came here—and in 1928 he married a woman from an upper-middle-class Czech American family. Well established in the farming center of Westmoreland, he and his wife became involved in a whole panoply of civic activities, including the twin causes of Indian independence and citizenship for Asian Indians in the United States.

Shortly after he was able to become a citizen, Saund was elected to a local judgeship, and in 1956 he was elected to Congress as a Democrat in a race that attracted national attention not only because of Saund's origin but also because his opponent was a famous aviator, Jacqueline Cochran Odum. Taking office in January 1957, Saund became the first Asian American congressperson. Saund's election caused a small sensation and was exploited by the United States Information Agency, which soon sent him on a tour of Asia as evidence of the growth of ethnic democracy in the United States. He was twice reelected but was defeated in 1962 after a stroke confined him to a hospital bed.[13]

THE STRUCTURE OF THE ASIAN INDIAN COMMUNITY

The great changes in the Asian Indian community have come since 1965. Rather than reinforce old communities or increase the status of members of the immigrant elite, that migration has created a new community, one that has few connections in ethnicity, class, occupation, or location with the majority of its early twentieth-century predecessors. These new immigrants have *not* been predominantly Sikhs, have *not* entered agriculture, and are *not* concentrated in the Far West.

By 1970 there were perhaps 75,000 Asian Indians in the United States, of whom fewer than a third represented the older communities and their natural expansion. At the first scholarly conference examining the new Asian Indian immigration, held in Chicago in 1976, it was predicted that the 1980 census might show as many as 250,000 persons of Indian origin.[14] That census—the first specifically to ask about Indian nationality and ethnicity and the first to denominate them "Asian Indians"—in fact found nearly 390,000. As noted, the 1990 census reported more than 815,000 Asian Indians, a growth of more than 1,000 percent in twenty years. To put the figures for 1990 into perspective, about every ninth Asian American was either an immigrant from India or the offspring of such a person.

Statistically, these Asian Indians present a profile somewhat different from that of Asian Americans generally. In 1990, when nearly 52 percent of Asian Americans lived in the Far West, only 21 percent of Asian Indians did. Part of this disparity was due to the fact that there is no significant Asian Indian community in Hawaii, but it was also because Asian Indians were more evenly distributed throughout the nation. A third of Asian Indians lived in the Northeast, and almost a quarter each lived in the South and Midwest. In age, Asian Indians were above the national median—34.8 years as opposed to the national 33.0—whereas all other Asian American groups except Japanese Americans were younger (from Chinese at 32.3 years to Hmong at 12.4 years). In terms of sex ratio, the once predominantly male Asian Indian migration has become more balanced, and there were 116.7 males per 100 females in 1990.

Asian Indian women, like almost all other Asian American women, have demonstrated significantly lower fertility than American women generally. In 1980 age-standardized rates for Asian Indian women, for example, showed 1,224 children per 1,000 women aged 15 to 44, compared to 1,358 for white women, a national figure of 1,429, and black and Hispanic figures of 1,806 and 1,817, respectively.[15] What these data reflect, as far as Asian Indian women are concerned, is class rather than ethnicity, education rather than national origin. The overwhelming number of Asian Indian women of childbearing age were foreign born.

The 1990 census indicated that of adult Asian Indians in this country, a startling 58 percent were college graduates, compared to 37 percent of all Asian Americans age 25 and older. The figure for all Americans of that age group was 20 percent.

An occupational profile of the Asian Indian population shows that 47 percent of foreign-born workers in the group were managers, professionals, and executives, as opposed to about half that—24 percent—for the white population. Even though many of these were not particularly well-compensated proprietors, the median income of full-time Asian Indian workers was reported as $18,079 in 1979, higher than the figure for whites or for any other Asian American group. The next most prosperous individuals, Japanese Americans, earned $2,000 less. Asian Indian family income, however, while ahead of that of whites, was close to the Asian American norm and lower than that for Japanese Americans because a significantly smaller percentage of Asian Indian women were in the labor force. For the group that the census calls "female family householders," only 58.2 percent of Asian Indian women were in the labor force, as opposed to 72.5 percent of such Japanese American women.

At the other end of the economic spectrum, Asian Indian families were very unlikely to receive public assistance; only 4.5 percent of these families received assistance in 1979. Only they among recent Asian immigrant groups had a figure below that for whites, which was 5.9 percent. Public assistance was received by 6.2 percent of Korean families, 6.6 percent of Chinese families, 10 percent of Filipino families, and 28.1 percent of Vietnamese families. (The last figure was higher than that for Hispanics, 15.9 percent, and blacks, 22.3 percent.) Incomplete data indicate that welfare dependence for immigrant groups goes down sharply with extended residence in the United States.

Data on Asian Indian families below the federal poverty line indicate this quite clearly. For all Asian Indian families with foreign-born wage earners (the vast majority of all Asian Indian families) only 5 percent were below the poverty line, a figure lower than that for the foreign-born of any other Asian American group. For those who emigrated before 1970, the Asian Indian poverty rate was 2.2 percent of all families; for those who came between 1970 and 1975, the figure was 3.2 percent; and for those arriving between 1975 and 1980, the poverty rate was 10.7 percent.

Asian Indian families seem remarkably stable. In 1980, for example, 92.7 percent of all Asian Indian children under 18 years of age lived in a two-parent household, a figure higher than that for any other Asian American group and significantly higher than that for white Americans, which was 82.9 percent. Asian Indian households tended to be small—2.9 persons on average—but, not surprisingly, households of recent immigrants were larger. In 1980, Asian Indian households composed of post-1975 immigrants had an average of 3.5 persons. Forty-five percent of the persons in these households were not members of one nuclear family; for all Asian Indian households such persons amounted to only 9 percent of the members.

Nathan Glazer has characterized the Asian Indian population as being "marked off by a high level of education, by concentration in the professions, by a strong commitment to maintaining family connections, both here in the United States and between the United States and India."[16] Parmatma Saran, on the basis of a 1977–1978 survey of 345 Asian Indian residents in the New York metropolitan area, has written, perhaps too sweepingly, about the Asian Indian experience in the United States. However, since New York had the largest single concentration of Asian Indians—68,000 persons (17.5 percent in 1980), with another 31,000 (7.9 percent) in New Jersey—that region is certainly not unrepresentative of the whole.

In Saran's sample, 73 percent of the men in the labor force could be classified as technical or professional. Among Asian Indian women in his sample, the profile was similarly high; nearly half—47 percent—were professional and technical.[17] The overwhelming majority of these people were recent immigrants who received all or most of their training in India, and thus they were part of what is often called the brain drain. The brain drain reflects the fact that many underdeveloped countries, as part of their modernization, train more professionals than can be employed profitably in those countries. A study in the early 1970s indicated that nearly 10 percent of doctors trained in India were practicing abroad, mainly in the United States and Great Britain.[18] (Large numbers today are also employed in the oil-rich states of the Persian Gulf.) Those with a Marxist bent fulminate about a "gift of labor to the imperialist countries,"[19] and those with a free-market bias talk about individuals making choices based on their perceptions of economic opportunity. What is all too often ignored is that settler societies—the United States, Canada, Argentina, Brazil, Australia, New Zealand, and South Africa—have from their inception drained talent and enterprise from the countries that nurtured them.[20] To cite an important but little-noted example, the extraordinary number of college graduates, largely from Cambridge, who helped settle New England in the early seventeenth century made persons with university educations more prevalent in the colony than in the metropolis.[21]

More recent students of patterns of Indian migration to New York have suggested that the flow in the 1980s was of persons less well trained. One of the more obvious phenomena in New York is the degree to which Asian Indians have begun to predominate in the newsstand industry. Many, if not most, of the thousands of kiosks in New York subways are owned and staffed by Asian Indians. Those who put in ten-hour, twelve-hour, and sometimes longer days below ground in the subway stands are often recently arrived and less-educated relatives of better-educated persons who came earlier and put their savings into profitable enterprises.[22]

In California's fabulous Silicon Valley, Asian Indian entrepreneurs, largely graduates of Indian Institutes of Technology, made important contributions during the 1990s. One study, by AnnaLee Saxenian, a professor of regional development at the University of California, Berkeley, showed that in 1998 774 high-tech firms with Asian Indian chief executive officers had $3.6 million in annual sales and employed 16,598 persons. Nativists who speak of immigrants as an economic drain must ignore such persons.[23]

On a national basis—where there are no systematic studies—one of the most startling occupational niches that Asian Indians have come to occupy has been hotel and motel operation, particularly the latter. One newspaper story estimated that two-fifths of all the motels in the Interstate 75 association—Interstate 75 runs between Detroit and Atlanta—are owned and operated by Asian Indians, often as a part of national franchises. Again, in many instances, these establishments are often owned by persons whose relatives run them. A very large percentage of the motels are run by one ethnic group, the Gujarati (persons from the northern Indian state of Gujarat), many of whom share the surname Patel. One joke prevalent in southern California talks about "hotel, motel, Patel." Other businesses in which Indians tend to cluster are restaurants and small clothing operations (the so-called sari shops), some of which cater to the ethnic community and some of which appeal to the fashion-conscious in the general community.

National occupational data, while not as impressive as that in Saran's New York sample, still show a profile of occupational achievement. According to the 1980 census, nearly half—47 percent—of all foreign-born Asian Indian workers were in the category of "managers, professionals, executives," nearly twice the rate for white Americans (24 percent) and significantly higher than that of any other segment of an Asian American group. (The next highest such segment was 33 percent for native-born Chinese Americans; foreign-born Chinese came in at 30 percent.)

This elite socioeconomic profile must not be thought of as an ethnic characteristic. India is the home of some of the most heart-wrenching poverty, and Indian immigrants to Great Britain have a very different profile. Compare Saran's New York sample with Arthur Helweg's Punjabi Jats in the small British city of Gravesend. The "vast majority" of the approximately 7,000 Asian Indians there in 1978 were in unskilled jobs. That was also probably true of most of the approximately 900,000 Asian Indians who then lived in the United Kingdom.[24]

THE BIRTH OF PAKISTAN AND BANGLADESH

The bloody partition of India in August 1947 created two new and independent nations, India and Pakistan, in place of the unified British colony of India. Both were multicultural, but most Pakistanis were Muslims and most

Indians Hindus. The communal strife that accompanied independence killed more than half a million persons; 7.5 million Muslim refugees fled to Pakistan from India, and 10 million Hindus left Pakistan for India. Further territorial division occurred in 1972 when, in the course of a brief war between India and Pakistan, what had been East Pakistan became the independent nation of Bangladesh. Recent demographic data shows India with 984 million people, 80 percent Hindu and 14 percent Muslim; Pakistan with 135 million people, 97 percent Muslim, and Bangladesh with 127 million people, 88 percent Muslim and 11 percent Hindu.

PAKISTANIS AND BANGLADESHIS IN AMERICA

Before late 1947, the relatively few immigrants from what are now Pakistan and Bangladesh are listed in American records as Asian Indians, and Bangladeshi who came to America between 1947 and 1972 are recorded as Pakistanis. In the 1990 census, about 100,000 persons reported that they were of Pakistani origin, and some 12,000 said that their origin was Bangladesh. Between 1990 and 1997, an additional 93,000 immigrants came from Pakistan and nearly 50,000 from Bangladesh in the same period. This group of perhaps 250,000 persons comprises a tiny fraction of the more than 5 million Muslims in the United States but represents the vast majority of Muslim immigrants from the nations treated in this volume. Very few Muslims have come to the United States from the largest nation in Southeast Asia, Indonesia, where nearly 200 million Muslims live.

There have been no systematic studies of the Pakistani and Bangladesh communities in America: Even in Leonard's detailed treatment of South Asian Americans there are only passing mentions. One place where a sizable Pakistani community has developed is in Chicago, where Asian Indians and Pakistanis share a business district along Devon Avenue; diplomatically, the city authorities have put up signs designating one segment of the district Jinnah Road and another Gandhi Marg, thus honoring a founding father of each nation.[25]

THE FUTURE

The future of the Asian Indian community in the United States is probably a bright one. In the 1990s, two movies, *Gandhi* and *A Passage to India,* and the television series *The Jewel in the Crown* generated interest in India, but in an India that no longer exists. Despite what one writer called "a rage for the Raj," most Americans are unaware of the Asian Indians in their midst. Their broad geographic distribution and the absence of ethnic neighborhoods have kept their social visibility low. But their rapid growth continues. The

1990 census recorded more than 800,000 Asians Indians, more than three times the 250,000 found ten years previously. At some midwestern universities, such as Ohio State, Asian Indians are the largest single group of Asian American students. All the evidence indicates that the Asian Indian population will grow faster than the Asian American population generally.

Indisputably, the Asian Indian community is putting down roots. In Cincinnati, for example, some 400 largely well-to-do, middle-class Indian families raised $700,000 to build a temple to serve as a community center as well as a place for religious observances. In Artesia, a suburb of Los Angeles, there is a four-block stretch that some residents now call Little India.[26] Enterprising Indian merchants have given a different flavor to this small, middle-class community, with stores selling Indian sweets, clothing, groceries, and jewelry. Only Jackson Heights in Queens and Chicago's Devon Avenue have more ethnic Indian stores and restaurants, according to a spokesperson at the Indian embassy in Washington.

Many of the merchants are relatives of the professionals who moved here earlier. Not as well-educated and lacking the professional qualifications, they have moved into the small-business sector, just as other Asians in previous eras made similar moves. They do not mind working long hours and are ardent advocates of the free-enterprise system. Some established merchants have complained about the growing competition—Indian stores are said to be taking away customers from the regular businesses—but others ask who would rent the stores if the Indians were not there.

Despite such evidence of continuing ties to India and Indian culture, evidence of increasing acculturation is also strong. Many observers, including a number of Asian Indian community leaders, have argued that Indians here have been particularly reluctant to make the crucial break with their past and become American citizens. Yet one sophisticated study suggests exactly the opposite. Elliott Barkan examined American naturalization patterns between 1951 and 1978. His results showed that not only have Asians in general been more likely to become citizens than most other resident aliens who arrived during those years, but also that Asian Indians were more likely to do so than members of other major Asian ethnic groups. Barkan calculated for the period from 1969 to 1978 the percentage of aliens who were naturalized during the fifth to eighth year of their permanent residence in the United States. Dividing all such persons into a simple Asian/non-Asian dichotomy, he reported that almost 65 percent of Asians became naturalized, as opposed to only 45 percent of non-Asians. The same data, when broken down into five main Asian ethnic groups, showed Indians with by far the highest naturalization rate, more than 80 percent. The next highest rate is that of the Filipinos, just over 60 percent.[27]

We should recognize that such rates do not necessarily represent a transfer of loyalties. As we have seen, current immigration law provides a strong incentive to acquire citizenship for newcomers wishing to practice chain migration, as both Asian Indians and Filipinos are currently doing. However, whatever the reasons, Asian Indian immigrants to the United States seem to have been extraordinarily eager to become American citizens. There is no reason not to believe that their patterns of acculturation will be similar to those of other modern ethnic groups, although their unique religious heritage may provide some new variations.

NOTES

1. For general historical surveys of Asian Indians, see Gary R. Hess, "The Forgotten Asian Americans: The East Indian Community in the United States," *Pacific Historical Review* 43 (1974): 576–596; H. Brett Melendy, *Asians in America: Filipinos, Koreans and East Indians* (Boston: Twayne, 1977); S. Chandrasekhar, ed., *From India to America* (La Jolla, CA: Population Institute, 1982); and Joan M. Jensen, *Passage from India* (New Haven, CT: Yale University Press, 1988).

2. U.S. Immigration Commission, *Reports of the Immigration Commission*, pt. 25: *Japanese and Other Immigrant Races in the Pacific Coast and Rocky Mountain States*, vol. 1: *Japanese and East Indians* (Washington, DC: Government Printing Office, 1911).

3. Mark Juergensmeyer, *Religion as Social Vision: The Movement against Untouchability in the 20th Century Punjab* (Berkeley: University of California Press, 1982), pp. 30–31, 383–389.

4. The literature on Gadar is extensive. We have used chiefly L. P. Mather, *Indian Revolutionary Movement in the United States of America* (Delhi: Chand, 1970); Arun Comer Bose, *Indian Revolutionaries Abroad, 1905–1922* (Patna, India: Bhavati Bhawan, 1971); Emily C. Brown, *Har Dayal: Hindu Revolutionary and Rationalist* (Tucson: University of Arizona Press, 1975); Don Dignan, *The Indian Revolutionary Problem in British Diplomacy, 1914–1919* (New Delhi: Allied Publishers, 1983); and Joan M. Jensen, "The 'Hindu Conspiracy': A Reassessment," *Pacific Historical Review* 48 (1979): 65–83.

5. D. S. Saund, *Congressman from India* (New York: Dutton, 1960).

6. Bruce La Brack and Karen Leonard, "Conflict and Compatibility in Punjabi-Mexican Immigrant Marriages in Rural California, 1915–1965," *Journal of Marriage and the Family* 46 (1984): 527–537; Karen Leonard, *Making Ethnic Choices: California's Punjabi Mexican Americans* (Philadelphia: Temple University Press, 1992).

7. Barbara M. Posadas, "Crossed Boundaries in Interracial Chicago: Filipino American Families since 1925," *Amerasia Journal* 8 (1981): 31–52.

8. Carl T. Jackson, *The Oriental Religions and American Thought: A Socio-Historical Study* (Westport, CT: Greenwood Press, 1981).

9. Wendell Thomas, *Hinduism Invades America* (Boston: Beacon Press, 1930).

10. William Roger Louis, *Imperialism at Bay: The United States and the Decolonization of the British Empire, 1941–1945* (New York: Oxford University Press, 1978).

11. Robert Shaplen, "One-Man Lobby," *The New Yorker*, Mar. 24, 1951, pp. 35–55. See also R. Narayanan, "Indian Immigration and the India League of America," *Indian Journal of American Studies* 2, no. I (1972): 1–30.

12. Bruce La Brack, "The Sikhs of Northern California: A Socio-historical Study" (Ph.D. dissertation, Syracuse University, 1980); Bruce La Brack, "Immigration Law

and the Revitalization Process: The Case of the California Sikhs," *Population Review* 25 (1982): 59–66.

13. Saund, *Congressman from India.*

14. Hekmet Elkhanialy and Ralph W. Nicholas, eds., *Immigrants from the Indian Subcontinent in the U.S.A.* (Chicago: India League of America, 1976).

15. Robert W. Gardner, Bryant Robey, and Peter C. Smith, *Asian Americans: Growth, Change and Diversity* (Washington, DC: Population Reference Bureau, 1985). This booklet is the source for all further unattributed population data.

16. Nathan Glazer, foreword, in Parmatma Saran and E. Eames, eds., *The New Ethnics: Asian Indians in the United States* (New York: Praeger, 1976), pp. vi–viii.

17. Parmatma Saran, *The Asian Indian Experience in the United States* (Cambridge, MA: Schenkman, 1983).

18. Rosemary Stevens and Joan Vermeulen, *Foreign Trained Physicians and American Medicine* (Washington, DC: Government Printing Office, 1972).

19. Hilbourne A. Watson, "Migration and Political Economy of Underdevelopment: Notes on the Commonwealth Caribbean Situation," cited in Saran, *Asian Indian Experience*, p. 23.

20. John Higham, "Immigration," in C. Vann Woodward, ed., *The Comparative Approach to History* (New York: Free Press, 1968).

21. Samuel E. Morison, *The Puritan Pronaos* (Cambridge, MA: Harvard University Press, 1936).

22. From a discussion by Johanna Lessinger at the conference "India in America: The Immigrant Experience," held at the Asia Society, New York, Apr. 17, 1986.

23. AnnaLee Saxenian, *Silicon Valley's New Immigrant Entrepreneurs* (Berkeley: Public Policy Institute of California, 1999) and Scott Thurm, "Asian Immigrants Help to Reshape Silicon Valley as Entrepreneurs," *Wall Street Journal*, June 24, 1999.

24. Arthur Wesley Helweg, *Sikhs in England: The Development of a Migrant Community* (Delhi: Oxford University Press, 1979).

25. Karen Isaksen Leonard, *The South Asian Americans* (Westport, CT: Greenwood Press, 1997).

26. "Indian Immigrants Gain Here," *Los Angeles Times*, May 19, 1987.

27. Elliott R. Barkan, "Whom Shall We Integrate? A Comparative Analysis of the Immigration Act (1951–1978)," *Journal of American Ethnic History* 3 (1983): 29–57.

Chapter 9

THE KOREANS

BACKGROUND

In 1970, there were an estimated 70,000 Korean residents of the United States; by 1980, the population had grown to 357,393; and the 1990 census indicates a total of 789,849. This growth is almost entirely due to immigration, meaning that Korean Americans are primarily a first-generation group. However, unlike the early Chinese, Japanese, and Filipinos, Korean immigrants often arrived in family groups, so even though all of the individuals were born in Korea, the family may have included infants, adolescents, and young adults along with the father and mother. As a consequence, intergenerational differences in terms of acculturation, identity, language facility and coming to grips with the dominant culture have an immediacy that was delayed for the older Asian groups. Parents, barely arrived in the United States, have sent their children to American schools and have been faced with the question of differences between their traditional ways and the norms of the new culture. The Chinese and the Japanese old-timers faced these issues much later—the early Japanese immigrant was a single male who sent for a wife from the old country after several years in the United States and whose children were then American born; the Chinese male immigrant remained even more isolated for many years. Therefore, whereas generational terms are meaningful for Japanese Americans, for Koreans they have a different connotation. An individual may have been born in Korea as an Issei, or first generation, but his arrival may have been as an infant or small child so that his socialization may be more like the Nisei or second generation. The difference is important enough so that terms such as "knee high," or 1.5 generation, have been used to identify this generation. Another factor compounding the difficulty of classification is the relative ease of flying to and from Korea, so that there is a constant movement between the two countries. In addition, Koreans from South and Central America are a part of the mix.

The following structure is not unusual in the current community: father and mother, born in Korea, following traditional, old-country patterns; eldest daughter, arriving with a Korean high school diploma, being more Korean than American; second daughter finishing high school in America and having more American than Korean ways; and youngest son, having gone through his entire schooling in the United States, being almost thoroughly American. But acculturation is seldom linear and predictable; parents may selectively adopt American ways, and the almost completely Americanized youngster may hold onto some old-country values. The mixture, referred to as *culture conflict,* can cause considerable discord within families.

KOREAN IMMIGRATION

There are a variety of ways of describing Korean immigration to the United States. One way is to view it in terms of waves, although only the current flow is large enough to warrant such a description. Korean political exiles were living in the United States as early as 1885,[1] but the first significant influx, albeit just a trickle, was to Hawaii (1903–1905); the second migration came after the Korean War (1950–1953); and the current immigration, which is still in progress, was the result of the 1965 Immigration Act. Each group of newcomers differed in demographic characteristics, the conditions surrounding their migration, and the kind of America they entered. Consequently, their adaptation and their experiences in America were different.

Background

Modern Korean history reflects the influence of three powerful neighbors—China, Japan, and Russia—and Korea's strategic location in proximity to them. The three countries struggled over who should have the most influence over Korea. China dominated Korea as a tributary state until 1868, when Meiji Japan began to contest her influence. China's defeat in the Sino-Japanese War (1894–1895) led to the Japanese replacing the Chinese overlords. Japan's aggressive policies drove Korea to appeal to other foreign powers who could serve to limit Japanese aggression, and this led to relationships with Russia and the United States.

American diplomatic relations with Korea started in 1882 with the Korean-American Treaty at Chemulpo (now Inchon). The treaty, also known as the Treaty of Amity and Commerce, called for free traffic between the two nations, including the permission for Koreans to reside, rent homes, and purchase land in America. Very few Koreans took the opportunity to come to the United States during this period.

Internal and international events soon led to the initial immigration of Koreans to Hawaii. In 1894 the Tonghak Rebellion, basically an antimodern revolt much like the Boxer Rebellion in China, failed because of the lack of unity and discipline. The rebellion served as a catalyst for the Sino-Japanese War, which was fought on the Korean peninsula. China's defeat gave Korea political independence but in essence conceded the country to Japan. From 1895 to 1905, Russia and Japan struggled over who should "protect" Korea; the Russo-Japanese War (1904–1905) saw Russia defeated, and in the Treaty of Portsmouth (1905), Russia recognized Japanese power over the nation. Japan annexed Korea in 1910.[2]

Hyung-chan Kim views the treaty with the United States and the two wars as the main spurs to Korean emigration to America.[3] Korea had earlier been known as the "hermit kingdom" because of the reluctance of its subjects to travel out of their country. However, the wars uprooted a large number of Koreans, forcing many to move to port cities in search of employment, which was scarce, and the treaty with the United States signaled a possible opportunity in a new land.

The First Wave

Hawaii was a natural target for the immigrants. Hawaiian sugar planters wanted to replace Chinese and Japanese laborers—especially the Japanese, who had become militant in their demands for better treatment. However, Wayne Patterson notes that the first proposal to import Korean labor was denied and that it took seven years, until 1903, for the first Korean laborers to arrive in Hawaii.[4] But in the next two years, 7,266 Koreans arrived in Hawaii, and another, 1,033 went to Mexico.[5]

The immediate trigger for emigration was a severe famine, bolstered by such additional factors as an epidemic of cholera, heavy taxes, and government corruption. The exodus was not solely to the New World; Koreans went to Manchuria, Japan, and Russia as well.

Although the first Korean immigrants to Hawaii were primarily from the lower classes, very few were peasants. The Korean peasant was very conservative—upholding Confucian tradition and staying on the land were high priorities, to the point that immigration was viewed as unthinkable and even immoral.[6] A goodly number of the immigrants had been converted to Christianity before they left Korea.

Life in early Hawaii was not easy, especially for women. One writer describes poverty, frustration, and less than human treatment.[7] Typical jobs were farm laborer, tenant farmer, cook, janitor, and launderer.

The migrants were neither integrated nor assimilated; plantation life was characterized by racial and ethnic segregation, hard work, low wages, and minimal contact with other groups. Interaction was further limited by language and cultural differences and a sojourner's orientation. There was no pressing need to think about entering the mainstream or cooperating with other groups. However, after Korea was formally annexed by Japan in 1910, there was no home country to which the migrants could return. The Japanese also prevented Koreans from leaving their country, so the number of Koreans in America remained static. Even though most early Korean newcomers arrived in Hawaii with a weak national identity, life in a strange land and the takeover of their homeland by Japan led many to adopt a strong nationalism.

One consequence was that emotional attachment to Korea became very strong. The immigrants started Korean-language schools in 1905, and their children were taught Korean values, customs, history, and geography as well. They also set up churches and patriotic societies, including military training centers to support Korean independence movements and an end to Japanese rule. They followed a government-in-exile model, putting the emphasis on military training and retaining old-country ways until such time as they could return to liberate their country from foreign domination.

It might be expected that a small group, cut off from the country of origin and unable either to go back or to be replenished by new immigration, would soon disappear as a distinctive entity. But just as in the case of the Japanese immigrants, the Koreans resorted to "importing" wives ("picture brides") from Korea, permitting family life for some and the beginning of an American-born generation. But the number of Koreans was very small; in 1930, they constituted only 1.8 percent (6,461) of the entire Hawaiian population of 347,799. Yet Adams reported that only 104 Korean males married non-Koreans in the period from 1912 to 1924.[8] Higher rates of exogamy would occur several generations later.

Details of the adaptation of the descendants of the early Korean immigrants to Hawaii are revealing. Factors such as small numbers, the lack of a cohesive community after the demise of the independence movements, acculturation, and the pull of the Hawaiian melting pot all had an effect. Harvey and Chung report that in addition to these factors, Koreans placed a high value on becoming American, being well educated, and entering the professions.[9] As a consequence, the children and grandchildren of the initial immigrant group have one of the highest interethnic marriage rates in Hawaii. Between 1960 and 1968, 80 percent of the Koreans married non-Koreans, compared to the 40 percent outmarriage rate for Hawaii's other ethnic groups during the same period. Korean brides generally chose

Caucasian grooms, whereas Korean husbands chose Japanese wives. The outmarriage rate rose even higher, to 90 percent, in the 1970s.[10]

But the rapid move toward acculturation and assimilation into the Hawaiian mainstream has not been without cost. High rates of separation and divorce, psychological problems, and other dysfunctional symptoms have been reported. The course of experience of Korean immigrants in Hawaii between 1903 and 1945 can be summarized as follows: political preoccupation, Christianity and the Christian churches, importation of brides, birth of a second generation, ethnic dormancy, rapid acculturation, and rising rates of outmarriage.[11]

A smaller group of Koreans migrated to the U.S. mainland; the 1930 census showed fewer than 2,000 in California. The irony of their situation—coming from Korea, which had been subsequently taken over by Japan; organizing to free Korea from Japanese rule; and yet being officially represented by the Japanese government—is seen in an incident described by Eunsik Yang. In 1913 a group of Korean laborers was attacked in Hemet Valley, California, by a white mob that had mistaken them for Japanese. The Japanese consul general in Los Angeles stepped in to protect the Koreans and asked for compensation on behalf of "their nationals," an offer that was rejected by the Koreans because they questioned the authority of the Japanese government.[12]

The assassination of Durham Stevens in 1908 further illustrated the feelings of Koreans about their relationship with Japan. Stevens, who had been appointed as adviser to the Foreign Affairs Department of the Korean government, made a number of statements that were printed in the *San Francisco Chronicle*. His points were (1) that Koreans had been exploited and corrupted by their own officials, (2) that they were illiterate and backward, (3) that if not for Japanese protection, they would be under Russian domination, and (4) that under the present Japanese resident general, they were happy and enjoyed life in every respect.

The Koreans in San Francisco were outraged over these remarks. Stevens was attacked by several Koreans and died two days later. Chang In-hwan was charged with the murder, was sentenced to serve twenty-five years in prison, and was released in 1919. He died in 1930, and in 1975 his corpse was flown to Seoul, where he lies as a patriot in the national cemetery.[13]

There were also a small but important number of Korean students and political exiles who emigrated to the United States. Many of them were from the upper classes and were admitted without passports because the American government sympathized with the plight of anti-Japanese Koreans who could not go back to their homes without fear of persecution. Nowadays they would be classified as refugees.

Probably the best known of these exiles was Syngman Rhee.[14] A controversial figure in the Korean American community, Rhee was nevertheless able to establish a base of support that gave him prominence and a position of leadership. After the defeat of Japan, the gaining of Korean independence, and the split between north and south, Rhee was elected the first president of South Korea in 1948. He had influential American supporters, including General Douglas MacArthur and other U.S. military authorities, who saw in Rhee a staunch conservative and a militant anticommunist. But Rhee's rule was wracked with problems, and he was forced from office in 1960. One writer observed, "Rhee's police state fell because of official corruption, favoritism, political oppression and fraudulent elections. . . . practiced in the name of patriotism and in the guise of anti-communism."[15]

The Second Wave

The second group of Koreans, who came between 1951 and 1964, was a heterogeneous one, consisting of wives of American servicemen (the Korean War took place in 1950–1953), war orphans, and students.

It is perhaps too easy to forget the destructiveness of the Korean War. The popular movie and TV series *M*A*S*H* merely hinted at the ugliness of the conflict; a more telling account by Choon Soon Kim indicated that destruction and disease were widespread.[16] There were an estimated 1 million civilian and 300,000 military casualties. On the civilian side in South Korea alone, the war was responsible for 300,000 widows, 230,000 wounded, 330,000 permanently handicapped, 100,000 orphans, and 1 million cases of tuberculosis. It is reasonable to assume that figures for North Korea were similar.

A total of 28,205 Korean "war brides" arrived in the United States between 1950 and 1975. Few studies are available on this generally invisible minority. They integrated and assimilated before they acculturated, and since most followed their husbands, they could be found throughout the United States. Many could be found clustered around army bases; one author remembers being greeted by a group of Korean wives at an isolated army base at Fort Huachuca, Arizona.

In one of the few studies made, Bok-Lim Kim evaluated the adjustment of Korean wives of American servicemen and noted some of their problems.[17] They suffered from culture shock, lack of education, isolation, problems of communication, and general alienation. Kim notes that some marriages were happy, but there were also cases of physical abuse, suicide, and attempted suicide, and the divorce rate among these couples was high. The wives were marginal, both to the dominant community and to the Korean community, and the high incidence of social problems may be attributed to that marginality.

Even less is known about Korean war orphans. Hurh and Kim, citing various sources, indicated that in 1950 some 24,945 children were institutionalized in Korean orphanages. Of these, 6,293 were adopted in the United States, mostly through the Holt Adoption Agency, between 1955 and 1966. Roughly 46 percent had white fathers, 41 percent were full Koreans, and the rest were black Koreans.[18]

Dong Kim conducted a nationwide study of adopted Korean adolescents. In general, they were place in white, middle-class, Protestant families in rural and small communities. Religious and humanitarian reasons were given as primary motives for adoption, and family relations were deemed as supportive. The children were reported to have healthy self-concepts, and the adoptions were generally considered successful.[19]

However, in a later report, the problem of racial differences was observed.[20] Although all of these children's surroundings and inputs were typically American, their physical characteristics set them aside from the mainstream. The adoptees were seen as Asian, yet they were almost totally cut off from their native contacts and culture. The implications of this "dual identity" with minimal ethnic support may be a cause of future problems.

The last group in the second wave consisted of a relatively large number of Korean students who came to the United States between 1945 and 1965. An estimated 5,000 are still in the country today, yet almost nothing is known about them. Questions as to how many went back, how many changed their resident status, how many married and whom they married, and how well those who stayed adapted remain topics for future research.

The Third Wave

The third wave was a result of the Immigration and Naturalization Act of 1965, and the Korean migration still continues. For the first time in American immigration history, flows from Asian nations have exceeded those from European countries. For example, in 1965, the three countries outside of the western hemisphere that sent the most immigrants were the United Kingdom, Germany, and Italy; in 1975, the three main countries of origin were the Philippines, Korea, and China. The Korean share of the total U.S. immigration rose from 0.7 percent to 3.8 percent between 1969 and 1973.

However, note that the number of Koreans living in other parts of the world is much higher. An estimated 1,255,000 Korean residents were living in Manchuria (northern China) in 1961, approximately 600,000 are residents of Japan, and a large but unknown number are living in central Asia (Russia). The United States is home to the second-largest community of Koreans abroad.[21]

The current immigration is family-oriented and includes a large proportion of housewives and children. It is a highly educated group and differs from earlier Korean immigrants in that most live in the cities. They are arriving at a time when ethnic and racial groups are asserting their identities, and there has been a shift in the American ethos away from monolithic assimilation and toward ethnic and cultural pluralism.

Researchers conducted interviews with a sample of U.S. visa applicants in Seoul in 1986. The majority anticipated some racial discrimination, as well as problems related to their limited English proficiency. They expected little improvement in their economic status in the short run but expected to do well over the longer term. They were prepared to work hard and felt that their efforts would eventually be rewarded. The three aspects favoring the United States over Korea were higher wages, rewards for hard work and ability, and a more favorable political environment.[22]

It is too soon to detail the pattern of adjustment of these Korean newcomers, although several trends are clear, among them expectations of economic success in the majority culture, retention of aspects of Korean culture, rapid flight to more desirable housing in the suburbs, and the development of ethnic business districts. Other expectations include permanent residence, a good education for their children, and the acquisition of American citizenship.[23]

Major barriers to participation in the mainstream include lack of familiarity with American society and the language handicap. In this the Koreans are not unique; almost all immigrants have had to deal with these differences.

In summary, the present-day Korean immigrant is contending with a multitude of issues, including cultural and linguistic differences, parent–child stresses, changes in roles, conflicts in norms and values, achieving a healthy identity in a predominantly white society, and varied levels of acceptance by both the majority and other minorities already living here.

OCCUPATIONAL ADJUSTMENT

Occupational adjustment for the new immigrant generally means downward mobility (very few are able to find jobs of equal status), segregation from the mainstream (the small businesses are generally in "Koreatowns" or other minority areas), and general isolation from the white community. Many are in the small-business sector, which means working long hours, weekends, and holidays. There is a constant struggle to lower labor costs to survive, and the struggle can lead to poor work conditions and to the use of family, extended family, and relatives.[24]

An interview with a Korean student at UCLA demonstrates the family business model. The student cannot remember a single time when his parents closed their small market for a full day—even Christmas and other holidays. Only during the Los Angeles riot of 1992 was the store closed—involuntarily. The student remembers working Saturdays and Sundays at the market and admits, "Whereas most people loved three-day weekends, I just dreaded them. That just meant another day at the store."[25]

For many young Koreans, the weekend was not for swimming, going to the beach, and relaxing—it meant another two days at the store. They envied youngsters who had time to study and to play and even families in which the parents held 9-to-5 jobs and had free evenings and weekends.

Many of the small-business enterprises are run by immigrants with solid educational or professional backgrounds whose difficulties with English have forced them to take a different path. They may start by taking menial jobs, scrimping and saving enough to buy a gas station, liquor store, convenience market, or laundromat. Stores that sell wigs and mom-and-pop groceries are also popular. According to a survey by the Korean Chamber of Commerce of Southern California, there were about 7,000 Korean-owned businesses in Los Angeles County in 1984.[26]

Although the Korean business community in Los Angeles is located in an area that is at least half Latino and only 12 percent Korean, it serves as the hub of the ethnic community. Here the Koreans—newcomers, elderly, oldtimers, and young—can find ethnic food and ethnic stores, run into old friends and meet new ones, and (perhaps most refreshing of all) not have to understand English.

However, there are growing concerns about the unrestrained growth of Koreatowns. Zoning regulations, the need to attract non-Korean clientele, ethnic segregation, the proliferation of shopping centers, inadequate parking, and such matters have had an effect on Korean business. One Korean leader commented on the need to funnel the energy and vitality of his group toward a better-planned and more orderly development. Perhaps, as the immigrants obtain citizenship and participate in the political process, a more sophisticated Koreatown may develop.[27]

Hurh and Kim report that the majority of Koreans employed in non–small-business occupations worked in segregated workplaces under unfavorable conditions.[28] Past skills and education may not be as important as how immigrants are integrated into the workplace and may be indicative of the split labor market facing many nonwhite immigrants. Such a market differentiates between jobs that provide adequate pay and chances for upward mobility and jobs that are lower paying and lead basically nowhere. Minorities are often stuck in the latter positions.[29]

Min, discussing ethnic enterprise, indicates that Korean immigrants possessed the same three factors—hard work and frugality, strong family and kinship ties, and group solidarity—as the earlier Chinese and Japanese immigrants. However, the Koreans may have a more individualistic outlook than the group-oriented Chinese and Japanese. Other factors pushing Koreans to the small-business sector include lack of opportunities in white-collar jobs and the perception that it was easier to start a small business in the United States than in Korea.[30]

Perhaps the greatest change for the newcomers is the ease of female and youth employment. Families that in Korea would never think of wives and children working now find that such opportunities, though low paying, are readily available. In some instances, wives and children find employment more easily than husbands and other male adults. The effect on family dynamics can be stressful. The temptation to make money is difficult to restrain, and problems of child care, latchkey children, and obsession with earning a living are difficult to avoid.

LOS ANGELES RIOT OF 1992

The uneasy relationship between Korean small businesses, primarily in southeast Los Angeles, and the surrounding black community exploded when a jury found four police officers not guilty of violating the civil rights of black beating victim Rodney King. The rioting and looting that erupted made Korean stores special targets. The media were especially provocative, repeatedly featuring images of armed Koreans guarding their stores. The impression at times was of armed conflict between Korean shopowners and the surrounding neighborhood. The aftermath of the riot left destruction, despair, feelings of hopelessness, and divisive intergroup tensions.

The effects of the riot were still being felt by the Korean community nearly a year later. More than half of the victims showed symptoms of post-traumatic stress, nearly half felt hopeless about the future, and only three out of ten had reopened their businesses.

Riot victims complained of nightmares, depression, anxiety, and fear. Ulcers, poor appetite, domestic violence, and child abuse were blamed on the riot. The Koreans felt that they had been victimized by the rioters and then again by an insensitive American bureaucracy when they sought government assistance.[31]

The movie *Falling Down* added to the Korean's problems. Jeana Park, executive director of Korean Americans for Justice, commented on the scene in which star Michael Douglas confronts a Korean store owner, accuses the man of taking his money yet lacking the grace to learn English, and then smashes the merchandise with a baseball bat. Particularly galling was the remark of a friend who asked Park whether the outcome would have been different if the store owner had been "an American." Park wanted to scream that the store owner *was* an American and had a rightful place in American society.[32]

Park also mentioned the case of Soon Ja Du, a Korean store owner, who shot and killed Latasha Harlins, a black teenager. The store owner thought that the youngster was leaving her store without paying; the subsequent trial and very light sentence added to the tension between the two communities.

THE CHRISTIAN CHURCHES

One of the unique characteristics of the Korean immigration has been the role of the Christian churches. Catholicism was introduced into Korea through China as early as 1784 but was banned soon after—the ruling class considered the new religion dangerous because it challenged the Confucian system of loyalties and ancestor worship that underpinned its rule.[33]

American influence began in 1884 when the Presbyterian Board of Missions sent a representative to Korea. During the Sino-Japanese War (1894–1895), missionaries devoted time and effort to alleviating the suffering of people caught in the conflict, and that unselfish devotion endeared them to the natives. Many Koreans adopted the Christian faith.

Adopting Christianity was also a means of identifying with and gaining foreign protection. Later it was also associated with a growing nationalism and an anti-Japanese stance. Even today, political resistance in Korea is often associated with the church communities. American missionaries were influential in persuading the first group of immigrants to go to Hawaii. The proportion of the early immigrants to Hawaii who were Christians or who later converted to the faith was large. One expert estimates that there were thirty-nine churches and 2,800 Christians in the period between 1903 and 1918 when the total Korean population was about 8,000. He hypothesizes several reasons for the strength of the church: It provided a group tie that was lacking in the community; the adherence to Christianity was a means of gaining sympathy from the white community; it served as a social outlet; and there were group pressures to belong.[34]

The churches also played several other roles for the first group of immigrants to Hawaii. They were active in the Korean independence movement and were also important in maintaining cultural traditions. They sponsored language schools, taught Korean history, and served as centers for recreational and social activities. They were pluralistic structures; membership was almost exclusively Korean, even though the religious practices were drawn from Anglo-European theology.

The Christian church continues to play an active role in the presentday Korean community. In southern California the number of Korean churches increased from 11 in 1965 to 215 in 1979. The results of a survey of religion indicated that 10 percent of Koreans were Catholic and the rest Protestant. Presbyterians were by far the most numerous denomination. The number of Buddhists was too small to be analyzed.[35]

Many of the reasons for the continued strength of the Christian churches in the Korean community have not changed. They provide for many needs—religious involvement, identity, and a resource for newly arrived immigrants. They also serve as a place for meeting people, obtaining peace of mind, and achieving self-improvement. But there are also some negatives—too much gossip, self-interest, schisms and conflict, and the constant solicitation of money.[36]

The Korean churches are central to the Korean community. It will be interesting to follow their development as acculturation and new opportunities arise. Will they remain separated from the dominant community, or will there be integration, especially as housing and other patterns of the ethnic community change?

The experience of the Japanese Christian churches in America may be instructive. The Japanese churches began as exclusively ethnic—services were held in Japanese in all Issei congregations. English-speaking services were introduced as the American-born generations began to take part—the church remained ethnic but served both Japanese and English groups.

Questions about the viability of the ethnic church are now being heard, with issues of integration and pluralism as focal points of discussion. But constant replenishment from the old country has not been a factor for Japanese Americans, so the outcomes for the Korean community may be different.

Also important will be the mobility of the ministry of the ethnic church. Will Korean clergy rise to positions of power and serve on the decision-making bodies of the host churches, or will they remain auxiliaries, outside the mainstream?

FAMILY AND KINSHIP TIES

Korean immigrant groups have always featured family, extended family, and other kinship ties. It is not unusual for former elementary school children in Korea to be reunited with schoolmates several decades later in Los Angeles, just as aunts, uncles, nephews, and nieces form extended family units in the new country.

The Koreans come from a "traditional culture," where tasks and roles were clearly defined. Wives were expected to stay at home and to bear responsibility for household tasks, while the husband served as the breadwinner. The husband was the final authority and had the power to enforce his decisions. Children were expected to be obedient and to defer to parental wishes.

Hurh and Kim studied family role expectations in Korean American families and found that even though many wives worked, the great majority of both wives and husbands adhered to the traditional role patterns brought over from the old country.[37] A substantial proportion of husbands did not perform household chores, even if their wives were employed. Explanations for the persistence of the traditional division of household tasks included past strong socialization to male-female roles, the relative isolation of most Koreans to American influences, the continued strong influences of traditional families, the long work hours of Korean husbands, and financial pressures. The authors concluded that given the present-day realities of most Korean families, the traditional roles of males and females have not been drastically altered. However, in interracial marriages, one common response of Korean females, as well as other Asian females, was that they did not wish to marry males who expected them to behave in traditional female pattern. They expected more egalitarian roles and had to look outside of the Asian community for such partners.

The most visible changes in family life center around children. The younger the child, the more likely he or she is to be influenced by the American culture. Going to an American school leads to acculturation, especially if the child attends an integrated school, where his or her ethnic group is in the minority, as has been the case for Korean children in America.

Bok-Lim Kim studied the adjustment of Korean schoolchildren to American schools in Chicago and Los Angeles and found a surprising amount of similarity between the two sites. The children reported a variety of difficulties in school, including reading, spelling, and mathematics, but almost 20 percent indicated that American schools were easy. Some children had encountered racial discrimination, which in part came from their inability to handle the English language. They showed a relatively strong identification with facets of the Korean culture; Korean food and a desire to visit the ancestral homeland were popular.[38]

Acculturation, especially if rapid, can lead to conflict with parents. Dress and hairstyles, music, dancing, movies, and other seemingly superficial aspects of a culture can lead to misunderstandings, raised voices, and a gulf between parent and child. Issues involving differences in values, clashing norms, and changing family roles remain as deeper problems.

A study conducted by the United Way in Los Angeles addressed some of the problems and social service needs of the Korean community.[39] It noted that Western-based value systems, based on individuality, autonomy, and competition, were in conflict with the old Korean ways of family-centeredness, interdependence, and harmony. Underemployment and intergenerational problems were also causes of concern.

The most pressing problem was language. Other common concerns were unemployment, health, services for youth, and the lack of adequate social services to meet the needs of newly arrived immigrants.

GEOGRAPHIC ADAPTATION

Although the majority of Koreans have settled in urban areas such as Chicago, New York City, and especially Los Angeles, they are, after the Asian Indians, the most dispersed Asian group in terms of geographic distribution. Part of the spread is related to job opportunities—at academic meetings, it is not unusual to run into Korean colleagues who are teaching in Iowa, Virginia, Georgia, and other states that have small Asian populations. Many of them are Korean-born and of the first generation, for whom matters of acceptance, isolation, ethnic concerns, and the socialization of their children have yet to be studied. The general wisdom is that Korean living outside of popular ethnic settlements will acculturate and integrate at a faster rate than those with many ethnic neighbors.

Michael Seipel studied the social integration patterns of Koreans in upstate New York. He noted that although they belonged to the Korean church and other ethnic organizations, they also belonged to a large number of nonethnic organizations. Most of these outside organizations were job-related; Koreans were absent in civic, political, and labor organizations. Most significant, none of the respondents held membership in organizations that represented leadership or power. Therefore, he concluded that although there is an impressive participation of Koreans in both ethnic and nonethnic organizations, the data can be misleading in that they are affiliated with organizations with only marginal community influence.[40]

One facet of Korean immigration is that although Los Angeles remains the biggest draw, Koreans have spread to other parts of the country. For example, Pan and Pae write about how the Korean immigrant community has flourished in Annandale, close to Washington, DC. There is a Koryo Bakery, a video store with Korean movies; there is the Jin Sung Garden Korean Barbecue restaurant, and a teenage group hunting for a Korean rap group's newest release. One immigrant responded that it was just like Korea—one could survive without a single word of English.[41] Similar remarks can be heard in Korean communities as far apart as Los Angeles, Chicago, and New York.

Koreans have developed the greengrocer image in New York City. Marketing fresh fruits and vegetables in an attractive fashion means long hours and the use of family labor in order to make a decent living. Park describes the business as a fresh breeze for single New Yorkers who do not have to travel to supermarkets for their fresh produce.[42]

The Washington, DC area's first Koreatown, called *hanin-town* by Koreans, is in Fairfax County. It is the home of dozens of Korean American lawyers, doctors, computer programmers, and other professionals; there are also twenty-seven Korean restaurants, nineteen Korean churches, sixteen beauty salons, ten weekly newspapers, nine acupuncturists, as well as clothing stores, cafes, and karaoke clubs. The Korean population in 1999 in the Fairfax County area was over 100,000, which made it the second most populous immigrant community after the Salvadorans. It was noted that area also has a large Chinese community as well as Asian Indians, Vietnamese, and Filipinos.[43]

Longtime white residents have mixed views about the demographic changes. Some welcome the new burst of economic opportunity, but others grumble about the changes, claiming that Korean businesses aren't doing enough to serve non-Koreans. This again is a familiar refrain in Los Angeles and other areas where Koreans, as well as other minorities, have gathered. But previous Asian groups have gone through similar experiences and time, acculturation, accommodation, and hard work have tended to result towards relatively peaceful resolutions.

CURRENT ISSUES

There are a number of issues facing the Korean population. Culture conflict between the old and new is a problem for most immigrant groups, especially in terms of male and female roles. The Confucian model is vertically structured with males on top, and the exposure to modern feminism can strain the traditional male-female roles, which may often erupt in domestic violence.

The Korean small business structure can be viewed from a middleman perspective. The businesses are caught in the middle between the white power structure and black customers. It is difficult to survive under the conflicting demands of both groups, and it is easy to become the target of scapegoating from all sides, including young Asian American activists.

Kim emphasizes that Koreans should be studied in a variety of locations in order to identify similarities and differences, or to put it into modern vernacular, Koreans in their own "hood." The young Korean growing up in New York will probably reflect the East Coast ambience compared to his peer growing up in Fresno, San Francisco, or Los Angeles. The family who first immigrated to South America will certainly bring a different experience from those who came to the United States directly.[44]

There is an interesting story concerning white-collar, middle-class Koreans, desperate to immigrate to the United States, paying as much as $30,000 each to work in chicken plants on the Eastern shore. If they are hired, they receive permanent U.S. residency for themselves and their families under a federal program designed to fill unskilled jobs. For some, it is the only legal means of coming to the United States. It is interesting to note that during World War II, Japanese Americans found jobs outside the concentration camps as chick sexers because of their ability to identify male and female chicks. Chickens have apparently played an important role for these two Asian groups.

A study by Miller, Sung, and Seligman studied the relationship of beliefs and Korean immigrant success. The findings indicate that success as defined as educational and financial attainment is associated with "work optimism," the belief that in the United States reward is proportional to choice and the ability to improve.[45] The idea that hard work, dedication, and effort reminds us of old-fashioned, traditional values and it will be interesting to see how long these values will remain in the 1.5 and future generations of Korean Americans.

One problem is that of Korean gang members robbing new immigrants. A newspaper report indicates that gang members are terrorizing

Korean business owners and residents in New York, New Jersey, and Connecticut. Authorities speculate that the bandits had carefully chosen their targets, deciding on houses occupied by Korean immigrants who spoke little English, and were isolated from neighbors.[46]

At the present time, the Koreans represent one of the more unusual groups in terms of marital assimilation. We will present data in Chapter 12; while Koreans are very low in marital assimilation, some Asian groups are assimilating at a higher rate.

SUMMARY

The three waves of Korean immigrants entered America with different motivations, populations, and resources, and the reception they received from the American society was likewise different. The first wave was numerically small—mostly single males, brought to work on Hawaiian plantations. They lived segregated existences, enforced by the American and Hawaiian oligarchy; they developed their own organizations, especially the Christian church. Expectations of returning to their homelands evaporated when the Japanese took over their country in 1910. The immigrants then turned their time, money, and energy toward the day when they could reconquer their homeland. They experienced little acculturation or integration into the Hawaiian society. The importation of "picture brides" meant the start of family life for some.

Their children and the following generations paint a more familiar immigrant picture. These Korean Americans moved away from the plantation. Many were not interested in freeing Korea; more pressing goals were acculturation, education, and job mobility. The boundaries between Hawaii's various ethnic and racial groups were open; in the absence of the social control and enforcement of a strong ethnic community, acculturation, integration, and intermarriage took place.

It is interesting to meet some of the descendants of the first wave. One such man has a Korean surname but an Anglo first name. He is a Los Angeles lawyer, the graduate of a prestigious mainland university, and can trace his background to the early arrivals. He is married to a Japanese American from Hawaii and, much to the astonishment of Koreans making up the third wave, has little knowledge of the Korean language or culture. Although his story is a rather typical American story—immigration, acculturation, integration, assimilation—it seems surprising to some people because it involves an Asian family rather than a European one.

Little evidence is available about the second wave. These immigrants came one by one—brides and students—so their experiences were much more individual. Some war-bride marriages failed; other such unions turned out successfully. Their children, mostly of mixed blood, have not come to public attention, so it can be presumed that they have quietly moved into the American mainstream through the usual route of acculturation, integration, and assimilation.

The third wave is the largest, and the migration continues. Although it is too early to make a final judgment, Hurh and Kim postulate an "adhesive adjustment."[47] The term reflects the immigrants' strong and persistent sense of attachment to the Korean culture while adopting some of the ways of the new culture. Bok-Lim Kim makes a similar assessment, using a bilingual, bicultural model.[48] She indicates that Korean parents have no intention of discarding the Korean language and their culture ways, yet at the same time they have a strong sense and positive orientation toward the majority culture. They want their children to learn English, to excel in school, and to become part of the American mainstream. The existence of these two cultural ways can lead to a healthy biculturality; however, it can also lead to marginality, conflict, and alienation.

The most optimistic sign is the America that the migrants of the third wave have entered. They came at a time when immigration laws did not single out Asians as "undesirables," when there was an emphasis on family reunification, equal opportunity, affirmative action, and small-business loans. Legal discrimination has disappeared; establishment of the rights of minorities and the popularity of ethnic pluralism have created a solid base from which to interact with the mainstream.

But as is common with other Asian American groups, there are reminders that life in the United States is not utopia. The Los Angeles riot of 1992 sent a particularly fearsome message—that unresolved economic and racial tensions could translate into violence and destruction. That disastrous event has awakened Korean Americans to the fact that understanding and working with the surrounding communities should have high priority. Eui-Young Yu argues that, in spite of the stresses, strains, problems, and successes, the Koreans of the Los Angeles area appear to be at the stage of community development that is typical of first-generation immigrants.[49]

NOTES

1. Hilary Conroy, *The Japanese Seizure of Korea, 1868–1910* (Philadelphia: University of Pennsylvania Press, 1960), p. 174.

2. Hyung-chan Kim, "Korean Community Organizations in America: Their Characteristics and Problems," in Hyung-chan Kim, ed., *The Korean Diaspora* (Santa Barbara, CA: Clio Press, 1977), pp. 65–83.

3. Ibid.

4. Wayne Patterson, "The First Attempt to Obtain Korean Laborers for Hawaii," in Kim, *Korean Diaspora*, pp. 9–32.

5. Yo-jun Yun, "Early History of Korean Immigration to America," in Kim, *Korean Diaspora*, pp. 33–46.

6. Won Moo Hurh and Kwang Chung Kim, *Korean Immigrants in America* (Cranbury, NJ: Associated University Presses, 1984).

7. Mary Paik Lee, *Quiet Odyssey* (Seattle: University of Washington Press, 1990).

8. Romanzo Adams, *Interracial Marriage in Hawaii* (Montclair, NJ: Patterson Smith, 1967).

9. Young S. Kim Harvey and Soon-Hyung Chung, "The Koreans," in John McDermott, Jr., Wen-Shing Tseng, and Thomas Maretzki, eds., *Peoples and Cultures of Hawaii* (Honolulu: University of Hawaii Press, 1980), pp. 135–154.

10. Harry H. L. Kitano, Wai-tsang Yeung, Lynn Chai, and Herb Hatanaka, "Asian American Interracial Marriage," *Journal of Marriage and the Family* 46 (1984): 179–190.

11. Harvey and Chung, "The Koreans."

12. Eun-Sik Yang, "Korean Community, 1903–1970: Identity to Economic Prosperity." Paper presented at the Korean Community Conference, Koryo Research Institute, Los Angeles, Mar. 10, 1979.

13. See Warren Y. Kim, *Koreans in America* (n.p.: Po Chin Chai Printing Co., 1971), and Bong-youn Choy, *Koreans in America* (Chicago: Nelson Hall, 1979).

14. Choy, *Koreans in America*, pp. 182–189. Choy describes Rhee as inept but popular, especially among Koreans living in Korea who were unacquainted with his record abroad.

15. Ibid., p. 194.

16. Choong Soon Kim, *Faithful Endurance* (Tucson: University of Arizona Press, 1988).

17. Bok-Lim Kim, *The Korean American Child at School and at Home* (Washington, DC: U.S. Department of Health, Education and Welfare, 1980).

18. Hurh and Kim, *Korean Immigrants in America.*

19. Dong Soo Kim, "How They Fared in American Homes: A Follow-Up Study of Adopted Korean Children," *Children Today* 6 (1977): 2–6, 31.

20. Dong Soo Kim and Sookja P. Kim, "A Banana Identity: Asian American Adult Adoptees in America." Paper presented at the annual program meeting of the Council on Social Work Education, Washington, DC, Feb. 17, 1985.

21. Hyung Chan Kim, "Korean Community Organizations."

22. Insook Han Park, J. T. Fawcett, Fred Arnold, and Robert Gardnes, *Korean Immigrants and U.S. Policy: A Predeparture Perspective* (Honolulu: East-West Population Institute, 1990).

23. Bok-Lim Kim, *Korean American Child.*

24. Kwang Chung Kim and Won Moo Hurh, "Social and Occupational Assimilation of Korean Immigrant Workers in the United States," *California Sociologist* 3 (1980): 125–142.

25. Sally Kim, "Growing Pains," [UCLA] *Daily Breeze*, Apr. 29, 1993, p. 10.

26. David Holley, "Koreatown Suffering Growing Pains," *Los Angeles Times*, Dec. 8, 1985, p. 1.

27. Ibid.

28. Hurh and Kim, *Korean Immigrants in America.*

29. Edna Bonacich, "A Theory of Ethnic Antagonism: The Split Labor Market," *American Sociological Review* 37 (1972): 547–559.

30. Pyong Gap Min, "Korean Immigrants in Los Angeles," in Ivan Light and Parminder Bhachu, eds., *Immigration and Entrepreneurship* (New Brunswick, NJ: Transaction Publishers, 1993) pp. 205–242.

31. K. Connie Kang, "Korea Riot Victims Suffer Stress Disorder," *Los Angeles Times,* Mar. 9, 1993, p. B3.

32. Jeana Park, "Portrayal of Store Owner Seen as Volatile Stereotype," *Los Angeles Times,* Mar. 22, 1993, p. F3.

33. Hyung-chan Kim, "The History and Role of the Church in the Korean Community," in Kim, *Korean Diaspora,* pp. 47–63.

34. Ibid.

35. Hurh and Kim, *Korean Immigrants in America.*

36. Ibid.

37. Ibid.

38. Bok-Lim Kim, *Korean American Child.*

39. United Way, *1984 Koreatown Profile Study Report* (Los Angeles: Koreatown Profile Committee, 1984).

40. Michael Myong Seipel, "Social Integration Patterns of Korean Americans in the Predominantly White Communities." Paper presented at the annual program meeting of the Council on Social Work Education, Washington, DC, Feb. 17, 1985.

41. Philip Pan and Peter Pae. "Immigrant community flourishes in Annandale." *Washington Post,* May 16, 1999, p. A1.

42. Kyeyoung Park, *The Korean American Dream: Immigrants and Small Business in New York City* (Ithaca, NY: Cornell University Press, 1997).

43. Peter Pae. "Talking Jobs to Immigrate." *Washington Post,* May 16, 1999, p. A1.

44. Kwang Chung Kim, ed. *Koreans in the Hood: Conflict with African Americans* (Baltimore: Johns Hopkins University Press, 1999).

45. Lisa Miller, Soo Hyung Sung, and Martin Seligman, "Beliefs About Responses and Improvement Associated with Success among Korean Immigrants," *Journal of Social Psychology* 139 (1999): 221–229.

46. "Gang Charged with Terrorizing Korean Immigrants," *Bergen Record,* December 18, 1999.

47. Hurh and Kim, *Korean Immigrants in America.*

48. Bok-Lim Kim, *Korean American Child.*

49. Eui-Young Yu, "Korean Community Profile," *Korea Times,* English sec., p. 1.

Chapter 10

THE PACIFIC ISLANDERS

The Pacific Islanders remained relatively isolated for many years, but the advent of World War II brought an end to their peaceful existence. Their strategic location meant that the massive military might of the warring nations led to a large-scale invasion of the Islands, not only of men but of weapons, large-scale technology, and modernization. But, as Colbert[1] writes, modernization also brought poverty, crime, corruption, youth anomie, drug abuse, degradation of the environment, and a drastic change in traditional cultural ways.

But proponents of the new ways counter by applauding the introduction of employment, a wage system, higher standards of health and living, up-to-date technology, science, and less dependence on ritual and superstition. Younger generations are more likely to prefer aspects of modernization such as Hollywood movies, television, fast foods, and more independence from parental control. It is a timeless struggle, not only on the Islands but throughout the world, when a more traditional generation and culture comes face to face with the new. And when the new generation becomes old, it will no doubt face the challenges of the younger generation.

But the idea that people would voluntarily leave sandy beaches, clear skies, warm weather, and the "romantic lifestyle" of tropic isles like Samoa for overcrowded freeways, poor housing, and urban living is difficult to believe. Yet such a migration is now taking place. It has meant that for some of the small island communities, a greater number of persons now live on the mainland than remain in their former homes. Perhaps paradise, as depicted in Hol-

Table 10.1   Pacific Islander Population, 1980 and 1990

Group	1980	1990
Polynesian		
Hawaiian	220,278	205,501
Samoan	39,520	57,679
Tongan	6,226	16,707
All other	2,186	3,998
Micronesian		
Guamanian	30,695	47,754
All other	4,813	7,216
Melanesian		
Fijian	2,834 ⎫	7,218
All other	477 ⎭	
Pacific Islander, not specified	469	4,519
Total	259,566	350,592

Source: U.S. Census.

lywood movies, is not sufficient to sustain life, or, more likely, the island image reflects a stereotype, not a reality. Economic incentives, joining family, and a better life for children sound rather mundane coming from migrants from tropical isles, but these reasons appear as powerful for them as for others who have immigrated to America. Relevant questions are then the same as for any immigrant group: Who are they, why did they come, how were they received, and what are their adaptive patterns in the United States?

Before 1980, Pacific Islanders were not measured as a specific group in the U.S. census. The 1980 census divided the Pacific Islander population into Polynesian, Micronesian, and Melanesian (see Table 10.1). The most numerous were the native Hawaiians, who comprised 85 percent of the Pacific Islander population, followed by the Samoans, Guamanians, and Tongans. The 1990 census indicated no change in the rankings but showed an increase of 35 percent in the number of Pacific Islanders in the fifty states. They amounted to less than fourteen hundredths of 1 percent (.00014) of the population. In this chapter, we will cover the Samoans, Guamanians, and Hawaiians; our observations may also be pertinent to other Pacific Islander groups.

SAMOANS

The Samoan Islands are located in the South Pacific, approximately 2,300 miles southwest of Honolulu and 1,600 miles northeast of New Zealand. There are nine major islands, which have high rainfall, high humidity, and a tropical climate. The islands are divided into two political entities, American Samoa and Western Samoa. American Samoa has been United States territory since 1900. Western Samoa, in this century, has been owned by Germany, Great Britain, and New Zealand, but has been independent since 1962. The population of American Samoa increased from 5,679 in 1900 to 46,773 by 1990. Western Samoa also saw a dramatic increase in population during the same period, from 32,815 to ca. 190,000. However, large-scale emigration during the past several decades has slowed the population growth.[2]

Samoan legends hold that the people originated on the islands, but social scientists believe that Samoa was populated by Asians who came over the ocean in canoes. They lived in isolation until 1816 when Christian missionaries arrived via Tonga and Tahiti. Because the chiefs accepted the Christian faith, the islanders also became Christians. They were soon followed by traders from Great Britain, Germany, and the United States; the influx of foreigners dramatically changed native ways of life.

Prior to foreign intervention, Samoans lived under *faasamoa*, a term that denotes their customs, culture, values, and traditions.[3] The people living on the various islands shared the same language and culture, and the family served as the main organizing unit. Family name and reputation were important; respect for brothers, sisters, and older persons was built into the structure so that *faasamoa* gave the people a sense of cohesiveness, pride, and identity.

Their social structure was hierarchical. Central to the social system was the family, with the children at the bottom, the parents above the children, and the chief at the top. In the village, the family was below the village council of chiefs; at the district level, the district council was made up of certain chiefs from each village. The stratification continued up to the national level and was called the *Matai* system, which acted as the basic governing unit. The system of governance was effective in keeping unity among the islands for thousands of years prior to the arrival of foreigners.

Britain, Germany, and the United States were the primary contenders for influence over the islands. The intrusion of the colonial powers forced changes in the Samoan way of life. Division of the islands and introduction of Western methods of education, individualism, working for wages, and a cash economy meant that the Samoans could no longer live in their traditional ways. The foreign powers stripped the local governance structures of their ability to exercise authority and control, and the Samoan system was supplanted by colonial administrators.

The effects of westernization on a small population, living in a restricted space, can only be described as dramatic. The native way of life became an anachronism; the world powers fragmented the islands, the various powers claiming different spheres of influence. Acculturation meant becoming more American in American Samoa, more English in

Western Samoa. This background led Sereisa Milford to assert that what-ever the reasons given for leaving the islands, the primary impetus was pro-vided by Western colonialism and imperialism.[4]

The Mead-Freeman Controversy

Samoa became prominent through the early writings of Margaret Mead, es-pecially in her book concerning adolescent sexuality.[5] Her view was that growing up in Samoa was akin to living in paradise—competition was lim-ited, and there was little guilt or inhibition in terms of sexuality. Derek Free-man attempted to unmask Mead's findings; retracing her footsteps several decades later, he concluded the opposite—that Samoans were by nature sexually inhibited, puritanical, aggressive, highly competitive, and prone to jealousy.[6] Pathological behaviors included assault, rape, suicide, and murder.

In an attempt to discover the "real" Samoa, Lowell Holmes conducted his own investigation, which generally supported Mead's findings. Perhaps the most acute observation on the controversy came from the wife of the prime minister of Western Samoa, who stated that neither Mead nor Free-man accurately represented the Samoan culture or its way of life. Both out-siders missed the subtlety of life in Samoa; it was neither the permissive paradise of Mead nor the aggressive society of Freeman. Another Samoan suggested that anthropologists study the tribal tensions and the sexual neu-roses on the island where he now lives—Manhattan.[7]

Migration

The first modern migration from Samoa occurred in the 1920s when Samoan members of the Mormon church were brought to Hawaii to help build the Hawaiian Mormon Temple at Laie, about 35 miles from Hon-olulu.[8] This first group of immigrants was guided by a primarily religious orientation, and most stayed on in Laie, in contrast to subsequent groups, who were more concerned with economic issues and tended to move on to Honolulu and other places where there were better economic opportunities.

In contrasting some of the differences between the native Hawaiians and the Samoans who made up the bulk of the population at Laie, Bernard Pierce noted that the Samoans were much more business-oriented than the Hawaiian population. He attributed these differences to prior contact that had enabled the Samoans to develop a business sense, including a desire to acquire goods, that had eluded the Hawaiians. He also noted that the Samoans were never apologetic about their culture, whereas the Hawaiians often made derogatory remarks about their own way of life.[9]

The second significant migration occurred after the U.S. Navy trans-ferred administration of American Samoa to the Department of the Interior in 1950. Many Samoans followed the Navy to Hawaii and then to the mainland. Others migrated to the United States seeking better jobs, better education, and reunion with relatives. Western Samoans, as citizens of an independent nation, must go through regular immigration procedures; Samoans from the American sector are able to travel to the United States without passports or visas.

Most Samoan Americans have settled in Honolulu, San Francisco, Los Angeles, San Diego, and Seattle. Outside Hawaii, they face a vastly different physical and cultural climate. As one Samoan told us, in Hawaii she never felt that she was a member of a minority group, but in Los Angeles she is clearly aware that she is part of a minority.[10] The Samoan Islands are in the tropics, where distances are short and the people are surrounded by kin. Skin color and language are not marks of difference, and there is an easy familiarity. Age is treated with respect, and family needs have the highest priority.

But in America, Samoan populations, primarily first-generation, are practically invisible and largely ignored by the dominant community. Because of their small numbers and the relative insignificance of their home islands in international affairs, they possess little political power. An additional handicap is that they are often lumped in with other Asian groups who are often more successful than they. They suffer disadvantages due to language barriers, lack of educational and occupational skills, and low income.

Most live in family and extended-family units and expect to have other kin join them in a chain migration. Although they are a first-generation community, there are many young children. Their median age of 20.8 years is far below the American median of 33.0 years. Their sex ratio is about evenly divided, 51.5 percent male to 48.5 percent female, and they tend to marry among themselves.[11]

In common with all Americans, finding a job and securing housing are among their highest priorities. Since most are unskilled laborers, wages are minimal. One solution, which is also reinforced by their past ways, involves an exchange of goods and services among kinfolk. Thus the family and the kinship network serve as important resources, and some of the Samoan ways can be preserved, tempered by the realities of living in urban America.[12]

The Samoan adaptation reflects a bicultural lifestyle. At work a man might dress and act like fellow Americans, but at home he may take off his shoes, put on a lava-lava (a long wraparound skirt), sit on the floor, and talk to others in Samoan. He may wait for the adolescents in the household to prepare the evening meal and expect his school-age children to take care of the younger members. Household decorations may reflect an island ambience.[13] It will be interesting to see how long this lifestyle will be retained as the younger, more acculturated generation achieves adulthood.

The demographic picture of the Samoans indicates that *faasamoa* may be affected by the large number of young children in the Samoan community. While the first-generation adults are engaged in Samoan-style oratory, exchange of gifts, and the Samoan chatter, younger children are expected to fall back to the outer circle. Thus in Samoa the children might hear and learn to participate from their peripheral positions; in urban America they are more likely to retreat to another room to watch television. Parents are also likely to encourage their children to speak English and to practice the behavioral patterns that will allow them to get ahead in the new culture. But as one Samoan told us, there remains less of an emphasis on higher education, especially when compared to the Chinese and Japanese. If a high school graduate is given the choice of getting a job and putting food on the table or spending the next four years in college, there is a tendency to choose the former.[14] Younger adults are likely to find that the old culture is less relevant and hinders their participation in the new society. Perhaps it will be up to future generations to appreciate the ways of the ancestral culture.

One of the special facets of the Samoans, which differentiates them from the other Asians, is athletic ability, coupled with large body size. As a consequence, Samoans have become prominent in football, at both the college and the professional level, and it is not uncommon to hear sports broadcasters struggling over a name like Tuiasasopo. One potential problem is that athletic role models may become too attractive; only a tiny proportion can succeed in professional sports.

GUAMANIANS

In many ways, the problems and adaptations of the Guamanians, Tongans, and other Pacific Islanders are similar to those faced by the Samoans. The absence of a Margaret Mead may have made the rest of the islanders less familiar than the Samoans—at best a mixed blessing.

Guam, Saipan, Tinian, and Rota are territories of the United States and constitute the commonwealth of the Northern Marianas. The native people are the Chamorros, and the islands are located about 1,500 miles east of Manila, 1,500 miles south of Tokyo, and 6,000 miles west of Los Angeles.

Guam was "discovered" by Magellan on his famous round-the-world expedition in 1521 and was under Spanish rule until Spain lost the Spanish-American War of 1898. It then became a United States possession. Spanish rule was characterized by a missionary zeal and attempts to change the life of the inhabitants in every way. But the Chamorros did not submit; there were revolts and high Chamorro resistance. As a consequence, the Spanish rulers virtually wiped out the native population. Early accounts placed their number at over 50,000, but by the first recorded census in 1710, only 3,539 survived. Eventually, the natives, composed primarily of females—most of the males had been eliminated—mixed with Filipino and Mexican exiles, as well as later arrivals such as Europeans and Japanese, so most modern Guamanians have a multiracial ancestry.

Guamanian immigration was aided by the 1950 Organic Act, which conferred American citizenship on the inhabitants of Guam. It has been a two-way migration—Guamanians have been coming and going in both directions—so precise numbers are difficult to ascertain. There are a number of reasons for the migration. One is military service: As early as 1938, young men volunteered for the Navy and ended their careers in West Coast cities such as San Francisco, San Diego, Seattle, and Los Angeles. Another group immigrated to attend American schools because there was a need for trained people to help in the administration of the islands. Prospective teachers, nurses, doctors, and lawyers left to be trained on the mainland, and many did not return. Then there were those who were dissatisfied with island life; they saw a dearth of educational and vocational opportunities, as well as inadequate public services, medical facilities, and job opportunities. Other reasons behind the immigration were destructive storms in 1962 and 1976 and overpopulation.

The immigrants had dreams of America similar to the images held by other immigrants. It was the land of opportunity, of milk and honey, of peace and tranquillity. A more practical reason was to join old friends and relatives.

The year 1970 was an important one for Guam, as for the first time its governor was elected. Prior to that time it had experienced a series of colonial administrations—the Spanish, the Americans, the Japanese, and the Americans again. The island was also opened to immigration; previously it had been under the protection of the U.S. military, and no one was allowed to come in. The opening up of the island meant increased foreign job competition, especially from Filipinos, Taiwanese, and Koreans.[15]

Chamorro values include a strong family, ancestor worship (despite a Catholic tradition), a fishing and farming lifestyle, and the authority of the mother in the home. The mother is the primary decision maker; families are close-knit, with parents, unmarried and married children, and aunts and uncles often in close proximity. Child rearing is viewed as a family responsibility. Faye Munoz cited the example of the role of one strong mother: A couple who had been married for twenty-eight years and living in California continues to seek the permission of the wife's mother if they wish to go out. If the mother says no, the couple will stay at home.[16]

Guamanian problems are similar to the problems faced by other islander groups. They are unsophisticated in the business and technological world. Whereas groups such as the Chinese, Japanese, Koreans, and Vietnamese have gone into restaurants, grocery, and liquor stores, few islanders can be found in small businesses. There are almost no Pacific Islanders in the professions; common jobs are in the unskilled and semiskilled sector, as custodians, cooks, and clerks.

Guamanians come from a culture with rich oral rather than written traditions. Children born in the United States and those who had left Guam before the age of 12 have difficulty with the native language, and elders fear that much of their history will fade away.

Older folks suffer from isolation—there is little integration—and they tend to know more about political activities and occurrences in the islands than in their present homes in the United States. Other problems include low pay, inadequate education, and difficulty in supporting large families. Guamanian immigrants do not understand their neighborhoods or the larger political system, and often they do not know where to turn for help or for personal, business, or social services; their former island networks, effective in their earlier lives, are less relevant here. Munoz indicated that although the Chamorros had been exposed to American influences since the turn of the century, their needs and priorities were deemed less important than the defense requirements of the United States.[17] As a consequence, they became dependent on America—paternalistic models, no matter how benign, often do that—and this left them unprepared for independent living once they gained their freedom.

HAWAIIANS

Of all of the Pacific Islander groups, the Hawaiian represents either the most successful or the least successful, depending on one's orientation. If the criteria for success include racial amalgamation and interracial mixing, then Hawaiians would certainly be deemed very successful. There are almost no "pure" Hawaiians left, although their disappearance cannot be attributed solely to racial amalgamation. However, if success is measured by pluralistic models—the ability of a group to retain its autonomy and culture and to remain racially "pure"—then the natives of Hawaii would certainly be classified as unsuccessful.

Hawaii was believed to have been colonized by Polynesian voyagers, mostly from the Marquesas Islands and Tahiti over 1,500 years ago. When Captain Cook, the famous English explorer, came to the islands in 1778, their more than 300,000 inhabitants had a thriving culture. It was a highly stratified system, reminiscent of medieval Europe, China, and Japan, with a class of chieftains (*aliis*) at the top; an elite group of specialists (*kahunas*) active in the arts, crafts, medicine, and religion at the next tier; and the commoners, who made up the majority of the population, at the bottom.[18]

Hawaii's past was marked with conflict. "Tribal" warfare and eventual bloody reunification of the islands under the control of King Kamehameha I left them unprepared for the "foreign" invasion. By the time the first New England Congregationalist missionaries arrived in 1820, one year after the death of Kamehameha, Hawaii had already undergone a change from the idyllic isle discovered by Cook several decades before. For example, Cook emphasized the strength, intelligence, and cleanliness of the natives who farmed, fished, and enjoyed athletic games and dances. But by the 1820s, commentators complained about the laziness of the Hawaiians, their apathy, and their poor health; the destruction of the native culture was already under way.[19]

The hospitality of the islanders—it was a place for happy refreshment after a long voyage—and the importance of trade were the key factors in their demise. Hawaiian chiefs rushed to trade with the *haoles* for fancy clothes, ornaments, and weapons and in their greed claimed rights to fishing grounds and fruit trees and often worked the commoners to death. Agricultural resources that were formerly consumed by the people were put up for sale to the visitors; the insatiable tastes of the chiefs for foreign goods resulted in heavier taxes. Hawaiian boys went sailing with the big ships; derelict haole seamen roamed the ports, encouraging swift trades in alcohol and sex. Then came the introduction of the "white man's diseases" from European sailors and traders—syphilis, gonorrhea, colds, pneumonia, smallpox, and cholera. The Hawaiians had to immunities to diseases with which they had had no experience; powerful, robust Hawaiians could succumb as easily to measles as to cholera.[20] Drunkeness was widespread, and in extreme cases, Hawaiians lost the will to live. From a relatively stable population of about 300,000 in 1778—before the coming of the white men— the natives were reduced to a population of about 57,000 in 1889. Within thirty years of Cook's arrival, indifference and apathy became a part of the Hawaiian way of life, to be replaced years later by overwhelming despair. The old social ties had largely disappeared, and group respect had been demolished.[21]

The Christian missionaries from New England also sped the process of social change by attacking the roots of the Hawaiian way of life. The native language, dress, dances, and art were downgraded, and the entire sociopolitical system of the islanders was constantly forced to change. But at least initially, the missionaries were moved by spiritual goals, whereas sailors and merchants came for lust and profit.

The Hawaiians were introduced to Western culture in the form of explosives, iron implements, a money economy, and Christianity. The single event that most dramatically changed the social system was the Great Mahele of 1848, which permitted the purchase of land by private persons.[22] Through a series of complicated manipulations, much of the land formerly under the king and chiefs ended up in the hands of a few white oligarchs.

After the Great Mahele, haole investments in land expanded, the growing of sugar and other enterprises grew at a rapid pace, and the demand for cheap labor changed the demography of the islands. In common with the Native Americans on the mainland, the native Hawaiians did not make good laborers—why should any man work from dawn to dusk, week after week, performing backbreaking labor for someone else when the fish were plentiful in the sea and the coconuts dropped from the tree? One visitor, commenting on Hawaiian labor, noted:

> If the overseer leaves for a moment, down they squat . . . and the longest-winded fellow commences upon a yarn . . . that keeps upon the others a broad grin. . . . as soon as he comes in sight, [they] seize their spades and commence laboring with an assiduity that baffles description, and perhaps all the while not strain a muscle.[23]

The importation of cheap labor thus became a high priority for the plantation owners. Chinese, Japanese, Koreans, and Filipino laborers were imported from Asia; smaller numbers of workers were also brought from such European areas as Scotland, Portugal, Spain, and Germany.

Beginning in the early 1840s, American residents in Hawaii, though a tiny minority, played an enormous role in Hawaiian politics. From 1842 to 1854, for example, an American, J. P. Judd, served as prime minister to Kamehameha III, and by the late nineteenth century, Americans dominated the Hawaiian economy as well. The United States made a series of commercial treaties with Hawaii and in 1887 received the exclusive right to establish a naval base at Pearl Harbor. The coming to power of the nationalist and traditionalist Queen Liliuokalani threatened the control of the American elite, and it overthrew her in a coup in 1893, aided by U.S. naval forces. A provisional government headed by Sanford B. Dole, the pineapple king, negotiated to have Hawaii annexed, but anti-imperialist President Grover Cleveland refused to allow it to take place. The Dole government continued in power until 1898, when, in the enthusiasm for expansion created by the Spanish-American War, Hawaii was annexed by a joint resolution of Congress. Although Hawaii had a population and economy worthy of statehood at the time of annexation, racism kept it in territorial status until 1959. American politicians rightly assumed that polyethnic Hawaii would send non-white representatives to Congress. As one southern legislator put it during a hearing on Hawaiian statehood in the 1930s, if Hawaii became a state, we'd have "a senator named Moto!"[24]

Lawrence Fuchs reports that there were at least three Hawaiis at the time of annexation. One was the haole society, characterized by monogamy, private ownership of land, Western dress, music and recreation, and Christianity. Whites owned most of the land, were in control of the economy, and ran the political system. Plantation life was primarily Asian—languages, games, worship, and attitudes toward family, property, and authority had the flavor of the Orient. Asians provided the labor; although in the majority numerically, they were divided by ethnicity and were economically dependent. Then there was what remained of the native Hawaiian culture, found in the more remote villages, where people prayed to Madam Pele, the Fire Goddess, to spread lava over the land to wash the foreigners into the sea.

The relative power of each of the groups was a good predictor of the type of Hawaii that was to emerge.

At the start of the twentieth century, Hawaii was full of contradictions, yet the oligarchy lived and managed them up to the time of the Japanese attack on Pearl Harbor, when the cumulative effect of public education, universal suffrage (which was decreed under American annexation), and World War II began to alter its structure. As Fuchs writes:

> A handful of haoles, intolerant of opposition, ran the Islands, but discontent was openly expressed in uncensored ethnic papers. The oligarchy, self-consciously Caucasian, made few open appeals to racial prejudice. The small group . . . nevertheless helped foster education. The small aristocracy, reaping the benefits of a plantation system, with its ruthlessness, was constantly torn between the desire for power and profit and the evangelism of both the Congregational church and the American dream of freedom and opportunity for all.[25]

But the toilers on the plantations and the native Hawaiians did not see the conflict—power and profit seemed always to prevail.

There were some gaps in the stratification system. One was the emphasis on education—a New England value—and children of former plantation workers acquired an education. Foremost were the children of Asian background; native Hawaiians were less so inclined. Another was that of miscegenation and intermarriage; even the early haoles married Hawaiian women of high rank. Members of important haole families—Bishop, Wilcox, Shipman, Campbell, and others—married Hawaiian women. As Fuchs speculates, their own traditions of intermarriage may have prevented them from attacking the marital practices of other groups. Native Hawaiians joined in this practice fully.

Although there were strikes and other symptoms of discontent, the haole oligarchy dominated the islands for the next forty years. Ethnicity became the primary means of identification—people thought of themselves as haoles, Hawaiians, Portuguese, Chinese, Japanese, Filipinos. Each ethnic group, shaped initially by the historical circumstances of its immigration, developed a distinctive way of life. The goal for the haole was to maintain control; for the Portuguese, to be considered a haole; for the Chinese, to be economically independent; and for the Japanese, to be accepted. The goal for the Hawaiians was to recapture the past.[26]

Of all the groups, the native Hawaiians had the most difficulty in adjusting to the competitive haole culture. Much of their past behavior did not fit into the newer society. For example, their sexual behavior and the casual use of property were looked on as criminal by haole norms. The islands had undergone too much change; a retreat to the past left the Hawaiians even further behind.

An attempt was made in 1920 to set aside public lands at nominal rents to persons of at least one-half Hawaiian blood through the Hawaiian Homes Commission. The legislation was an attempt to "rehabilitate" the

Hawaiian people and for them to regain possession of their land. But as Fuchs reports:

> The rehabilitation idea did not produce a Hawaiian renaissance. It was, after all, too much to ask. The haole religion, family structure, sex mores, land system, property relationships . . . were fundamentally different from what was known in ancient Hawaii. The Hawaiian Homes Commission Act represented one more, perhaps the major, futile Hawaiian effort to recapture the past.[27]

An understandable and all too common response to frustrated lives is the phenomenon of scapegoating. Hawaiians were no exception. Rather than venting their hostility against the powerful haole, the natives began blaming the "orientals" for their plight. They helped the haoles write land laws discriminating against the Chinese, then turned their animus against the Japanese. But even though they disliked both the haoles and the Asians as groups, the natives maintained many individual friendships and continued their traditions of sex and marriage without discrimination.

Intermarriage meant that Hawaiians and part-Hawaiians became diffused throughout the population. They carried on the spirit of *aloha*—in spite of animosity and hostility toward groups, individuals were treated with friendliness and generosity. As a consequence, the picture of Hawaii as a racial paradise has a degree of validity, given the ethnic and racial diversity of its population.

Alan Howard recorded a rise in ethnic militancy in the 1970s led by younger, relatively well-educated Hawaiians with an interest in the native language, traditional art and music, and a revitalized ethnic identity. Their basic theme was their alienation from their land and the abuse of the environment by the "foreigners." It included valuing group affiliation over individual achievement and maintaining social relations over accumulating wealth.[28]

At a conference sponsored by the Council of Hawaiian Organizations, a number of goals were listed. First was to achieve self-determination, followed by establishing a land base for use by native Hawaiians. Other goals were to address educational needs, to achieve economic independence, and to strengthen the family and the old spirit of cooperation. The leaders saw the haole immigration as the primary cause for the disruption of the Hawaiian lifestyle.[29]

Haunani-Kay Trask writes that their country was stolen from them, along with their citizenship, their lands, and their independence.[30] In many ways there are similarities between the experiences of Native Americans and Hawaiians. Both were "conquered," and both wish to restore and affirm historic water, fishing, hunting, gathering, and access rights. Their opponents object to special rights for both Native Americans and native Hawaiians.

Present-day Hawaii has not been kind to the native Hawaiians, who have the highest poverty rates, the shortest life expectancy, and the highest infant mortality in the state. They have more heart disease and cancer and comprise a high proportion of the prison population. Their educational level and political sophistication remains minimal, so that their future power in the state is likely to remain low when compared to some of the more active Asian American groups. However, leaders in the community have become more active in asserting their rights by advocating for a Hawaiian nation, regaining control of their lands, and petitioning the United Nations for Hawaii to be placed on the decolonization list. The image of Hawaii as the island of aloha, romance, and harmony is certainly not in the experiences of the natives.[31]

Hawaiians have emigrated to the mainland, but their actual numbers are difficult to assess. Many are of mixed ancestry, and their experiences are as diverse as their backgrounds.

COMMON PROBLEMS

A number of similar problems are faced by all immigrants from the Pacific Islands. They represent a group with 1,200 distinct languages[32] and cultures so different from one another that there is no easy way to classify them. For most islanders, the problems are more pronounced when they leave home for life on the mainland. The native Hawaiians are unique in that they are the only ones to have been "invaded"—they lost their lands, power, culture, and identity because they lacked restrictive immigration laws and other practices that would have kept them in a position of dominance. Instead, they integrated and assimilated at a rapid pace, so that by the end of the 1980s, very few of the "pure" remained.[33]

Some of the problems faced by all Pacific Islanders in America are these:

1. The vast differences between the education and skills necessary to survive in a modern technological society and the culture of the islands.
2. Loss of status, rank, and prestige. Former leaders may end up in unskilled laboring jobs; very few find employment in the white-collar and professional sector.
3. Low wages and high expenses. Many Islanders have large families and are obligated to take care of them. Most contribute regularly to their churches.
4. Problems of roles and identity. Identities that are closely tied to the family, kinship groups, and villages are weakened in the new culture. Hierarchical roles, especially of the male, are threatened.
5. Unrealistic stereotypes of the islands that foster an exotic, romantic image or one of heavy-drinking revelers.

6. Placement under the banner "Asians." Pacific Islanders' backgrounds are vastly different, and this lack of differentiation places the islanders at a disadvantage when competing for federal funds and other forms of assistance.
7. Attempts to recapture a past that may be beyond their ability to control.

The problems for the Pacific Islanders are more sociocultural than those caused by discrimination and oppression. What was functional in a small island economy may not be useful in an urban, technological society. Further, unlike some other Asian groups, their numbers are too small and their resources too slim to develop a structurally separate community and a parallel "opportunity structure." Community resources that may have been supportive in the islands may not be effective in helping them capitalize on opportunities available in the mainstream American society.

The most encouraging sign is that islander immigration comes at a time when overt discrimination has largely disappeared. There are still problems associated with membership in a different "race" in a race-conscious society, but the relatively small size of the group should enable them to acculturate at a rapid pace. Their cultural ties, especially in terms of their language, are not functional in any international sense, so by the second and third generations it may quietly disappear. However, it is hoped that their strong family ties and the ethos of helping one another will be retained and become integrated into the larger society.

NOTES

1. Evelyn S. Colbert, *The Pacific Islands: Paths to the Present*, (Boulder, CO: Westview Press, 1997), provides brief histories of many islands.
2. Ramsey Shu, "Kinship Systems and Migrant Adaptation: Samoans of the United States," *Amerasia Journal* 12 (1985): 23–47.
3. Sereisa Milford, "Imperialism and Samoan National Identity," *Amerasia Journal* 12 (1985): 49–56.
4. Ibid.
5. Margaret Mead, *Coming of Age in Samoa* (New York: Morrow, 1928).
6. Derek Freeman, *Margaret Mead and Samoa: The Masking and Unmasking of an Anthropological Myth* (Cambridge, MA: Harvard University Press, 1983).
7. Lowell D. Holmes, *Quest for the Real Samoa* (S. Hadley, MA: Bergin & Garvey, 1987).
8. Bernard Pierce, "Acculturation of Samoans in the Mormon Village of Laie, Territory of Hawaii" (master's thesis, University of Hawaii, June 1956).
9. Ibid.
10. Interview with Sereisa Milford, Sept. 9, 1986, at UCLA.
11. Ramsey Shu and Adele Satele, *The Samoan Community in Southern California: Conditions and Needs* (Chicago: Asian American Mental Health Research Center, 1977).

12. Lydia Kotchek, "Of Course, We Respect Our Old People, But . . . : Aging among Samoan Migrants," *California Sociologist* 3 (1980): 197–212.

13. Ibid.

14. Ibid.

15. Faye Munoz, "An Exploratory Study of Island Migration: Chamorros of Guam" (Ph.D. dissertation, UCLA, 1979).

16. Ibid.

17. Ibid.

18. Alan Howard, "Hawaiians," in Stephan Thernstrom, ed., *Harvard Encyclopedia of American Ethnic Groups* (Cambridge, MA: Harvard University Press, 1980), pp. 449–452.

19. Bradd Shore, "Pacific Islanders," op. cit., pp. 763–768.

20. Lawrence Fuchs, *Hawaii Pono: A Social History of Hawaii* (New York: Harcourt, Brace, 1961).

21. Ibid.

22. Ibid.

23. Ibid., p. 24.

24. Ibid.

25. Ibid., p. 42.

26. Ibid.

27. Ibid., p. 72.

28. Howard, "Hawaiians."

29. Shore, "Pacific Islanders."

30. Haunani-Kay Trask, "Politics in the Pacific Islands: Imperialism and Native Self-determination," *Amerasia Journal* 16 (1990): 1–19. See also Haunani-Kay Trask, *From a Native Daughter* (Monroe, ME: Common Courage Press, 1993).

31. Mindy Pennybacker, "Should the Aloha State Say Goodbye? Natives Wonder." *Nation* 263 (5) (August 12, 1996): 21–25; Noreen Mokuau and Jon Matsuoka, "Turbulence Among a Native People: Social Work Practice with Hawaiians," *Social Work* 40 (1955): 465–473.

32. Linda S. Parker, *Native American Estate* (Honolulu: University of Hawaii Press, 1989).

33. I. C. Campbell, *A History of the Pacific Islands* (Berkeley: University of California Press, 1989).

Chapter 11

THE SOUTHEAST ASIANS

The Vietnam War created a different set of relations with Southeast Asia. What was once a forgotten and neglected area became a high priority for military action and its effects still linger today, especially because it introduced new Asian populations to our country. They came involuntarily, did not meet visa and quota requirements, and many were totally unprepared for life in the United States. Initially, there were special programs to help them fit into the new country, but by the end of the century, most programs had run their course.

However, because of the circumstances leading to their arrival, studies on their adaptation, including different cultural styles, have become one topic of inquiry. For example, a front-page article in the *Los Angeles Times* discussed child brides among the Hmong. Every winter in the Central Valley of California, Hmong men search for brides, often as young as 12 and 13 years of age. There is a male saying, "If you marry a girl your age, by the time she has given you enough children, she will look twice your age."[1]

Early marriage has made Hmong mothers among the most prolific in the world, with an average fertility rate of 9.5 children per woman. One concern among U.S. authorities is that the Hmong have the highest welfare rate of any group in the United States. Another concern is that many young girls who have been doing extremely well in school drop out at an early age in order to marry and to have children.

The pressure "to do something" is high, even though it is difficult to conceive of any intervention that would be effective concerning marriage rituals that have long been a part of the ancestral culture. California law defines sex with anyone under 15 as a felony, and court permission is necessary for marriage under 18 years of age, but the legal system is stretched too thin to pursue a crime rooted more in culture than in vice.

But there is concern regarding this practice, for it runs counter to the norms of the dominant society. Questions of how long this practice might continue and if it will have an effect on the future of the Hmong, especially the young girls, are legitimate concerns. For example, one female respondent said, "Hmong females have no rights. . . . We're just supposed to have babies, be housewives, do what the husband says to do. It's a very sad life."[2]

But if research among the Hmong on this issue were to be conducted thirty or forty years from now, there is a high probability that acculturation would have taken place and marital practices would be more in keeping with dominant-group norms, so that the only remark might well be that once upon a time in the 1990s, there was this quaint custom of taking child brides. The unfortunate consequence of publicizing such "culture conflicts" is that it may tend to reinforce stereotypes of the "strange and alien ways" of the newcomers rather than understanding such conflicts as issues that all immigrants have had to resolve.

Southeast Asians who have entered the United States as refugees include the Vietnamese, Laotians (Lao and Hmong), Cambodians (Kampucheans), and ethnic Chinese. Their refugee status was one result of U.S. intervention in Vietnam after World War II and the subsequent fall of South Vietnam to the communist forces from Hanoi. Before we examine each of these Southeast Asian groups, we will study the differences between a refugee and a "regular" immigrant and discuss briefly the history of U.S. policy toward refugees.

WHO IS A REFUGEE?

A refugee is a person who flees his or her native country for safety in a time of distress. Thus refugees are a special kind of immigrant; however, they face the same questions that all newcomers must address. Do they attempt to become a part of the mainstream? Are their goals acculturation, integration, and assimilation? Or do they wish to retain a separate identity, maintaining pluralistic structures and awaiting the day that they can return to their homelands? What are the attitudes of the majority group toward them? What are the reactions of other minorities?

Although the major difference between the refugee and the immigrant relates to the type of entry into our country, there are other differences worth noting. In a push-pull model of migration, the refugee is more likely to be pushed out of his or her home. There is often a move from one site to another; an additional element is some type of persecution, based on race, religion, or political ideology. There is a strong dimension of fear and crisis.

Very few refugees have the luxury of thinking about the long-term consequences of their migration. Many harbor the hope of eventually returning to their homes, and hence there is a temporary quality to their migration.

But if past behavior of Russians, Jews, and Cubans is any indication, few refugees will return home. Most students of migration, beginning with Ravenstein, argue that "push" immigrants are less likely to return than "pull."

There is general agreement that the term *refugee* was first applied in the late 1600s.[3] However, the sight of populations fleeing from political and other disasters was a common one long before that time. At one period, refugees were regarded as desirable and made welcome since they brought with them technological, industrial, military, commercial, and agricultural skills. At present, it appears that refugees representing less wealthy and less skilled populations are less desired, especially if they are racially and culturally different from the host society. But the rapid changes in the political and economic spheres over the past several decades have created a massive refugee population, so it can be justifiably argued that the twentieth century is the century of the refugee.

The increased use of the passport during World War I, identified by Neal Ascherson as one of the more noxious but lasting mementos of that war,[4] created "stateless persons" and compounded problems of mobility across national boundaries. The Russian Revolution and the steady stream of refugees fleeing from German fascism in the 1930s further contributed to population movement. World War II saw the displacement of many populations from their previous homes; current conditions creating refugees include changes in government, wars, civil strife, and instability.

Although there is general agreement that a refugee is one who flees a country in a time of distress, the question of who is a "true" refugee remains difficult to ascertain. Economic migrants, fortune hunters, opportunists, and those who have consciously planned on immigration are mixed with those who were forced to flee for their lives because of a change in the political structure. Bruce Grant acknowledges the crisis conditions leading to forced migration, but he also notes that some refugees fled to the United States and other countries for a reason common to most immigration—the hope for a better life compared to limited opportunities at home.[5] But no matter what the circumstances, refugees share a common background. They have cut ties with the country of their birth, and they are venturing into a new land with little formal preparation. There are questions of how to make a living, how to fit, and how to manage. Will their norms and values be congruent and functional in the new setting? How helpful will their new hosts be in the transition?

U.S. POLICY TOWARD REFUGEES

Prior to 1980, the United States policy toward refugees was on an ad hoc basis. The Displaced Persons Act of 1948 allowed individuals uprooted by World War II and those fleeing Soviet persecution to immigrate; the

Refugee Relief Act of 1953 offered asylum to victims of national calamities and those fleeing communism. After the Bay of Pigs incident, Congress acted to regularize and make permanent the immigration status of all Cubans who had arrived in this country since January 1, 1959, by granting them refugee eligibility through the Migration and Refugee Assistance Act of 1962. Amendments to the Immigration and Nationality Act of 1965 established parole authority for granting asylum on an individual basis. Cuban refugees entering the country between 1961 and 1971 and 100,000 refugees from Indochina in 1976 came under the parole provisions.

In 1980, President Carter signed the Refugee Assistance Act, which for the first time formulated an explicit policy for refugees. It moved beyond Cold War priorities and established annual admission levels of 50,000 and allowances for upward increases. It recognized the principle of asylum and regularized mechanisms for distributing federal aid to refugees and for reimbursing states, local governments, and private voluntary agencies for their refugee-related expenses.

THE TWO WAVES OF SOUTHEAST ASIAN REFUGEES

Two waves of refugees are generally identified.[6] Many in the first wave were military personnel, civil servants, teachers, farmers, fishermen, employees of the Americans, and Catholics. They recognized that their middle- and upper-class lifestyles would not be compatible with a communist regime; they feared reprisals and personal harm, so escape was a necessity. Educational attainment was generally high; nearly half of the household heads were born in northern Vietnam and had fled to the south after the French defeat at Dienbienphu in 1954. The immigration was primarily in family groups, although there was also a sizable number of unaccompanied single males. There were extremes in wealth; some came with substantial sums of money, while others fled with scarcely more than the clothes on their backs.[7]

The second wave consisted of refugees who arrived in the United States after 1975. Poor agricultural harvests, the economic drain of continued fighting in Laos and Cambodia, loss of jobs, and generally poor economic conditions contributed to the push. Many also feared being sent to "reeducation" centers and work camps and being forcibly moved away from their urban environment. Increased hostilities between Vietnam and China created an additional problem for the ethnic Chinese residing in Southeast Asia; their loyalty was questioned, and their property was expropriated.

To sum up, the first wave was generally composed of refugees from the more "advantaged" backgrounds than the second. In the first wave, 49 percent were under 36 years of age; in the second wave, 58 percent. Family size was four in the first group and four to five in the second. Forty-one percent were Catholic and 40 percent Buddhist in the first wave; 29 percent were Catholic and 47 percent Buddhist in the second. In terms of education, 48.8 percent of the first wave attended over four years of college, compared to 29.1 percent of the second. The first wave was generally more familiar with Western ways and culture than the second, although the latter also included members of the intelligentsia who had been unable to leave earlier.[8]

The recency of the migration of Southeast Asians can be garnered from the following statistics. Prior to 1970, there were approximately 20,000 Vietnamese in the United States, and the number of Cambodians and Laotians was too small to be counted. By 1980, there were 415,235 Indochinese, of which 78 percent were Vietnamese, 16 percent Cambodians, and 6 percent Laotians. In 1990, these figures had risen to 614,547 Vietnamese, 239,096 Laotians (149,014 Lao and 90,082 Hmong), and 147,411 Cambodians. Although there were official attempts to scatter the refugees throughout the country, the majority have migrated to the Sunbelt states. California has the most Asian refugees, followed by Texas and Washington. By 1990 a significant percentage of these groups was American-born. Twenty percent of Vietnamese were in this category: They had a median age of 6.6 years.

SarDersai provides a historical look at the Southeast Asians. The region is not a cohesive unit of similar backgrounds.[9] There are at least four different religions: Islam, Hinduism, Buddhism, and Christianity. Five non-Asian powers have ruled the region: the British in Burma and Malaya; the Dutch in Indonesia; the French in Laos, Kampuchea, and Vietnam; the Americans in the Philippines; and the Portuguese in Timor. Only Thailand remained free. Japan had control of the area during World War II.

As a consequence, each of the colonies had different spheres of administration, education, trade, and currency, and, most important, these differences created barriers against easy and effective communication.

THE VIETNAMESE

Background

Foreign influences on Vietnam have included the Chinese, French, Japanese, and American. The history of Chinese immigration to Southeast Asia extends over 2,000 years. Some came by land, to Cochinchina and Cambodia; more came by sea, to Vietnam. The Chinese influence has been long and pervasive, yet relationships between the two cultures have seldom been positive. The Chinese lived in their own segregated communities and were subject to numerous repressive measures.[10]

The French entered Vietnam in 1777 at a time when European powers were colonizing most of the world. Their initial influence was primarily cultural and religious. Their conquest of the region began in 1858 under Napoleon III. France saw the growing influence of the British and Dutch in this area and seized the opportunity by aiding the ruling families to suppress peasant uprisings. The Treaty of 1787 gave the French exclusive trading rights and access to the ports. French Catholic missionaries became a significant factor in the country, and the ruling group, fearing a foreign takeover, passed an edict of death against the missionaries. The French responded by landing troops but did not gain control over Vietnam until the 1890s. Civil liberties, such as the freedom of speech, participation in the political process, and travel, were denied the Vietnamese.[11]

There were continuous rebellions against French rule. The most significant was the Revolutionary Youth Movement, which was founded by Ho Chi Minh in 1925 and evolved into the Vietnamese Communist Party in 1930. The strikes and rebellions that occurred during the worldwide depression of the 1930s were crushed by the French; most of the surviving resistance leaders went underground.

The Japanese moved into Vietnam in 1940. For the most part they tolerated and cooperated with existing French colonial institutions, substituting Asian imperialism for European. The defeat of Japan in August 1945, the last episode of World War II, left a power vacuum that was partially filled by the Viet Minh, led by Ho Chi Minh, who had resisted the Japanese and would resist the French, the Americans, and, eventually, his ideological cousins, the Chinese. All, in his eyes, were foreign intruders.[12]

The French, with American assistance, reoccupied Vietnam, but their defeat at Dienbienphu accelerated a departure that had been sure to come. In an international conference at Geneva, Switzerland, in 1954, France conceded the independence of Vietnam and the neighboring countries of Laos and Cambodia. Free elections were to be held in all of Vietnam in 1956, but these never took place. Instead, two rival regimes, the Republic of Viet Nam (South Vietnam) and the Democratic Republic of Viet Nam (North Vietnam), evolved under a Catholic Nationalist, Ngo Dinh Diem, and the Communist Ho, respectively. An artificial division at the seventeenth parallel with a demilitarized zone, similar to the Korean model, was declared but proved unavailing. In both North and South Vietnam, separate but highly suspect elections were held, although few scholars now doubt that Ho had much more support throughout the country than Diem, whose religion in a nation overwhelmingly Buddhist and whose Western support in a highly nationalistic country tarnished his credentials. Throughout the period from 1945 to 1975, a bloody civil war went on in Vietnam, with each side receiving significant foreign support.

The United States entered this conflict almost imperceptibly. Aid was given to the French by the Truman administration (1945–1949), and by the end of the Eisenhower administration (January 1961) there were approximately 600 American advisers in Vietnam. When President John F. Kennedy died in November 1963, there were more than 16,000 American soldiers in Vietnam, and they were beyond the advising stage. Under President

Lyndon B. Johnson the number grew to almost 475,000 at the end of 1967, not counting perhaps 60,000 men in the offshore fleet and another 33,000 stationed in Thailand. Only when the generals asked for another 206,000 men did Johnson stop the troop buildup, but not the war or the bombing that went with it. Although it was clear by 1968, if not before, that the war could not be won without sacrifices that neither the American government nor its people were willing to make, the fighting went on until April 1975 and was extended into the former French colonies of Laos and Cambodia.

Loss of life was tremendous. In addition to more than 50,000 Americans, perhaps 2 or 3 million Vietnamese were killed. (These figures do not count the postwar bloodbath in Cambodia.) This carnage created many millions of refugees, internal and external. Within South Vietnam one official estimate was that just between 1965 and 1968, as many as 3 million people became refugees. Many were housed in squalid refugee camps with minimal sanitary facilities; others crowded into Saigon and other cities. By 1969, South Vietnam had changed from an 85 percent rural country to one that was nearly half urban.[13]

Although tens of thousands of Vietnamese had come to the United States before 1975, the total U.S. withdrawal from Vietnam in early 1975 set off the first part of the second wave of Southeast Asian refugees. Between then and the end of the year, more than 130,000 were admitted. That number dropped to 17,000 over the next two years. Then, starting in 1978, it surged again as hundreds of thousands of so-called boat people sought desperately to leave Southeast Asia. Not only Vietnamese and ethnic Chinese but also Cambodians and Laotians began to fill the refugee camps in the countries of first asylum, particularly Thailand. The United States agreed at first to accept 7,000 a month from the camps and then doubled this to 14,000. This second part of the second wave peaked during the fiscal year October 1, 1979–September 30, 1980, when over 166,000 Southeast Asian refugees were admitted, some 70,000 of whom were not from Vietnam. In all, from April 1975 to September 1984, more then 700,000 Southeast Asians were admitted to the United States. They represented about one Asian American in seven at that time. And it should be noted that only about half of all Southeastern Asian refugees came to the United States. At the end of 1981, according to the United Nations High Commissioner for Refugees (UNHCR), China had taken more than a quarter of a million, France and Canada more than 80,000 each, Australia nearly 60,000, West Germany over 20,000, and Great Britain some 16,000.[14]

In Transit

Peter Rose describes a number of ways that refugees arrived in the United States.[15] For some, there was an initial move from their homes to first-asylum camps in Thailand, Malaysia, and the Philippines. Papers had to be checked and essential information transmitted to New York. Next came a search for sponsors. The selection of a sponsoring agency was more or less arbitrary, unless friends and relatives could be found. When a match had been made and medical clearances obtained, the next move was to a transit center. Special chartered planes would take the refugees to West Coast airports. A final trip would then be made to a prearranged residence in a nearby city.

For others, there were additional waystations prior to reaching America, such as the Refugee Processing Centers in Indonesia and the Philippines. The purpose of these stations was to regulate the flow of refugees and to orient them to the manners and mores of their future homes. For example, at Bataan in the Philippines, caseworkers updated files and assigned all refugees between the ages of 16 and 55 to English-as-a-second-language (ESL) classes. Refugees were required to attend eight weeks of ESL classes, as well as four weeks of cultural orientation classes, before moving on to their final destination.

These temporary centers were under the jurisdiction of the UNHCR and the local governments, with the United States playing no official role but providing most of the funding. Since other countries were also involved, the curriculum was not limited to the English language and the American culture. Language training and learning a new culture are difficult steps under the best of conditions; an evaluation of the courses indicates neither outstanding success nor dismal failure.[16]

A recital of the bureaucratic steps that a refugee must go through hides the pain, suffering, and anxiety that each person experiences. Stories about the boat people and their experiences of starvation, drowning, rape, and robbery were not uncommon. Although almost every refugee has undergone terrible experiences, those of the boat people, escapees from Vietnam trying to get to Thailand or Malaysia by sea, were perhaps the worst. In 1981 vicious attacks on these helpless people by pirates reached epidemic proportions; some 80 percent of all boats were apparently attacked at least once. One survivor later told her story in Seattle. Vo Thi Tam was the wife of a former officer in the South Vietnamese air force. After he had been released from "reeducation" by the new government, he and Vo, who was pregnant, decided to try to escape. Somehow they became separated; Vo still does not know what happened to him or whether he is dead or alive. Here is her story:

> When we reached the high seas, we discovered, unfortunately, that the water container was leaking and only a little bit of the water was left. So we had to ration the water from then on. We had brought some rice and other food that we could cook, but it was so wavy that we could not cook anything at all. So all we had was raw rice and a few lemons and very little water. After seven days we ran out of water, so all we had to drink was the sea water, plus lemon juice.

Everyone was sick and, at one point, my mother and my little boy, four years old, were in agony, about to die. And the other people on the boat said that if they were agonizing like that, it would be better to throw them overboard so as to save them pain.

During this time we had seen several boats on the sea and had waved to them to help us, but they never stopped. But that morning, while we were discussing throwing my mother and son overboard, we could see another ship coming and we were very happy, thinking maybe it was people coming to save us. When the two boats were close together, the people came on board from there—it happened to be a Thai boat—and they said all of us had to go on the bigger boat. They made us all go there and then they began to search us—cutting off our blouses, our bras, looking everywhere. One woman, she had some rings she hid in her bra, they undressed her and took out everything. My mother had a statue of Our Lady, a very precious one, you know, that she had had all her life—she begged them just to leave the statue to her. But they didn't want to. They slapped her and grabbed the statue away.

Finally they pried up the planks of our boat, trying to see if there was any gold or jewelry hidden there. And when they had taken everything, they put us back on our boat and pushed us away.

They had taken all our maps and compasses, so we didn't even know which way to go. And because they had pried up the planks of our boat to look for jewelry, the water started getting in. We were very weak by then. But we had no pump, so we had to use empty cans to bail the water out, over and over again.

That same day we were boarded again by two other boats, and these, too, were pirates. They came aboard with hammers and knives and everything . . . we could only beg them for mercy. . . . So these boats let us go and pointed the way to Malaysia for us.

That night at about 9:00 P.M. we arrived on the shore and we were so happy finally to land somewhere that we knelt down on the beach and prayed, you know, to thank God.

While we were kneeling there, some people came out of the woods and began to throw rocks at us. They took a doctor who was with us and they beat him up and broke his glasses, so that from that time on he couldn't see anything. . . . They searched us for anything precious that they could find, but there was nothing left except our few clothes and our documents. They took these and scattered them all over the beach.

Then five of the Malaysian men grabbed the doctor's wife, a young woman with three children, and they took her back into the woods and raped her—all five of them. Later, they sent her back, completely naked, to the beach.

After this the Malaysians forced us back into the boat and tried to push us out to sea. But the tide was out and the boat was so heavy with all of us on board that it just sank in the sand. And so they left us. . . .

In the morning, happily, the local police came, and Vo and the other survivors were taken to a refugee camp from which she—one of the lucky ones with relatives already in the United States—was soon able to come to the United States as a refugee.[17]

William Liu interviewed refugees who discussed their experiences in temporary camps in Guam and Camp Pendleton. Problems included boredom and the lack of counseling and guidance. One of the most serious complaints was the lack of serious concern about mental health needs. The refugees also criticized the assumption that they would assimilate to American ways without difficulty; they feared that resettlement policies might lead to the breakup of family and extended-family units; and they resented the lack of sensitivity to Vietnamese cultural values and existing social networks.[18]

In summarizing the experience of the first wave, Liu indicated that from the point of view of education and skills, the refugees were desirable immigrants. However, he predicted that they would face problems of status loss because so many would have to settle for lesser jobs than in their pre-settlement lives.[19]

LAOTIANS: HMONG AND LAO

Refugees from Laos may be divided into two distinct groups: the highland and lowland Laotians. The highland Laotians are primarily Hmong, but include peoples called Mien, Tai Dam, and Lao-theung. The lowland Laotians are ethnic Lao whose experience in the United States is similar to that of other less modernized refugees from the region. Our treatment here will focus on the Hmong whose experience is quite different. The Hmong are a people indigenous to China who spread southward into the hills of Laos early in the nineteenth century. Some Hmong (the word means "free man") also populated parts of Thailand and Vietnam. They are referred to in Chinese history as a race who lived in the mountains, speaking a particular language, wearing special clothes seen nowhere else, and dating as far back as 3,000 years. Modern authorities have described them as an industrious, independent, and peace-loving people who became involved in the Vietnam War primarily because of their strategic location.[20]

Background

Laos was influenced by the French brand of colonialism, though the French invested even less in terms of transportation, education, or health care in Laos than they did in Vietnam. The Japanese occupied the nation during World War II, but it was reoccupied by the French in 1946. In 1954 the Geneva Accords established Laotian independence under the Royal Lao government. However, a political split in 1949 resulted in the creation of the Progressive People's Organization, a forerunner of the Pathet Lao and an ally of the Viet Minh. Thus, by the time the Royal Lao government came to power, the Pathet Lao was in control of perhaps half the countryside.

The escalation of the war in Vietnam affected Laos; the country was used as a major supply line for North Vietnam (the Ho Chi Minh Trail ran the length of eastern Laos). There was massive American bombing there, and by 1970, two-thirds of Laos had been bombed, creating more than

600,000 refugees. The CIA trained counterguerrilla forces among the Hmong; their missions included collecting intelligence on North Vietnamese movements and rescuing American personnel, especially downed American pilots. An estimated 15,000 Hmong were killed in combat. They gained the reputation of being courageous and knowledgeable jungle fighters.[21]

The fall of Vietnam and the withdrawal of American forces saw thousands of Hmong fleeing Laos. They fled to different parts of the world—to the United States, to France, to French Guiana, a few to Canada and Australia, and many more to Thailand. As late as 1983, more than 76,000 Laotians were in Thai refugee camps; more than 75 percent of these were mountain people.[22]

Resettlement

The experiences of the Hmong in transit were similar to those of other Southeast Asian refugees. At first the resettlement programs attempted to scatter them throughout the United States, but most voluntarily moved to the warm-weather states, though a group of perhaps 10,000 has settled in and around Minneapolis. The northeastern cities were too cold, and rents were too high. Other areas proved too isolated and lonely. Even understanding sponsors could not take the place of extended family and familiar faces.

One story relates how many Hmong relocated to the Fresno area. There was a rumor that a Hmong family became prosperous by raising cherry tomatoes in Fresno. Word got around, and the combination of climate, fertile agricultural land, and a community of fellow ethnics drew many Hmong to the San Joaquin Valley. In 1985 an estimated 20,000 of the 60,000 Hmong were reported as living in the valley, approximately 15,000 of them in Fresno.[23] The story is familiar to groups who have little access to reliable information and are dependent on rumors and personal information networks. Stories of one of their group "making it" are often followed by a mass migration to that area, with the hope that similar good fortune awaits them.

Peter King and David Holley in 1985 focused on some of the problems the newcomers faced. The Hmong came as an immigrant group with very few tools with which to adapt to the American society. They had no written language until the 1950s, when missionaries came to their villages. They strongly believe in evil spirits, they trust their shamans, and they distrust modern medicine. The arrival of the Hmong has strained social service agencies. Nearly nine out of ten Hmong were reported to be on welfare, and the clustering of the population has created several ethnic ghettos. Although Fresno lies in the heart of an agricultural area, it is the home of agribusiness, not the kinds of small family plots that characterized the former Hmong homes in the highlands. Furthermore, in the old country there were no taxes and few bills. In Fresno, at the first of the month, everything comes due.[24]

The situation has reached the point where no direct resettlement is allowed from Thailand to Fresno, yet it is estimated that perhaps one-half of the Hmong refugees who enter the United States will end up in the Fresno area. Bad feeling against the refugees runs high; minority groups who previously suffered prejudice and discrimination also feel threatened by the newcomers.

King and Holley also report several unusual cases involving the Hmong. One was the suicide of a Hmong who was apparently overcome with shame and confusion following arrest for a traffic violation; another was the attempted prosecution of some Hmong men as criminals in what to them was the customary way of claiming a bride. There were also mysterious deaths of middle-aged men who just went to sleep and never woke up.[25]

Faderman, in interviews with a variety of Hmong, provides a sensitive account of the problems of the older and the younger individuals. The elderly narrate how lost they have become. They had never used a flush toilet, nor were they familiar with radio and television. They despair of ever learning English; they are afraid to drive and have to be driven by the young. They have become increasingly dependent on their American born and educated children where roles are reversed; in the old country they were in charge and were in control; here they suffer the humiliation of ignorance, dependence, and alienation.

The young have their own issues. There is the complex process of becoming an American and being saddled with immigrant parents. There is the conflict of cultures; of shamanism and modern medicine; of gender and parent–child relations and how to deal with conflicting demands between the old and the new. Her young interviewees appear to have bought the American dream, fantasizing about big houses and fancy cars and struggling for the MBAs and medical degrees. Some even talked about big gang heists. Then there are the other young who came here as adolescents who speak of feeling lost and betrayed. They feel unprepared, and their meager exposure to American education does not prepare them for life in a world so different from the one they experienced in the old country.[26] Perhaps the only solace for the Hmong is that these experiences are typical of most immigrant groups.

Tou-Fou Vang offered a more cheery perspective. He reported in 1981 that on the whole, the Hmong were being successfully resettled. Goals of self-sufficiency had been accomplished, and the majority were holding manual jobs. The major problem was the English language; Vang emphasized that long-term goals could not be fulfilled without a mastery of English.[27]

The Hmong arrive with a strong family and clan system. By tradition the families are large, and they follow a model of male dominance in which the role of the wife is devotion to her husband and clan and kinship ties are strong. The clans serve as mutual aid associations, and the household, rather than the individual, serves as the primary unit.

Older Hmong still dream of going home to the Southeast Asian high-lands. Many are forced to rely on their children for an understanding of American ways, of which they do not necessarily approve. It is likely that the younger Hmong will take the initial steps toward understanding the new society; the older ones may be forced to tolerate the new ways or simply give up.

CAMBODIANS (KAMPUCHEANS)

The Khmer are the majority group in Cambodia, constituting about 85 percent of the population; Chinese and Vietnamese make up most of the rest. They are primarily Buddhist and similar to the Laotians in terms of their kinship systems, animist beliefs, modes of production, and world views.[28]

Background

Khmer culture has been influenced by the Thais, Vietnamese, Chinese, and Burmese. It was also influenced by the West, first through the Spanish and the Portuguese, later the French, and then the Americans.

Cambodia was at one time one of the great civilizations in Southeast Asia. Centered in the royal city of Angkor, the empire lasted from 802 to 1432, when it became a part of the Vietnamese and Siamese kingdoms. It remained a vassal state until the French took control in 1863. French rule was indirect and used indigenous authorities when possible. French investment was very small. By 1939, only four Cambodians had graduated from senior high school, and in 1941, of a population of nearly 3 million, there were only 537 students in the secondary schools. There were a number of rebellions against the French; in 1916 as many as 100,000 peasants demonstrated against the French in Phnom Penh.

Cambodian independence was declared by Prince Norodom Sihanouk in 1944 when Southeast Asia was still controlled by the Japanese. In 1946, Cambodia was declared an autonomous state within the French union, but the French retained control. In 1955, Sihanouk defeated a French-backed candidate and remained prime minister. Problems with the United States led to an increased dependence on Soviet and Chinese aid. There was also increased cooperation with the North Vietnamese, and by 1966, Cambodia was indirectly involved in the Vietnam War. The North Vietnamese and the Vietcong were regularly using the border area for food and as a sanctuary from South Vietnamese and American air attacks. Prince Sihanouk was aware of the situation but tried to pursue a course of neutrality. His country was caught between Communist China and North Vietnam on one side and the United States and South Vietnam on the other. However, according to Robert Shaplen, Sihanouk's gravest fear was to be taken over by the Vietnamese.[29] When Cambodia came under formal control of the Provisional Revolutionary government in 1969, the American response was to begin bombing Cambodia, including a program to defoliate the rubber trees.

In 1970, General Lon Nol, with the approval of the United States, overthrew Sihanouk's government. Relations with North Vietnam and the Viet Minh were broken off. Between 1970 and 1975, the United States dropped over half a million tons of bombs. The war created more than 3 million refugees.

Lon Nol's rightist government controlled the urban areas, but the extreme-left wing Khmer Rouge controlled the countryside. In 1975, just before the American exodus from Vietnam, the Khmer Rouge under Pol Pot entered Phnom Penh and overthrew Lon Nol. Pol Pot, born Saloth Sar, was a mysterious figure. He spent some years in Paris with a Khmer student group called the Marxist Circle, which had loose ties with the French Communist Party. He took over leadership of the Vietnamese Communist Party's Cambodian branch in 1962 and charted a course that would be independent from Vietnam.

Pol Pot's victory was followed by a reign of terror, which ended with the murder of at least 1 million Cambodians by Cambodians and the forced relocation of many others. The book *The Killing Fields* and the motion picture made from it depicted this horror graphically. More than 150,000 Cambodians fled to Vietnam and 33,000 to Thailand. Pol Pot's primary targets were intellectuals, government officials, and urban dwellers, but Cambodians of all classes suffered.

In 1978, Vietnam, by then under communist control and aided by the Soviet Union, which sought to control Chinese expansion in the area, invaded Cambodia and replaced the Pol Pot regime with a new puppet government. The invasion was followed by another mass exodus from Cambodia. An estimated 100,000, fearing the traditional enmity between the Khmer and the Vietnamese, fled to Thailand. Continued famine, along with the Vietnamese offensive, drove nearly 500,000 to first-asylum refugee camps along the Thai border.

In Transit

Paul Strand and Woodrow Jones estimated that in 1985 close to 300,000 Cambodians remained in Thailand, and along its borders, 94,000 were in Thai holding centers, and another 200,000 lived in border camps under the control of three Cambodian resistance factions.[30] There were also about 30,000 refugees, most of them ethnic Chinese, living in Vietnam.

Bosseba Kong, a refugee herself, described the incidents leading to the removal of her upper-class family from Phnom Penh.[31] She was attending a private school for girls run by Catholic nuns when the 1970 overthrow of Sihanouk occurred. The majority of the students at the school were Vietnamese, and because of the enmity between the Cambodians and the Vietnamese, the school was closed. Kong was not Vietnamese and was able to transfer to a high school in Cambodia. She planned to go to France for a college education. In 1975 the Khmer Rouge began to move forces into Phnom Penh, already overcrowded with refugees. Foreigners and upper-class Cambodians began to leave. Kong's father sent her and the rest of the family to Saigon. Kong arrived there in March 1975, when the South Vietnamese government was disintegrating and the American embassy was evacuating its employees. Her father rejoined the family by taking the last plane out of Phnom Penh, just as the Khmer Rouge took over the city.

But the situation in Saigon became critical, so the family then moved to Vientiane, the capital of Laos. Life there was peaceful, but because the future seemed uncertain, Kong's father decided to leave Laos. The entire family "sneaked out" of Laos into Thailand—they had been informed that Cambodian passports would not be recognized. They were able to make it safely to Oudong Air Base and then to Outapao Air Base, where many Cambodian refugees lived. From there it was a wait of several weeks before boarding a plane in June 1975 for El Toro Air Base, then to the Marine Corps Base at Camp Pendleton, and finally to a small town on the outskirts of Los Angeles under the sponsorship of the Presbyterian church.

Early Adaptation

The change from a peaceful, privileged life in Cambodia to eventual arrival in the United States covered almost every life situation that a person could experience. There was danger, anxiety, and fear, interspersed with happy moments and new experiences. The clash between norms, lifestyles, and cultures was constant. No matter where Kong and her family went, it called for adjustment and adaptation. Homesickness was a problem, and even today many refugees feel that their real home is Phnom Penh.

Judy Pasternak described the life of Tea Chamrath, who is also a refugee from Cambodia but holds a different orientation.[32] Tea learned English, got a job as a mapmaker, saved money, and brought his family to America. But Tea, a former marine commander in Cambodia, was not a typical immigrant. His plans did not include a future in the United States; his desire was to go back to Cambodia to fight. He read everything that he could about current events in Southeast Asia and joined with other Cambodians who planned to topple the regime in Phnom Penh. Many of his fellow refugees were former high-ranking military officers under Prince Sihanouk.

Resisters such as Tea, although fiercely militant in their desire to retake their homeland, were generally seen by Americans as doughnut makers, welfare counselors, and owners of small markets and jewelry stores. They seemed ordinary immigrants, just trying to make a living. Tea reportedly left for Southeast Asia, but no word was heard from him after the fall of Phnom Penh to the Vietnamese.

The situation in Cambodia is a case study of frustration and failure. No one seems to have won. The biggest losers have been the peasants. Millions have died or fled; those who remain exist under conditions of extreme hardship.

ADAPTATION

Since the arrival of the refugees is still so relatively recent, it is difficult to provide systematic evidence about their adaptation. We hypothesize seven interrelated factors that will affect the adaptation of the Vietnamese, as well as the other Southeast Asian refugees, to the United States:

1. Goals
2. Cohesion of the ethnic community and family
3. Compatibility of the ethnic culture with host society norms and values
4. Role of the federal government and voluntary agencies
5. Reception by the host society
6. Ethnic identity
7. Occupation and education

Goals

The goals of a group are related to motivations for immigration and subsequent experiences upon arrival in the new country. Refugees, as discussed earlier, are not voluntary immigrants and therefore may regard their stay in a country as temporary, awaiting the day that they can return home. However, the return home is obviously quite different from the quest of the sojourners; refugees must await the reinstatement of a favorable political regime. In many ways they may represent a government in exile, although for most the term may be too formal and unrealistic. The government-in-exile model, an experience that was a part of the early Korean migration, has also seen its counterparts in the Lithuanian, Latvian, Polish, and Cuban experiences, as well as that of the White Russian refugees from the Bolshevik Revolution of 1917. We have talked to members of several of these communities who have attempted to keep alive the native culture through the celebration of historic events and rituals. Some have even formed cabinets and appointed ministers and carry on as if they were part of a government. The strongest incentive to retain their old ways is the hope that one day they will be able to return to their homeland in triumph.

The initial policy of the U.S. government was to settle the refugees in widely scattered sites so that they would assimilate rapidly. This policy also sought to avoid intense competition for jobs in specific localities, which would arouse a backlash by American workers. There was also pressure to resettle the refugees as rapidly as possible, however unsuitable the situation, in order to place them in the category of "voluntary migrants" who would be able to take care of themselves and become "American."[33] Policymakers ignored the possible social and psychological consequences of separation, although there is little question that scattered individuals will integrate and assimilate at a higher rate than those residing in ethnic enclaves. The separation policy generally did not work; after a few months, many refugees moved away from their sponsors to live in California, Texas, and Louisiana. Their concentration in urban areas has provided the social networks that have been characteristic of the development of other Asian groups.

Beth Baldwin reported on two surveys conducted of the Indochinese in Orange County in California in 1981 and 1984. The 1984 report indicated that the longing to return to their native countries had not decreased and that a lesser percentage had applied for citizenship in 1984 than in 1981. There was a higher tendency to identify themselves in ethnic terms, such as Vietnamese, Lao, or Cambodian, rather than American. Baldwin speculated that the changes may be due to a difference in stages, whereby concerns for survival, which were of high priority at the beginning, were superseded by questions of past heritage.[34]

For many old-timers, the desire to return to the homeland will remain paramount, and acculturation and integration may be unrealistic goals. However, the younger refugees are acculturating more rapidly, are more desirous of becoming American citizens, and are more optimistic about their future in the United States.[35]

It is likely that refugees who have done well economically, educationally, and socially will be more likely to set goals of integration and assimilation. Younger refugees will also acculturate and become "American" at a rapid pace, and they will question the norms and values of their parents, just as children of other immigrants have done. It may be difficult for parents to teach their children "Vietnamese ways" and even more difficult to socialize them for a return to the old country as time in America lengthens.

It should be noted that one can be a "success" without acculturating, integrating, and assimilating. An individual can retain an ethnic identity, practice the ethnic culture, and participate primarily with fellow ethnics and still be a good American citizen or resident alien.

Cohesion of Ethnic Community and Family

The initial attempt by the federal establishment to separate and scatter the refugees throughout the country may have been based on good intentions, but it failed to take into consideration the valuable roles played by ethnic communities and families. Initially, there were no established Southeast Asian communities, but since 1975 over 500 mutual assistance associations have been created within the refugee communities.[36] They encompass cultural, religious, and political groups. Other organizations fulfill professional needs and serve senior citizen and youth groups. They provide social, religious, and fraternal support; education and language development; job training; and cultural orientation. As resources are meager, they have not developed to the point of providing jobs and business opportunities on a large scale to fellow refugees. Yet there are signs of the development of such economic assistance. For example, the area in Orange County, California, known as Little Saigon is made up of Vietnamese noodle shops, grocery stores carrying Asian foodstuffs, boutiques, Chinese herbal medicine shops, and a variety of professional offices.[37] Little Saigon provides a place where the refugees can speak the same language and experience the ambience of their home country. Another community has grown up in Anaheim, where there are shops and a club with the ambience of Saigon, including Vietnamese music and familiar food.[38]

Perhaps the most important function of an ethnic community is to provide social and psychological support for a population that has been forced to adapt to a strange land with different customs. It is a familiar story; most immigrants have gone through this stage. At one time the development of such communities was frowned on. The ethnic ghetto was considered a hindrance to Americanization and the "melting pot," but recent trends have been toward the encouragement of ethnic diversity and pluralistic structures. However, these ethnic communities are not all peaceful enclaves; there are intragroup conflicts based on political ideology, competing ambitions for leadership, status distinctions, and the question of who can serve as spokespersons for the group.

Refugees who arrived in family units—extended family included—had a number of practical advantages, such as emotional support and multiple incomes. They came from a culture, similar to other Asian groups we have discussed, with hierarchical family structures with the male at the head. A constant problem with such structures is that the role of the male head may be threatened. If the man who used to be the head of the family can't find a job or obtains one inferior to his employment in Vietnam, his role and status are threatened. In addition, the wife may be forced to work and may end up in a better-paying job than her husband. One Vietnamese wife believes that the new pressures, roles, and equality have caused the divorce rate among Vietnamese couples in America to rise rapidly. She added that to be successful in the business world, she had to be aggressive, assertive, and efficient, but when she was with her own people, she wished to be a Vietnamese woman—shy, patient, and resilient.[39]

Children are also caught in the familiar conflict between disparate cultural norms. In school they are taught to express opinions and ask why, whereas at home their parents want them to be more traditional and do what they are told. It will be interesting to see how the children will handle the question of culture conflict; it may well be that the experiences of earlier Asian groups such as the Chinese and the Japanese will serve as the model. Generational differences will no doubt appear as length of time in the United States increases.

Compatibility of Ethnic Culture with Host Society Norms and Values

Asian cultures generally fit into the dominant society through conformity and lack of overt conflict. In addition, the Vietnamese brought with them cultural values that were highly adaptive to the American society.[40] They came with a strong sense of the family, they wanted a better life for their children, and they had a high degree of achievement motivation. Vietnamese culture encourages responsibility, discipline, and hard work; prefers that adversity be faced with courage and stoicism; and places a high value on education.

Role of the Federal Government and Voluntary Agencies

One of the features of the resettlement of the refugees has been the role played by the federal government and private voluntary agencies. Without cooperation between the public and private sectors, the enormous job of moving and placing the refugees could not have been done.

Sponsorship has included commitments to provide food, clothing, and shelter until the refugees became self-supporting. Sponsors were to help in finding employment, arranging for schools and medical services, and providing advice and counsel.

Liu, although acknowledging the positive contributions by both the public and private sectors, writes that government bureaucracies, operating in their customary fashion, showed little sensitivity to the culture of the Vietnamese, partly because very few Asians were involved in the program.[41] Further, they adopted an assimilation strategy and delegated the resettlement task to a variety of private agencies that operated in a nonuniform manner. The lack of coordination often caused confusion and conflict, both among the refugees and among the various agencies.

Federal financial assistance to the refugees has been helpful in the period of transition but has caused a variety of problems for the states, for it involved a time limit. In 1984, California had 300,000 to 350,000 of the 696,000 refugees taken into the United States since the 1975 fall of Saigon.[42] A significant portion of the California refugees—some 140,000—were on welfare. The state's cost climbed from zero in 1980 to $84 million in 1983 and an estimated $140 million in 1984. It should be recalled that the federal government provided total reimbursement for public assistance for the first three years, after which it was left to the state and local authorities to assume up to one-half of the costs, the same share that they assume for non-refugee populations on welfare.

Reception by the Host Society

Alden Roberts compared the attitudes of Gulf Coast residents and northern Californians regarding the refugees. Among Americans in the Gulf states, 77 percent disapproved of marriage to a Vietnamese, and 11 percent would exclude refugees from the country. Californians were more tolerant then the Gulf Coasters. Among a refugee sample, most perceived some prejudice, with the younger, more educated respondents reporting racism more often than the older, less educated, and less affluent members of the group.[43]

Earlier studies also report conflicts between Americans and Vietnamese. In Texas and Florida, American fishermen have been upset by the fishing techniques of the Vietnamese.[44] Blacks and Chicanos have complained about the special assistance given to the refugees, thereby decreasing the resources available to their own minority communities.[45] Baldwin's survey indicated that Orange County residents were just as dissatisfied with refugee resettlement in 1984 as they were in 1981.[46] The feeling that "they must be getting a government handout" is strong,[47] and resentment that American taxpayers have paid for the progress (or nonprogress) of the refugees persists.

Skinner and Hendricks noted that certain conflicts involved the Vietnamese with other ethnic minorities.[48] In a number of universities, blacks and Chicanos confronted school officials with complaints that the refugees were receiving a disproportionate amount of financial aid, thereby decreasing their share. Similar conflicts have arisen in the area of public housing and other government services.

The experience of the refugees supports the views of Lipset and Raab, who identified several groups who would feel threatened by an influx of refugees.[49] The "once hads," often called nativists, would be threatened by any influx of foreigners, whereas the "never hads," made up of the disadvantaged, including minority groups, would complain of a double standard in funding priorities and competition for jobs.

Studies of refugees in Australia, Canada, and France seem to echo the experiences in the United States. Nancy Viviani, writing about the Vietnamese migration to Australia, reported growing antipathy toward all immigrants in that country.[50] Polls taken in the 1980s revealed that 45 percent of respondents believed that immigration was too high and that 48 percent believed that Asian immigration was too high. Economic issues, including unemployment and inflation, were major concerns. There was also a feeling that the entry of the refugees would threaten the homogeneity of the country. Viviani believes that the fear of racial conflict stems in part from the unresolved issue of the treatment of the Australian aborigines.

Louis Dorais, studying the refugees in Quebec City, emphasized linguistic and cultural adaptation.[51] The presence of an educated bicultural elite, a relatively high level of economic integration, and positive expectations from the government contributed to the adaptation process.

Another Canadian study indicated that education, both academic and vocational, and length of residence were positively related to adjustment. Policy recommendations included an emphasis on education, patience, directing refugees to nonmetropolitan areas, and a focus on the elderly.[52]

The attitudes of a sample drawn from a small city in France indicated a slight favorable response for the refugees to maintain their heritage and language, rather than losing them to assimilation. On attitudes toward specific immigrant groups, the North African Arabs were the least favored, the Southeast Asians the most favored.[53]

It is apparent that the issues facing the Southeast Asians are strikingly similar to the issues faced by other immigrants from Asia. Past immigrants confronted racism, cultural differences, government bureaucracy, language difficulties, generational differences, and clashes in values. Questions about goals, including acculturation, "melting," integration, and biculturalism, remain issues for the older Asian immigrant groups and their progeny; the Southeast Asians have just started their journey into the American society.

Ethnic Identity

Identification as an ethnic minority provides certain advantages in the areas of employment, housing, health, education, and access to loans. It is what Milton Gordon labels corporate pluralism.[54] Skinner and Hendricks cite a 1979 speech before the National Coalition for Refugee Resettlement in Washington, DC, that examined some of the negative effects of ethnic minority labeling: Are the Vietnamese expected to assimilate as a minority group, which includes low-level jobs and a "job ceiling" above which they are not expected to compete? Does minority status reinforce a designation as outsiders? Does the categorization maintain a status quo rather than bring about fundamental social change?[55] Without ethnic minority status, groups are free to compete with each other and to confront established economic and political institutions.

But it should also be emphasized that the Vietnamese, like other migrants from Asia, are physically identifiable and cannot merge into the dominant culture as easily as have those of European descent.[56] Minority status may be forced on them, just as being "recognized" as an Asian remains a reality for the Chinese and the Japanese, even of the fourth and fifth generations.

Occupation and Education

The most obvious sources of satisfaction for any migrating group will be to find decent jobs and a good education for the next generation. Baldwin reported that in the prime employment group, defined as those between the ages of 25 and 54, some 45 percent of the men and 28 percent of the women were employed full time in Orange County.[57] Lack of English skills and the unavailability of child care were cited as the main obstacles to employment. Vietnamese have found employment as assembly line workers, technicians, machine operators, and office workers.

There have been problems of underemployment and the lack of Vietnamese in supervisory positions. Intraethnic conflict can occur—especially in cases of previously lower-status employees in the home country giving orders to former high-ranking army officers or males taking orders from females. Prior to the influx of refugees, Hispanics held many of the local assembly line positions, and accusations of job infringement have been reported by employers.[58]

Barry Stein compared the occupational adjustment of Vietnamese refugees with non-Asian refugee groups.[59] He found that in the same period, four to eight years after arrival, the Vietnamese were doing better than Cuban refugees and not as well as the Hungarian refugees of 1956 and the refugees from Nazi Germany. There was much downward mobility, but he believed that this pattern would be ameliorated by time, acculturation, language improvement, retraining programs, hard work, and determination. The early years are the most critical, for if problems are not solved early, discouragement follows, and refugees may resign themselves to dependence on the public welfare system.

The language barrier appears to be the most immediate problem for refugees. It creates misunderstandings and hinders effective communication. Further, because refugee status arose from politicomilitary decisions and events and not from conscious decisions to emigrate, solutions may have to include more than individual motivation. The economic disadvantages and psychological struggles of populations caught in events beyond their control place them in a different position from that of the voluntary immigrant.

Precise data about education are difficult to obtain because of the new-ness of the migration, but there is a general belief that the Southeast Asians, especially the Vietnamese, will do well in school. One young girl has even won a national spelling contest, and there are enough students attending major universities to form a Vietnamese Students Association. We are per-sonally acquainted with several ethnic Chinese families from Vietnam whose children are attending or have graduated from American universi-ties. It is a remarkable educational record for families that entered the coun-try so recently and with a language handicap.

Current Adaptation

James Freeman's interviews with a number of Vietnamese—not generals, leaders, or celebrities but common folks—provide a number of pertinent generalizations concerning the Southeast Asian experience.[60] Culture con-flict was a strong theme—the refugees were grateful for the basic freedoms found in America, but they felt that they were in, but not yet a part of, the American culture. Differences in customs and lifestyles were common; there was also a tremendous ignorance on the part of government agencies, which often lumped all of the various Southeast Asian groups together. They were pushed into English classes and job-training programs that were often unsuitable; children who did not understand English were often la-beled mentally retarded. Laotian speakers were brought in to assist refugees who spoke no Lao; Freeman himself writes that although he had lived in Southeast Asia, he never fully understood nor appreciated the lifestyles, customs, values, and traditions of the area.

Freeman believes that the refugees have been good to America, that they have provided an invigorating force, and that America is better off be-cause of their contributions. He concludes:

> For many people who were born in Vietnam, life in America, despite its posi-tive features, also retains its heavy burdens: the necessity to adjust to a world that is not "at ease," the memories of war, flight from oppression, and rela-tives left behind; the dream of returning to an idealized homeland that no longer exists. The successes of the Vietnamese-Americans are all the more re-markable when they are considered in light of what these people have endured.[61]

The cultural interaction between Americans and the refugees is sum-marized by Robert Proudfoot, who lists twenty-six areas of frustration for both sides. They include American bureaucracy, cultural and value differ-ences, unrealistically high expectations of success, unprepared sponsors, the lumping together of all refugees, too rapid an influx of refugees, inadequate health screening, and enormous language barriers.[62]

Proudfoot also summarizes a number of steps that would help refugees to adapt to American society. They include strengthening the already existing family units, working toward self-help mechanisms in the community, examining programs for teaching and learning English, and understanding the clash of values.

Young-Yun Kim, examining the adaptation patterns of Cambodian, Laotian, Hmong, and Vietnamese refugees, indicated that a key variable was English competence.[63] In general, English competence meant higher participation in interpersonal and mass communications, as well as better psychological health and functional fitness.

SUMMARY

Southeast Asian refugees are extraordinarily diverse. They bring a variety of backgrounds, differences in culture and history, and a heterogeneity of skills and experiences. Yet there is a tendency to lump them together as "refugees from Southeast Asia." That may conjure up the stereotypical image of boat people, of the refugee girl who won the national spelling bee, or of large families struggling to make ends meet in urban slums.

They do share some commonalities, however. The usual combination of variables that have affected all newcomers to the United States—motivations, skills and aspirations, and the strength of community and family—will determine part of their future. Another part of the equation, as for all migrating groups, will be the reaction of the dominant society, which also includes other minorities, both Asian and non-Asian.

What little evidence we have concerning the refugees indicates that many are having a difficult time. Chapter 12, in which we cover empirical data on such variables as employment and income, shows that the Southeast Asians are behind white Americans and the more established Asian groups. It would be surprising if such were not the case. The conditions of emigration—panic, inadequate time, little planning; problems in transit; life in temporary centers; then entrance into a modern, industrial society—would strain the adaptive capacities of most individuals.

Tom Owan, discussing the problems of refugees with human services workers, suggests three themes—all relevant to how we deal with *all* people who are different.[64] First is to be sensitive to the various cultures and life experiences and to recognize both similarities and differences. Communication patterns, feelings, and emotions may not be expressed in the American manner, so assumptions based on the American culture may be misleading. Second, culturally relevant frames for understanding must be studied, identified, and used. Patience and flexibility will be rewarded. Finally, there is a need for competent and well-trained personnel who can provide the assistance that the newcomers need. The sink-or-swim philosophy that has guided immigrant policy in previous eras may have to be rethought as we move from a resource-rich to a resource-limited society.

NOTES

1. Mark Arax, "The Child Brides of California," *Los Angeles Times,* May 4, 1993, p. A1.

2. Ibid.

3. Michael Marrus, *The Unwanted: European Refugees in the Twentieth Century* (New York: Oxford University Press, 1985).

4. Neal Ascherson, "No Place for Them," *New York Review of Books,* Feb. 27, 1986, p. 5.

5. Bruce Grant, *The Boat People* (New York: Penguin, 1980).

6. Liem T. Nguyen and Alan B. Henkin, "Refugees from Vietnam," *Journal of Ethnic Studies* 9, no. 4 (1982): 101–116.

7. William Liu, *Transition to Nowhere* (Nashville, TN: Charter House, 1979); Darrel Montero, *Vietnamese-Americans: Patterns of Settlement and Socioeconomic Adaptation in the United States* (Boulder, CO: Westview Press, 1982).

8. Nguyen and Henkin, "Refugees."

9. D.R. SarDesai, *Southeast Asia, Past & Present,* 2nd ed. (Boulder, CO: Westview Press, 1989).

10. Darrel Montero and Ismael Dieppa. "Resettling Vietnamese Refugees: The Service Agency's Role," *Social Work* 27, no. 1 (1982): 74–82.

11. Paul J. Strand and Woodrow Jones, Jr., *Indochinese Refugees in America* (Durham, NC: Duke University Press, 1985).

12. Ibid.

13. Jean Lacouture, *Ho Chi Minh: A Political Biography* (New York: Viking, 1968).

14. George Herring, *America's Longest War,* 2nd ed. (New York: Knopf, 1986).

15. Peter I. Rose, "Southeast Asia to America: Links in a Chain, Part II," *Catholic Mind,* (March-April 1982): 11–25.

16. Ibid.

17. Joan Morrison and Charlotte Fox Zabusky, *American Mosaic: The Immigrant Experience in the Words of Those Who Lived It* (New York: Dutton, 1980), pp. 447–448.

18. Liu, *Transition,* p. 118.

19. Ibid., p. 170.

20. Jeremy Hein, *From Vietnam, Laos, and Cambodia: A Refugee Experience in the United States* (New York: Twayne Publishers, 1995).

21. Nguyen and Henkin, *"Refugees."*

22. Ibid.

23. Peter H. King and David Holley, "Indochinese Find Haven, Pain in the U.S.," *Los Angeles Times,* May 1, 1985.

24. Ibid.

25. Ibid.

26. Lillian Faderman, with Ghia Xiong, *I Begin My Life All Over: The Hmong and the American Immigrant Experience* (Boston: Beacon Press, 1998).

27. Tou-Fou Vang, "The Hmong of Laos," in *Bridging Cultures: Southeast Asian Refugees in America* (Los Angeles: Asian American Community Mental Health Training Center, 1981).

28. Strand and Jones, *Indochinese Refugees.*

29. Robert Shaplen, "A Reporter at Large: The Captivity of Cambodia," *New Yorker* (May 5, 1986): 66–105.

30. Strand and Jones, *Indochinese Refugees*.

31. Bosseba Kong, "The Resettlement of a Cambodian Family in the United States" (master's thesis, UCLA, 1984).

32. Judy Pasternak, "For Cambodian Refugees, War Is Still Going On," *Los Angeles Times*, Mar. 24, 1985 (Westside Section).

33. Liu, *Transition*.

34. Beth C. Baldwin, *Capturing the Change* (Santa Ana, CA: Immigrant and Refugee Planning Center, 1982).

35. Ibid.

36. Beth C. Baldwin, *Patterns of Adjustment* (Orange, CA: Immigrant and Refugee Planning Center, 1984).

37. Kathleen Day and David Holley, "Vietnamese Create Their Own Saigon," *Los Angeles Times*, Sept. 30, 1984.

38. David DeVoss, "A Long Way from Home," *Los Angeles Times*, Jan. 5, 1986.

39. Day and Holley, "Vietnamese Create Their Own Saigon."

40. Peter I. Rose, "Links in a Chain: Observations of the American Refugee Program in Southeast Asia," *Catholic Mind*, (March 1982): 2–25; Peter I. Rose, "Southeast Asia to America," *Catholic Mind* (March-April 1984) 11–25.

41. William Liu, *Transition*, p. 173.

42. Penelope McMillan, "Indochinese Refugees a Costly Load for Counties," *Los Angeles Times*, Sept. 16, 1984.

43. Alden E. Roberts, "Racism Sent and Received: Americans and Vietnamese View One Another," *Research in Race and Ethnic Relations* 5 (1988): 75–97.

44. Paul D. Starr, "Troubled Waters: Vietnamese Fisherfolk on America's Gulf Coast," *International Migration Review* 15 (1981): 1–2.

45. Kenneth Skinner and Glenn Hendrick, "The Shaping of Ethnic Self-identity among Indochinese Refugees," *Journal of Ethnic Studies* 7, (3) (1977): 25–41.

46. Baldwin, *Capturing the Change*; Baldwin, *Patterns of Adjustment*.

47. Day and Holley, "Vietnamese Create Their Own Saigon."

48. Skinner and Hendricks, "Shaping of Ethnic Self-identity."

49. Seymour M. Lipset and Earl Raab, *The Politics of Unreason* (New York: Harper & Row, 1969), pp. 23–24.

50. Nancy Viviani, *The Long Journey* (Melbourne, Australia: Melbourne University Press, 1984).

51. Louis J. Dorais, "Refugee Adaptation and Community Structure: The Indochinese in Quebec City, Canada," *International Migration Review* 25 (1991): 551–573.

52. R. Montgomery, "Predicting Vietnamese Refugee Adjustment to Western Canada," *International Migration* 29 (1991): 89–117.

53. Wallace E. Lambert, Fathali M. Moghaddam, Jean Sorin, and Simone Sorin, "Assimilation vs. Multiculturalism: Views from a Community in France," *Sociological Forum* 5 (1990): 387–411.

54. Milton M. Gordon, *Human Nature, Class and Ethnicity* (New York: Oxford University Press, 1984).

55. Skinner and Hendricks, "Shaping of Ethnic Self-identity."

56. Andrew Lam, "Goodbye, Saigon—Finally," *New York Times*, Apr. 30, 1993.

57. Baldwin, *Patterns of Adjustment*.

58. Day and Holley, "Vietnamese Create Their Own Saigon."

59. Barry N. Stein, "Occupational Adjustment of Refugees: The Vietnamese in the United States," *International Migration Review* 13, no. 1 (1979): 25–45.

60. James M. Freeman, *Hearts of Sorrow* (Stanford, CA: Stanford University Press, 1989).

61. Ibid., p. 98.

62. Robert Proudfoot, *Even the Birds Don't Sound the Same Here* (New York: Peter Lang, 1990).

63. Young-Yun Kim, "Communication and Adaptation: The Case of Asian Pacific Refugees in the United States," *Journal of Asian Pacific Communication* 1 (1990): 191–207.

64. Tom Owan, ed., *Southeast Asian Mental Health* (Bethesda, MD: National Institute of Mental Health, 1985).

Chapter 12

THE PRESENT STATUS OF ASIAN AMERICANS

CENSUS DATA

Two 1993 Census Bureau publications provided a more detailed picture of the ten most numerous Asian American groups based on the 1990 census.[1] While these data are useful, they are not organized in the same way as that from the 1980 census, so direct comparisons are not always possible. Thus, in the previous edition, we relied on 1980 data that had been more fully analyzed. The Asian American groups treated in the 1993 volumes were Chinese, Filipino, Korean, Asian Indian, Japanese, Vietnamese, Cambodian, Laotian, Hmong, and Thai Americans. There were 6.9 million Americans in those ten groups, a 99 percent increase over 1980. Almost two-thirds of them, 66 percent, lived in five states: California, New York, Hawaii, Texas, and Illinois.

In this edition, we will use two primary sources of data to ascertain the present status of Asian Americans: the 1990 census and 1996 and 1997 U.S. Census reports. The figures in this chapter are from the 1990 census. 1996 and 1997 data, often structured in a different way, may be found in the Appendix. Reader's may find updates on the Census Bureau web site.

Foreign Born

Nearly two-thirds of these Asian Americans were born in foreign countries. Not surprisingly, the greatest percentage of foreign born were among Vietnamese, Laotian, and Cambodian Americans, while the lowest proportion of foreign born was in the Japanese American population.

Median Age

The median age of Asian Americans was 30 years, younger than the national median of 33 years. Only 6 percent of Asians were 65 years of age or older compared with 13 percent for the total population. However, there were wide differences in median age within the Asian American population. Japanese Americans had the highest median age—36 years—while the Hmong median age of 12.5 years was the lowest. The data showed that, overall, Asian American males had a median age of 29 years, while that for Asian American females was 31 years, a difference due in part to the longer life expectancy of females.

The Family

The average Asian American family contained 3.8 persons compared to a national average of 3.2 persons. Asian families were larger partly because of the higher percentage of two-parent families. Again, there were wide variations among the several groups. Hmong American families averaged 6.6 persons, while Japanese American families had 3.1 persons. The proportion of Asian American families with both husband and wife present was 82 percent, above the national proportion of 79 percent. As one would expect, the percentage of Asian American families headed by females was significantly below the national average, 12 percent versus 17 percent, but 26 percent of Cambodian American and 20 percent of Thai American families were headed by females.

Education and Language

Although the generalization that Asian Americans place high value on education is largely accurate, their educational attainment varies significantly by ethnic group. Filipino, Japanese, Asian Indian, Korean, and Thai Americans reported high school completion rates of over 80 percent while the refugee groups from Southeast Asia show completion rates below 50 percent. Asian American men had higher high school graduation rates than Asian American women, 82 percent versus 74 percent. At higher educational levels 38 percent of all Asian Americans were college graduates compared with 20 percent of the general population.

More than half, 56 percent, of all Asian Americans 5 years of age and older did not speak English very well, and more than a third, 35 percent, lived in what the census bureau calls "linguistically isolated" households, those in which all persons over 14 years of age either speak only a language other than English or speak English poorly. The linguistic data reflect the fact that about five-eighths of all Asian Americans, 63 percent, were foreign born. Groups that contain few foreign-born individuals, such as Japanese Americans, and groups that come from countries in which English is widely spoken, such as Filipino and South Asian Americans, were the least linguistically isolated.

The World of Work

The reports indicate that 67 percent of Asian Americans were in the labor force, slightly higher than the national participation rate of 65 percent. Filipinos, Asian Indians, Thais, and Chinese had the highest participation rates. The proportion of Asian American families with three or more workers was 20 percent, compared with a national average of 13 percent. Filipino Americans with 30 percent, and Vietnamese Americans with 21 percent, had the highest percentage of such families.

Asian Americans were more likely to be in technical, sales, administrative support, managerial, and professional jobs than the total population: 32 percent as opposed to 26 percent. Within the Asian American groups the proportions varied widely: 37 percent of all Korean American workers were in such positions as opposed to only 5 percent of Laotian Americans. Occupation is closely linked to educational achievement.

Income and Poverty

In 1989, the last full year covered by the 1990 census, the per capita income of Asian Americans was $13,806, slightly below the national per capita income figure of $14,143. But median Asian American family income of $41,583 was significantly higher than the median income for all families, which was $35,225. This was partly because, as we have seen, more Asian American family members worked, and partly because more Asian Americans had very high educational qualifications.

Despite family income and educational attainment, 14 percent of Asian Americans were classified as living in poverty as opposed to 13 percent of the national population. Foreign-born Asian Americans had a higher rate of poverty, 16 percent, than native-born, 10 percent, and Asian immigrants who had arrived in the 1980s had a much higher poverty rate, 22 percent, than those who had arrived before 1980, only 8 percent. The Southeast Asian refugees had the highest rates of poverty: 26 percent of Vietnamese Americans, 35 percent of Laotian Americans, 43 percent of Cambodian Americans, and 64 percent of Hmong Americans were in poverty status. At the other extreme only 6 percent of Filipino, 7 percent of Japanese Americans, and 10 percent of Asian Indian Americans were recorded as poor.

HIGHER EDUCATION

The influx of Asian Americans into higher education has changed the composition of student bodies all across the nation. In every region Asian American students are "overrepresented," that is, there are many more of them than their incidence in the population would predict. In the early 1990s one author spoke at well-attended meetings to celebrate Asian American weeks or months at campuses in Kansas, Wisconsin, Indiana, and Ohio. The ethnic mix of students varied from one campus to another. At Ohio State University, for example, Asian Indian students far outnumbered any other Asian group, while at the University of Cincinnati, Chinese students were the most numerous.

But the influx was most noticeable at California universities. For example, enrollment figures for new freshmen at UCLA between 1989 and 1992 show that in 1989 white Americans had the highest percentage of entering freshmen, with 41.8 percent, followed by Asian Americans, with 25.3 percent; by 1992, the groups had reversed positions: Asian Americans had the highest percentage, with 34.0 percent, followed by white Americans, with 32.8 percent (see Table 12.1). Enrollment for other groups over the same period remained relatively steady.[2]

Application and admission figures for 1993 for specific Asian American ethnic groups at UCLA are shown in Table 12.2. Chinese Americans had the highest application and admission rates among the Asian Americans, followed by the Korean, Thai, Filipino, and "East Indian" Americans. The lowest application figures for an Asian American group were for Japanese Americans, once the most visible group on the UCLA campus.[3] Their low numbers reflect a lack of replacements, due to both low immigration and smaller family size.

The rise in Asian American enrollments has led to changes on other college campuses. Asian American students at the University of California at Irvine demanded an Asian American Studies program, and the University of Connecticut opened an Asian Center. Though the development of the center was not smooth, one dean said that the Asian American students had changed the University of Connecticut for the better.[4]

SAT

College entrance is influenced strongly by a number of tests; the Scholastic Aptitude Test (SAT), now called the Scholastic Assessment Test, has been one of the most important. Asian Americans do extremely well on the quantitative part of the examination—in fact, better than any other group. In 1985, Asian Americans' math scores averaged 520 (out of 800); the comparable figure for whites was 490. Asian Americans' scores on the verbal section was 404, below the white average of 449 but still higher than for other comparison groups.[5]

Doctoral Degrees

The number of Asian Americans receiving doctoral degrees from 1975 to 1984 remained constant at approximately 1,000 per year. When analyzed in the context of their relatively small numbers, the number of Asian Ameri-

Table 12.1 Ethnic Composition of Entering Freshmen at UCLA, 1989–1992

Group	Fall 1989		Fall 1990		Fall 1991		Fall 1992	
	Number	Percentage	Number	Percentage	Number	Percentage	Number	Percentage
Native American	50	1.2	35	0.9	60	1.5	45	1.4
Black American	345	8.6	235	6.5	235	6.0	255	7.7
Asian American	1,020	25.3	1,285	35.7	1,455	36.9	1,130	34.0
Pacific Islander American	15	0.4	10	0.3	15	0.4	15	0.5
Chicano/Mexican American	530	13.1	435	12.1	450	11.4	470	14.1
Latino/Other Spanish American	240	5.9	160	4.5	195	5.0	170	5.2
Filipino American	145	3.6	140	3.9	180	4.5	135	4.0
White American	1,690	41.8	1,290	35.9	1,350	34.2	1,090	32.8
Other	5	0.1	10	0.2	5	0.1	10	0.3
Total	4,040	100.0	3,600	100.0	3,945	100.0	3,320	100.0

Source: UCLA, Office of Academic Planning and Budget, Oct. 27, 1992.

Table 12.2   1993 Admission Figures, by Asian American Ethnic Groups

Group	Applications	Admissions	Admission Rate (percent)
Pacific Islander American	81	35	43
Filipino American	915	289	32
Japanese American	570	236	41
Chinese American	3,235	1,574	49
Korean American	1,639	672	41
Thai/Other Asian American	1,441	589	41
East Indian/Pakistani American	633	271	43
White American	8,216	3,026	37

Source: UCLA, Office of Academic Planning, June 2, 1993.

cans receiving the doctoral degree was the highest of all minority groups. However, William Trombly observed that faculties of colleges and universities were still primarily white and would continue to be unless there were a drastic change in the ethnic and racial mix of the PhDs being produced.[6]

Does Education Pay?

Figures for educational level and income for white, Hispanic, black, and Asian Americans in California are shown in Table 12.3. White Americans make more than any of the other groups at every level. Based on census data, the figures show that Asian Americans are closest to parity with white Americans statewide, followed by black Americans and Hispanic Americans. The disparity persists at every level: For every dollar that white Americans made, Asian Americans made 82 cents; black Americans 74 cents; and Hispanic Americans, 59 cents.[7]

FAMILY

A common perception is that Asian Americans come from cohesive, intact families. There is evidence to support this contention: The number of divorces is small, especially among first-generation immigrants. Census figures indicate that Asian American divorce rates are well below their proportion in the population.[8]

However, acculturation and generational changes have led to different expectations and motives for marriage, resulting in a rise in the number of separations and divorces. Table 12.4 shows the percentage of households headed by women based on the 1980 census. The White and Japanese American figures were identical (10.1 percent); the Asian Indian percentage

Table 12.3   Educational Level and Income by Ethnicity in California, 1989

	Income ($)			
Educational Level	*White*	*Hispanic**	*Black*	*Asian*
No high school diploma	26,115	16,487	21,678	18,517
High school diploma	27,376	21,121	22,040	21,608
Bachelor's degree	44,426	33,817	34,290	33,758
Master's degree	52,787	41,431	42,254	45,550
Doctorate	59,348	46,873	54,205	53,792
Professional degree**	77,877	41,029	61,015	59,603

*Hispanics can be of any race

**Includes medical and law degrees

Source: U.S. Census data, analyzed by Richard O'Reilly and Maureen Lyons, *Los Angeles Times.*

was much lower (6.4 percent); and the Chinese (11.1 percent), Filipino (12.3 percent), and Korean (11.2 percent) American figures were slightly higher.

Asian American households are more likely to include multiple wage earners. In California, white American households with three or more workers totaled 12 percent, whereas the Japanese (19 percent), Chinese (20 percent), Korean (14 percent), and Filipino (24 percent) Americans all had higher percentages.[9] These figures are reflected in family income data. Thus although Asian American household income may be high, it often combines the income of several individuals.

Table 12.4   Percentage of American Households Headed by Women, by Ethnic Group, 1980

Group	Percentage with Female Head of Household
White	10.1
Black	29.8
Hispanic	18.1
Japanese	10.1
Chinese	11.1
Filipino	12.3
Korean	11.2
Asian Indian	6.4
Vietnamese	14.2

Source: Robert W. Gardner, Bryant Robey, and Peter C. Smith, *Asian Americans: Growth, Change and Diversity* (Washington, DC: Population Reference Bureau, 1985), p. 21.

It should be noted that Asian Americans have come from societies where the employment of women for wages outside the home was not a common practice. The need for additional income, better job opportunities for females and youngsters, and changing norms through acculturation have influenced household employment patterns.

There have been some negative consequences of multiple family employment. Aside from the lack of time and energy to devote to child rearing, there has been a rise in the number of latchkey children, children of working parents who can't be home after school and therefore give the children the keys to the family home.

Problems of intergenerational conflict between "old-fashioned parents" and their Americanized children are as old as immigration itself. But Asian American families generally do not ask for outside counseling, which can lead to the faulty assumption that they are problem-free.

OCCUPATION AND EMPLOYMENT

One of the most critical areas for evaluating the adaptation of Asian Americans is that of occupation and employment. The primary goal of most immigrants has been to better their economic status; hence one measure of their success is their ability to find jobs. The problem for many newly arrived immigrants, especially those with advanced or professional degrees, is the initial inability to find employment appropriate to their past experiences.

Figures from the 1980 census on selected occupational categories indicate wide variation within the group. For example, 49 percent of Asian Indian Americans were in the managerial group, compared to only 12 percent of Samoan Americans. There were relatively even distributions in most of the other categories. In general, the older, more established Asian Americans—the Chinese, Japanese, and Asian Indians—were distributed in more prestigious and higher-paying occupations than the newly arrived Pacific Islanders and Vietnamese. In terms of modal employment, the Japanese, Filipinos, Koreans, Hawaiians, and Guamanians were in the technical sector; the Chinese and the Indians, in the professional sector; and the Vietnamese and Samoans in the laborer sector.

The overrepresentation of Asian Americans in the small-business sector continues. Thirty-seven percent of Asian American businesses are in California, and of these, 76 percent have no paid employees; that is, they are run by family members. Sixty-eight percent of the Asian American firms are in retail or the provision of services.

Bruce Cain and Roderick Kiewiet, in their study of minority-owned businesses in California, made the following generalizations about Asian Americans.[10] The businesses are primarily sole proprietorships, using family and other unpaid employees, and profits are generally small. They tend to be concentrated in eating or drinking establishments (8 percent), food stores (6 percent), and health services (11.8 percent). The Chinese are disproportionately in the retail, wholesale, and finance areas and are not active in transportation or construction. Japanese businesses are more concentrated in construction and finance and less in the areas of retail and services. Filipino firms are in transportation, finance, and services. Korean enterprises are primarily in retail and not in finance. The Koreans have also become greengrocers—they operate about 1,000 of the 1,200 independent grocery stores in New York City.[11] In another virtual monopoly, a Los Angeles Police Department vice detective reported that twenty-two of the twenty-five massage parlors in Los Angeles (a figure that seems somewhat low) were operated by Koreans.[12] Asian Indians are noticeable in motels and newsstands.

The basic advantage of Asian American business owners over Hispanics and blacks is that they have greater family resources, including labor and income, and are therefore able to draw on a larger capital and employee base. They also serve a wealthier ethnic constituency.

However, there have also been drawbacks to business in the Asian American community. Language problems and dependence on ethnic clientele have limited growth and expansion. Concentration in traditional minority areas where per capita wealth is lower is another limiting factor, and the general reluctance of some Asians to take advantage of Small Business Administration (SBA) government loans is another handicap.[13]

The phenomenon of "ethnic succession" can be observed in the small-business sector. A small mom-and-pop grocery store may have been started by a Jewish couple, then sold to Japanese Americans, who in turn sold the business to a Korean couple. Older, more established minorities tend to move out as better opportunities arise; their place is then taken by newer immigrant groups. This is called *ethnic succession.*

UNEMPLOYMENT

Unemployment figures based on "men in the labor force who reported some unemployment during 1979" and drawn from the 1980 census show that some Asian Americans do better than white Americans, while others do not. Compared to white norms (17 percent), the Japanese (14 percent) and Indians (14 percent) had lower rates of unemployment, whereas the Chinese (19 percent), Filipinos (19 percent), and Koreans (21 percent) had higher figures. The exceptionally high rate of unemployment for Vietnamese (33 percent) indicates serious problems in that refugee community. The average length of time for Asian unemployment was generally less than for non-Asians. With the exception of the Vietnamese, the Asian rates were lower than the rates for the black (26 percent) and Hispanic (24 percent) American minorities.[14]

INCOME AND POVERTY

A variety of income figures can be drawn from the U.S. census: individual income, family income, figures based on the mean, and figures based on the median. It should also be noted that Asian Americans are concentrated in high-income states, such as California and New York, where the cost of living is also high.

Table 12.5 compares full-time Asian American worker median income for 1979 as reported in the 1980 census.[15] Compared to white workers ($15,572), the Japanese, Chinese, and Asian Indians had higher median incomes, whereas the Filipinos, Koreans, and Vietnamese had lower median incomes. The percentage of families at the poverty level also showed differences. Compared to rates for whites, the Japanese and Filipinos had lower rates of poverty, the Asian Indians about the same, and the Chinese, Koreans, and Vietnamese higher.

In terms of median family income, when compared to the white median, Asian American income was as follows: The Japanese, Asian Indians, Filipinos, and Chinese were above; the Koreans about equal; and the Vietnamese and Pacific Islanders below. As we have previously noted, family income figures are related to higher labor force participation by family members.

In August 1992, the *Los Angeles Times* profiled poverty in Los Angeles County. Among white Americans representing 41 percent of the county's population, 17.7 percent lived in poverty; Asian Americans, with 10.2 per-

Table 12.5   White, Black, Hispanic, and Asian American Worker Incomes and Family Poverty Levels, 1979

Population	Median Income of a Full-Time Worker ($)	Percentage of Families Below Poverty Level
White	15,572	7.0
Black	11,327	26.5
Hispanic	11,650	21.3
Japanese	16,829	4.2
Chinese	15,753	10.5
Filpino	13,690	6.2
Korean	14,224	13.1
Asian Indian	18,707	7.4
Vietnamese	11,641	35.1

Source: U.S. Census.

cent of the population, had 9.5 percent in poverty; black Americans, representing 10.5 percent of the population, had 15.5 percent in poverty; and Hispanic Americans with 37.8 percent of the population, had 56.8 percent in poverty.[16]

The basic generalization is that, with the exception of the newly arrived refugees, Asian Americans are doing relatively well in terms of income. However, as with any group, there are many who live on marginal incomes. There are the aging populations, dependent on Social Security (some are not eligible owing to employment in noncovered areas and others arrived in the country too late in life to be covered); individuals without families; the chronically sick; and people who cannot work for a variety of reasons. The notion that "Asians have made it" makes it extremely difficult for those on the margins to get the care and the attention that they need.

CORPORATE REPRESENTATION

Not many Asian Americans have risen to positions of authority and power in corporate America. Figures are difficult to obtain, but a major complaint among Asian Americans has been the lack of upward mobility into positions of power.

Table 12.6 shows the number of Asian American officers and directors in the largest U.S. business firms in 1985. Of the 29,000 officer and director positions, 159, or 0.5 percent, were held by Asians. Asians made up 3 percent of the members of the boards of directors of chambers of commerce at selected California sites. It is interesting to note that in Gardena and Mon-

Table 12.6   Corporate Success of Asian Americans: High-Level Management Positions Held

Position	Number of Positions	Number Held by Asian Americans	Percentage Held by Asian Americans
Officers and directors of 1,000 largest U.S. firms	29,000	159	0.5
Board of directors of chambers of commerce			
State of California	26	0	0.0
Los Angeles	41	2	4.8
San Diego	76	1	1.3
San Jose	27	0	0.0
Monterey Park	22	7	31.8
Gardena	27	3	11.1

Sources: The Corporate 1000: A Directory of Who Runs the Top 1,000 U.S. Corporations (Washington, DC: Washington, DC Monitor, Inc. 1985); individual chambers of commerce.

terey Park, suburbs of Los Angeles with high concentrations of Asian Americans, there is a high proportion of Asian board members.

POLITICS

Asian Americans, especially the Japanese, have exercised political power through the Democratic party in Hawaii. One Chinese American, Hiram K. Fong, two Japanese Americans, Daniel K. Inouye and Spark Matsunaga, and one Hawaiian, Daniel K. Akaka, have served in the U.S. Senate, and one, George Ariyoshi, has been governor. Patricia Saiki, a Republican, was first elected to the U.S. House of Representatives in 1986. Asian Americans continue to play an important role in the state.

Republican S. I. Hayakawa was the only Asian American to represent California in the U.S. Senate. A (temporary?) high-water mark was reached after the 1992 elections when two Japanese American Democrats, Norman Mineta from San Jose and Robert Matsui from Sacramento, and a Korean American Republican, Jay C. Kim, from suburban Los Angeles, all represented California in the U.S. House of Representatives. After the 1998 election, only Matsui remained, although, as noted earlier, Mineta, who had retired from Congress, was appointed to President Clinton's cabinet in 2000. As the following results from the November 1992 elections show, Asian Americans on the mainland are slowly beginning to find their places in the political sun at the grass roots. Tony Lam, 57, became the first Vietnamese refugee to hold an elective office in this country, winning a seat on the City Council in Westminster, CA. Nao Takasugi, a Japanese American Republican from Thousand Oaks in suburban Los Angeles, became the first Asian American in the state legislature since 1976. In Washington State, Velma Veloria, a Democrat who emigrated from the Philippines in 1961, won a seat in the state legislature. Of these, only Lam had a large ethnic base as Westminster, in Orange County, is the home of "Little Saigon," the largest Vietnamese refugee enclave in the nation. But even he needed many non-Vietnamese American votes to win. Only in Hawaii do Asian Americans dominate politics demographically. The general situation of elected Asian American officials was illustrated by Mike Matoma, a Sansei who is mayor of Carson, a Los Angeles suburb, who told a reporter at a 1993 meeting of the National League of Cities at which black, Hispanic, and Asian elected officials had separate caucuses, "The National Black Caucus had several hundred at their general membership meeting. The Hispanic elected officials had less, but they still had several hundred. When the Asians got together, we had 15, because throughout the United States we can only identify 60 to 70 people that are elected officials."[17]

Michael Woo, a Chinese American, was elected to the Los Angeles City Council and placed second in the race for mayor in 1993. The winner, Michael Riordan, received 67 percent of the white vote, whereas Woo garnered the majority of the vote of blacks (86 percent), Hispanics (57 percent), and Asians (69 percent). Because the great majority of Los Angeles voters are white, the strong minority showing was not sufficient for Woo to become the first mayor of Asian ancestry to head a large city.[18]

Although almost all elected Asian Americans have been from western states, Shien Biau Woo, a Shanghai-born physics professor-turned-politician, was elected lieutenant governor of Delaware in 1984, the highest state office won by an Asian American on the mainland at that time. 12 years later, in 1996, a Chinese American, Gary Locke, was elected governor of the state of Washington.

Increasing numbers of Asian Americans are running for office, and it is no longer unusual to see Asian American names on the ballot.

Although the majority of Asian Americans are registered Democrats, in Los Angeles County, they are less predominantly so than blacks and Hispanics. In common with these other minorities, they tend to have a relatively low level of voter registration. However, as a group they appear to be more politically conservative than other minorities.[19]

NATURALIZATION

It has been argued that because of their attachment to their homeland and difficulty in acculturating, Asian immigrants have been reluctant to make the final break with their past by becoming American citizens. Yet one sophisticated study we have of naturalization data suggests exactly the opposite. Elliott Barkan examined American naturalization patterns between 1951 and 1978 (see Table 12.7). His results showed that Asians in general have been more likely than most other persons to become naturalized U.S. citizens within a short time after they become eligible. The tendency for Japanese immigrants to have a lower naturalization percentage than the other four main groups most probably reflects the fact that, unlike many recent immigrants from elsewhere in Asia, few Japanese are involved in contemporary chain migration. For persons so engaged, of course, citizenship is a valuable tool, placing one's relatives in a higher preference category than relatives of a resident alien and qualifying a wider group of relatives to come to the United States. There is also the desire to become "American" as quickly as possible; loyalty and patriotism are not uncommon qualities among many immigrants from Asia.

SOCIAL PROBLEMS

By social problems, we refer to crime, delinquency, alcohol abuse, mental disorders, mental illness, and similar behaviors that are generally viewed as "bad" or dysfunctional. The reasons behind these problems may vary widely.

Table 12.7   Response to Citizenship: Percentage of Aliens Nationalized during Their Fifth to Eighth Year of Residence, Fiscal Years 1958–1978

Samples	1958–1968	1969–1978	1958–1978
All persons	50.98	50.16	50.56
Europeans	54.71	44.57	51.00
North Americans	41.12	42.81	42.17
South Americans	58.24	40.93	45.06
All persons but Asians	51.96	44.42	48.46
Asians	43.28	64.50	58.80
Chinese	43.90	75.70	66.17
Japanese	37.94	42.85	39.62
Koreans	28.84	58.20	53.11
Filipinos	28.74	60.93	55.18
Indians	53.61	81.11	78.56

Sources: U.S. Department of Justice, *Annual Report of the Immigration and Naturalization Service* (Washington, DC, 1951–1978), tab. 44; Elliott R. Barkan, "Whom Shall We Integrate? A Comparative Analysis of the Immigration and Naturalization Trends of Asians before and after the 1965 Immigration Act (1951–1978)," *Journal of American Ethnic History* 3 (1983): 48.

Crime and Delinquency

The early Chinese and Japanese were victims of a number of negative stereotypes. They were accused of living in filth, harboring disease, being heathens, and, worst of all, being less than human. Their sexual habits were compared to those of animals; questions of character and honesty were constantly raised. Yet scholarly studies conducted in the 1930s showed low rates of crime and delinquency among "orientals" in California, and statistics from the FBI fifty years later still showed that arrests of Asian Americans for serious crimes remained well below their proportion in the population.[20]

Nevertheless, concern about crime and delinquency in the Asian American communities runs high. Unemployed youth with limited language facility and minimal skills may be more prone to illegal actions, and publicity about "criminal elements, such as the *yakuza* of Japan, triads from China, and Korean and Vietnamese gangs, indicates that Asian American communities are not problem-free.

A California Youth Authority training seminar discussed gang activity among Asian Americans.[21] A member of the Los Angeles Police Department claimed that there were close tie-ins between gang activity in California and organized crime from some Asian countries. In addition, white-collar entrepreneurial crime has surfaced in the Asian Indian community.

Asian gang activity has been increasing in the Los Angeles area. For example, they have been suspected in carjackings, terrorist threats, extortion, and killings in the San Gabriel Valley, and officials have launched investigations into Asian organized crime in Southern California.[22] Another report detailed the actions of teenage gangs who extorted money from other teenagers. All persons involved were of Asian descent, and the extortionists were able to act with impunity because their victims were too frightened to report them.[23]

Eui-Young Yu analyzed juvenile delinquency in the Korean community in Los Angeles. High on the list of activities were gang fighting, runaways, and burglary. He noted that the major community organizations were largely operated and controlled by first-generation immigrants and that as a consequence, programs for the younger generation were inadequate.[24]

Alcohol Abuse

The abuse of alcohol is a social problem. Heavy drinking is known to occur among Japanese, Korean, and Filipino males, but very little seems to spill over into major problem behavior.[25] Since drinking mostly is done with friends during rituals and celebrations, it may be quite different from drinking to combat frustration, anger, and alienation. However, it is a cause of concern, particularly continued heavy drinking among young adult males (see Table 12.8). Research evidence concerning drug addiction among Asian Americans is scarce; it is probable that drug use will more or less reflect the ambience of the local communities.

Mental Health

A major problem in discussing mental health and mental illness is the lack of valid empirical data. What information is available generally supports the notion that although Asian Americans have as many problems as any

Table 12.8 Alcohol Consumption by Asian American Males (percent)

Types of Drinkers	Chinese (N = 122)	Filipino (N = 81)	Japanese (N = 75)	Korean (N = 57)
Heavy drinkers	17.2	33.3	44.0	26.3
Moderate to light drinkers	61.5	41.9	41.3	33.3
Infrequent drinkers or abstainers	21.3	24.7	14.6	40.4

Distribution is significant at the .001 level: N = number

Source: James Lubben, Harry H. L. Kitano, and Iris Chi, "Heavy Drinking among Young Adult Males," paper presented at the Fourth Conference in Asian American Studies, San Francisco State University, Mar. 20, 1987.

other group, very few use mental health facilities. There is a definite cultural element in the way that most Asians are seen by mental health professionals and why Asian Americans, as well as most other minority groups, do not avail themselves more of professional facilities.[26]

Tran Minh Tung, writing from a Southeast Asian perspective, identified some of the problems of diagnosis when seeing Asian patients:[27]

1. Asians do not freely discuss emotional conditions, especially if they are negative. Grief and depression may be expressed in muted form—obliquely and indirectly. Problems are often understated.

2. Asians may appear modest, discreet, and self-deprecating. They may not volunteer details about themselves and do not want to be seen as boastful. They may be reticent about negative items pertaining to self, family, or community.

3. There is special discretion when talking about one's family. A description of relationships and the emotional interplay among family members is difficult to obtain. Direct accusatory or hostile comments about parents or elders are unusual.

4. Very little voluntary information on sexual matters will be given. There is special difficulty between females and male professionals. Indirect information is more easily handled.

5. Physical symptoms and bodily discomfort are more acceptable areas for discussion than psychosexual matters.

6. All symptoms should be carefully examined for cultural relevance and meaning. Talking with dead parents and ancestors is not necessarily a sign of mental illness.

Clearly, cross-cultural differences complicate any assessment of mental health. Immigrants and refugees face enormous problems of adjustment; it is astonishing that most of them adapt to culture shock with few signs of overt breakdown. It may very well be that negative conditions, no matter how bad, may still be seen as relatively better than what they left behind. For some, there is also the option of returning home.

MASS MEDIA

One of the least successful aspects of the Asian American experience has been the portrayal of Asian Americans in the print and film media. Starting with the villainous stereotypes in early movies, progress can be measured only in inches. The evil Jap of World War II and the communist gooks in Korea, China, and Vietnam—faceless, fanatic, maniacal, willing to die because life is not valued—are endlessly recycled with changes in nationality as our foreign policy changes. A recent flurry of Hollywood films with a favorable approach to Asian Americans, the most notable of which was the adaptation of Amy Tan's popular novel, *The Joy Luck Club,* may change the pattern, but unfavorable images still predominate.[28]

Asian American filmmakers have attempted to portray the Asian American experience in more realistic terms; films such as *Dim Sum, Chan Is Missing,* and *Hito Hata* have achieved a limited success. Edward Iwata notes that some Asian American filmmakers try to shun the Asian American label and wish to be judged solely on their merits. Storytelling, thematic content, visual style, technique, and creative and financial control are important goals.[29]

Gotanda, a major Asian American writer, faces a common dilemma of most ethnic artists. Theaters expect certain themes about Asian Americans, and scripts out of the perceived norms are rejected.[30] He also notes that in film and television, Asian Americans are shut out. Aside from Pat Morita and a few houseboys and assistants, Asian Americans are rarely seen. A sitcom featuring Asian Americans would help.

The dilemma for Asian Americans in show business relates primarily to their visibility; non-Asian audiences may not accept Asian Americans in dominant group roles. In addition, productions that are relevant to minority group life may appeal to a limited audience.

The stereotypes of the dominant culture are not always negative—one author, when approached for his picture by a national newspaper, was asked if he would put on a kimono—but still they are stereotypes. Perhaps it is unrealistic to expect Asian Americans eventually to appear randomly in American productions as heroes, villains, lovers, and ordinary people, but it certainly would be a sign of progress to move in that direction.

Asian females in the anchor role on newscasts have become a relatively common sight. In Los Angeles, Tritia Toyota, Joanne Ishimine, and Wendy Tokuda appear nightly, and Connie Chung has been a national figure. The lack of Asian American males in similarly visible positions is especially noticeable.

MARITAL ASSIMILATION

A common rhetorical question—"Would you want your daughter to marry one?"—was once a critical consideration in maintaining separation between races. The expected answer was no, and for years the question reflected the deep-seated fears of mongrelization in both dominant and minority groups. Antimiscegenation laws codified these fears; prejudice, reinforced by stereotypes, discrimination, and segregation, maintained distance between races. But today the question has lost much of its relevance, and the standard answer might even be, "Why not?"

Table 12.9 shows the rates of outmarriage, defined as marriage out of one's own group, for Chinese, Filipino, Japanese, Korean, and Vietnamese Americans in Los Angeles County for various years from 1975 to 1989. The highest rates of outmarriage occurred in 1977, with 49.7 percent of Chinese,

63.1 percent of Japanese, and 34.1 percent of Koreans marrying a person of different ethnicity. (Figures for Filipinos and Vietnamese were unavailable at that time.)

The percentage decrease in the number of Chinese outmarriages may be deceptive, in that there has been an increase not only in the number of Chinese who outmarry but also in the number who marry other Chinese. The number of Japanese outmarriages decreased from 719 in 1984 to 588 in 1989, but the rate remained consistent at 51 percent. The Korean trend is unusual; there was an increase in the number of outmarriages between 1984 and 1989; however, there has also been a large increase in the number of inmarriages, so the rate of outmarriage fell back to extremely low levels (8.7 to 11 percent) in comparison to the other Asian American groups. The rise in the number of Vietnamese intermarriages may indicate a long-term trend.[31]

Data from Hawaii indicate high rates of outmarriage between 1970 and 1980: 75 to 82 percent for Chinese, 47 to 59 percent for Japanese, and 83

Table 12.9 Outmarriage Rates for Chinese, Filipinos, Japanese, Koreans, and Vietnamese in Los Angeles County, 1975–1989

Ethnicity	Year	Marriages	Outmarriages Number	Percent	Percentage Outmarrying by Gender Women	Men
Chinese	1989	1,836	622	33.9	63.0	37.0
	1984	1,881	564	30.0	56.6	43.4
	1979	716	295	41.2	56.3	43.7
	1977	650	323	49.7	56.3	43.7
	1975	596	250	44.0	62.2	37.8
Filipinos	1989	1,384	565	40.8	74.2	25.8
Japanese	1989	1,134	588	51.9	58.3	41.7
	1984	1,404	719	51.2	60.2	39.8
	1979	764	463	60.6	52.7	47.3
	1977	756	477	63.1	60.6	39.4
	1975	664	364	54.8	53.6	46.4
Koreans	1989	1,372	151	11.0	74.8	25.2
	1984	543	47	8.7	78.6	21.4
	1979	334	92	27.6	79.6	20.4
	1977	232	79	34.1	73.4	26.6
	1975	250	65	26.0	63.1	36.9
Vietnamese	1989	555	147	26.5	54.4	45.6
	1984	560	34	6.0	74.7	25.3

Source: Los Angeles County Marriage License Bureau.

to 92 percent for Koreans. Between 17 and 34 percent of outmarriages in Hawaii were to other Asians.[32]

The rise in marital integration is due to a combination of historical factors, demographic variables, the overthrow of discriminatory legislation, loosening controls of the family, better opportunities in employment and education, gaining of more equal status, desegregation of housing, and the rise of individual preferences in marital choices. The most powerful predictors of outmarriage were generation and sex. Females of the third or later generation tend to outmarry at a high rate.

One other phenomenon that is on the rise is the purchase of "Oriental brides" by non-Asians through mail order, reportedly a booming business.[33] Lonely American males pay a fee and are given pictures of prospective brides from Asian countries, especially the Philippines. Some Asian groups have reacted quite negatively to the practice, charging that these foreign women are being dehumanized and exploited. Defenders of the system maintain that it gives the women an alternative to a life of poverty.

There also are social clubs where majority-group males can meet "lovely Oriental females." Ads in Los Angeles and some other West Coast city newspapers advertise such clubs; male members include a high proportion of middle- to upper-status professional whites.[34] It may well be that males are looking for the stereotypical Asian female—good at housekeeping, service-oriented, willing to stay home, and sexy.

1997 CENSUS

The data for the 1997 U.S. Census reports were gathered from the March 1998 Current Population Survey. It is not as thorough as the decennial census counts and contains sampling variability and other sources of error. It also acknowledges the variations among the Asian American and Pacific Islanders in terms of socioeconomic characteristics, culture, and recency of immigration. Therefore, data users should exercise caution when interpreting aggregate data for this population.

Income[35]

The 1997 data, released in 1998, provides an overall picture of Asian American and Pacific Islander (AAPI) household income, individual income, poverty, college completion levels, and family data. The chief of the Census Bureau's Housing and Economics Statistics Division reported that the household income of $45,249 was the nation's highest. However, the average size of Asian and Pacific Islander households (3.17 people) compared with white households (2.58 people) worked out to an income of $18,569 for each individual, compared to $20,093 for each white household member.

The median household income for Asian Americans ($45,249) was followed by whites ($38,972), Hispanic origin ($26,628), and African Americans ($25,050).

The Asian and Pacific Islander group trailed the white population in per capita income. White per capita income in 1997 was $20,425; AAPI was $18,226, followed by African Americans at $12,351 and Hispanics at $10,773.

Poverty

The number and percentage of AAPIs who were poor was 1.5 million. (14 percent); for whites, 24.4 million (11 percent); for African Americans, 9.1 million (26.5 percent); and 8.3 million (27.1 percent) for Hispanics. The poverty threshold for a family of four was $16,400 in annual income.

Educational Attainment[36]

One-half of AAPIs ages 25 to 29 had attained a bachelor's degree in 1997 compared to 29 percent for Whites, 14 percent for African Americans, and 11 percent for Hispanics. For all persons 25 years and older, AAPIs had the greatest proportion of college graduates with 42 percent, compared to 25 percent for whites, 13 percent for African Americans, and 10 percent for Hispanics.

Other Data[37]

- AAPI children under 18 years of age were more likely to live with both parents (84 percent) than non-Hispanic white children (77 percent).
- AAPI population was about 10.1 million, or 4 percent of the total U.S. population.
- Of the 2.3 million AAPI families, eight in ten were married couples.
- Fifty-six percent of AAPI households had three or more persons in them.
- Eight in ten AAPIs 25 years and older had at least a high school education and about four in ten had at least a bachelor's degree.

Admissions Data, UCLA, Fall 1999[38]

The effects of Proposition 209 in California has had an effect on minority enrollment at the University of California. In 1992, African American freshmen enrollment was 7.7 percent; the percentage African American students in the admitted class of 1999 was approximately 3 percent. The Chicano/ Latino admissions rate for 1992 was 14.1 percent; in 1999, it was 10.5 percent.

The percentage of Asian Americans entering as freshmen in 1992 was 34 percent; in 1999 it was 42.3 percent. White students comprised 32.8 percent in 1992 and 33.5 percent in 1999. It is clear that Asian Americans have been most active in using higher education as one route to mobility.

SUMMARY

To sum up, there are numerous ways of assessing the status of Asian Americans. Those who had goals of amalgamation and participation in the mainstream have made progress, especially in recent decades. Incomes have risen; occupational levels have advanced; immigration laws have been liberalized. Many Asian Americans have entered colleges and universities. Marital assimilation has taken place, and each generation appears to be more American than the next. The repeal of discriminatory laws has allowed Asian Americans to become naturalized, to live where they wish, and to run for and be elected to public office. Many own homes. Infant deaths are low, and Asian Americans live longer.

Discrimination exists, but it is subtle. Mobility to the upper echelons of management and power has yet to be achieved in any consistent fashion. Instances of *isolate discrimination* serve as reminders that all is not fully well, that Asian Americans can still be the targets of racial attacks and scapegoating.

For pluralists, continued immigration has reinvigorated ethnic communities. English is not the preferred language for many, especially since such a large percentage are foreign-born and are recent arrivals. There are areas in the country where one can remain comfortably ethnic, where ethnic newspapers, ethnic television, ethnic churches, and a large number of ethnic organizations continue to thrive. One can retain the ethnic culture, speak the ethnic language, share ethnic foods, and live a life within an ethnic enclave, with minimal contact with the dominant community. The most significant change is that the current pluralism is voluntary, whereas in previous eras ethnic communities arose in response to the lack of opportunities in the larger community.

Asian American communities may be as dynamic as dominant communities, and thus changes are a part of life. American-born youngsters will change the culture of their communities. Some will integrate and amalgamate, some will follow a bicultural path, and some may opt for remaining primarily ethnic. Some new immigrants will stay in their enclaves; others will use the ethnic community as a waystation toward eventual participation in the mainstream. In the final analysis, ethnic communities have served and will continue to serve many purposes, just as they have played a significant role for other immigrant groups. But the major key to their survival is the dominant community. Assimilation or pluralism lies primarily in the hands of the more powerful larger community. Their immigration laws will determine the makeup of future populations; their control of laws, wealth, resources, and power will be the primary impetus for whatever changes may occur.

NOTES

1. U.S. Dept. of Commerce, Bureau of the Census. *We the Asian Americans*. (Washington, DC: Government Printing Office, and U.S. Dept. of Commerce, Bureau of the Census, 1993); *Asians and Pacific Islanders in the United States* (1990 CP-3-5). (Washington, DC: Government Printing Office, 1993). Data from the latter are based on sample tabulations and may vary slightly from what the Census Bureau calls "100-percent tabulations."

2. Office of Academic Planning and Budget, *Undergraduate Persistence Report* (Los Angeles: University of California, January 1993 and June 1993).

3. Ibid.

4. Katherine Farish, "Asians Get a Home at UConn," *Hartford Courant*, Apr. 6, 1993.

5. *New York Times*, Aug. 3, 1986.

6. William Trombly, "Faculties Still Largely White," *Los Angeles Times*, July 6, 1986.

7. Shawn Hubler and Stuart Silverstein, "Schooling Doesn't Close Minority Earnings Gap," *Los Angeles Times*, Jan. 10, 1993.

8. "Divorces," in *Vital Statistics of the United States, 1982, Vol. 3: Marriage and Divorce* (Hyattsville, MD:, U.S. Department of Health and Human Services, 1986), table 2-18.

9. Bruce E. Cain and D. Roderick Kiewiet, *Minorities in California* (Pasadena: California Institute of Technology, 1986).

10. Ibid.

11. John Greenwald, "Finding Niches in a New Land," *Time*, July 8, 1985, pp. 32–33.

12. Robert W. Gardner, Bryant Robey, and Peter C. Smith, *Asian Americans: Growth, Change and Diversity* (Washington, DC: Population Reference Bureau, 1985).

13. Cain and Kiewiet, *Minorities in California*.

14. Gardner et al., *Asian Americans*.

15. Ibid.

16. "Profile of Poverty," *Los Angeles Times*, Aug. 17, 1992, p. A20.

17. *New York Times*, June 3, 1993.

18. Richard Simon, "Anglo Vote Carried Riordan to Victory," *Los Angeles Times*, June 10, 1993, p. A25.

19. Don Nakanishi, *The UCLA Asian Pacific American Voter Registration Study* (Los Angeles: Department of Education, University of California, 1986).

20. Walter G. Beach, *Oriental Crime in California* (Stanford, CA: Stanford University Press, 1932); H. K. Misaki, *Delinquency of Japanese in California* (Stanford, CA: Stanford University Press, 1933); Edward K. Strong, Jr., *The Second-Generation Japanese Problem* (Stanford, CA: Stanford University Press, 1934); Harry H. L. Kitano, "Japanese American Crime and Delinquency," *Journal of Psychology* 66 (1967): 253–263; Federal Bureau of Investigation, *Uniform Crime Reports for the United States, 1980–1985* (Washington, DC: Government Printing Office, 1986).

21. "Asian Gangs," California Youth Authority Training Seminar, Camarillo, CA, Mar. 4, 1986.

22. Vicki Torres, "Eight Arrested, Guns Seized in Raid on Asian Gangs," *Los Angeles Times*, May 13, 1993, p. B3.

23. Denise Hamilton, "Asian Extortion Gang at School Revealed," *Los Angeles Times*, June 9, 1993, p. B1.

24. Eui-Young Yu, *Juvenile Delinquency in the Korean Community in Los Angeles* (Los Angeles: Korea Times, 1987).

25. See Linda Bennett and Genevieve Ames, eds., *The American Experience with Alcohol* (New York: Plenum Press, 1985), especially Harry H. L. Kitano, Herb Hatanaka, Wai-tsang Yeung, and Stanley Sue, "Japanese American Drinking Patterns," pp. 346–358; Harry H. L. Kitano, Herb Hatanaka, and Wai-tsang Yeung, "Alcohol Consumption among Chinese in the United States," pp. 359–371; and Joseph Westermeyer, "Hmong Drinking Practices in the United States," pp. 373–391.

26. Stanley Sue and H. McKinney, "Asian Americans in the Community Mental Health Care System," *American Journal of Orthopsychiatry* 45 (1975): 11–18.

27. Tran Minh Tung, "Psychiatric Care for Southeast Asians: How Different Is Different?" in Tom Owan, ed., *Southeast Asian Mental Health* (Bethesda, MD: National Institute of Mental Health, 1985), pp. 5–40.

28. Patti Iiyama and Harry H. L. Kitano, "Asian Americans and the Media," in G. Barry and C. Mitchell-Kernan, eds., *Television and the Socialization of the Minority Child* (New York: Academic Press, 1982), pp. 66–90.

29. Edward Iwata, "Asian Movies Take Flight," *Los Angeles Times,* May 13, 1993.

30. Jan Breslauer, "Swimming Against the Tide," *Los Angeles Times,* Jan. 3, 1993.

31. Harry H. L. Kitano, Diane Fujino, and Jane Takahashi, "Interracial Marriage: Where Are the Asian Americans and Where Are they Going?" in L. Lee and N. Zane, eds., *Handbook of Asian American Psychology* (Thousand Oaks, CA: Sage, 1997).

32. Ibid.

33. "Asian American Women," seminar held at the Asian American Studies Center, University of California, Los Angeles, Nov. 3, 1986.

34. Ibid.

35. U.S. Bureau of the Census, *Income and Poverty.* U.S. Department of Commerce, Economics and Statistics Administration, 1997.

36. U.S. Bureau of the Census, *Education, Educational Attainment.* U.S. Department of Commerce, Economics and Statistics Administration, 1997.

37. U.S. Bureau of the Census, *Asian and Pacific Islander Population.* U.S. Department of Commerce, Economics and Statistics Administration, 1997.

38. Diana de Cardenas, "Fall Admits: Diversity Stable, Los Angeles." *UCLA Today,* April 5, 1999, pp. 1, 6.

Chapter 13

ADAPTATION OF ASIAN AMERICANS

This final chapter will present a variety of models dealing with the experiences of Asian Americans as well as important areas of concern, such as interracial marriage and the mass media.

MODELS OF ADAPTATION

Emory Bogardus, studying Chinese, Japanese, Filipino, and Mexican immigrants in the 1920s, discerned a race relations cycle.[1] The cycle began with curiosity, followed by economic welcome, industrial and social antagonism, legislative antagonism, fair-play tendencies, quiescence, and second-generation difficulties. The model closely fits the experiences of the early Asian immigrants, especially the Chinese and the Japanese.

Robert E. Park had earlier proposed his own cycle, consisting of competition, conflict, accommodation, assimilation, and amalgamation.[2] However, after studying race relations in Hawaii in the 1930s, he concluded that there were three possible outcomes of the relations between groups: a caste system, complete assimilation, or permanent minority status. His model also described the experiences of Asian groups up to that time but did not accurately predict the changes that eventually occurred, especially in Hawaii.

Banton[3] summarizes the main features of Park's perspective:

1. Migration brings together, often in unequal relations, people who are racially different.
2. Because of competition, individuals become conscious of the features by which they are assigned different statuses.
3. People who are in the most dominant positions are unwilling to allow "equal opportunity" for those in less desirable positions. Instead, they tend to look down upon those less fortunate as "inferiors."

Tamotsu Shibutani and Kian Kwan contended in the 1960s that assimilation—defined as a change of mental perspective such that the immigrant perceives the world from an American point of view—is inevitable unless one group exterminates the other.[4] Given the relative degree of power of the dominant group and "voluntary immigration," the model has a degree of validity, although conditions such as the openness of the society, equality, and time since arrival should also be taken into account. Social barriers, such as legal discrimination, can extend inequality indefinitely.

Milton Gordon produced more detailed schema concerning assimilation into American society.[5] He saw seven stages—cultural, structural, marital, identificational, attitude receptional, behavioral receptional, and civic. Stated more simply, the variables leading to assimilation are taking on American ways, or acculturation; integrating into the structures of the dominant society; marrying into the dominant group; identifying as an American; and being accepted without prejudice, discrimination, or value conflict. Although Gordon has been criticized for advocating an assimilationist perspective, many of his variables are appropriate in any analysis of immigrant group adaptation.

There are a number of other models that differentiate between European immigrants and those of color. Robert Blauner wrote about these differences in 1972.[6] Colonized minorities (Native Americans, African slaves) did not immigrate voluntarily; they were forced to acculturate, were ruled and controlled by outsiders, and were subjected to racism. Therefore, the model of voluntary immigration, acculturation, integration, and eventual assimilation, which was the experience for many Europeans, has only limited relevance to "colored" minorities.

Pluralism emphasizes the maintenance of ethnicity and sees America as composed of a mixture of various groups. Analogies to a symphony orchestra or to a salad bowl are used to illustrate the model. Michael Walzer in 1980 saw racism as the barrier to a fully developed pluralism; ethnic groups are not all equal, so pluralism can mean continues disadvantage and inequality.[7] A country committed to pluralism is limited to providing opportunities to ensure that all citizens, without differentiation, share equally. It cannot, however, prevent people from moving from a more disadvantaged ethnic group to the resource-rich dominant group.

Philip Gleason in 1980 focused on some of the difficulties associated with a pluralistic position.[8] The notion of a rich and harmonious society in which each ethnic group is spending time and money to advocate its own needs and priorities has yet to be realized. Further, the notion of the common good or common goals is difficult to achieve under this model.

Cheng and Bonacich in 1983 viewed race and ethnic relations in the context of the world economy.[9] Capitalistic economies require cheap labor; cheap labor (migrant workers, immigrant laborers) lies at the periphery of the economic system. Racial and ethnic minorities are often located on the periphery; these outsides have little economic control over their lives; they are at the mercy of economic currents and political decisions. Race relations, from this perspective, are less a result of white racism and more a function of political and economic decisions.

The idealistic "melting pot" model saw a blend of all groups to create a new American society. However, in practice, it became an Anglo conformity model; rather than a variety of groups melting equally to form the "new" society, melting meant giving up the old in order to become an American. Then there is the question of what culture one is supposed to melt into. Is it to New England, New York, the South, the Midwest, the Mountain and Plains culture, the Northwest, or California? And we also have urban and rural differences, so that adds another dimension to the question of melting into what American culture. Does the newly arrived Korean immigrant melt into the Korean community in Los Angeles, or is melting into an ethnic community not considered as melting?

Asian Americans have problems that are common to immigrants and to the general society. There are gangs of alienated groups of adolescents, problems of the elderly, culture conflict, conflicts between generations, employment and health, mental health and mental illness. One major problem with Asian Americans is their reluctance to ask for help; their hesitation in using the public and private social services can be interpreted that they are problem-free, when in reality their hesitation is due more to cultural restraints.

PREJUDICE AND DISCRIMINATION

The variables most closely tied to shunting the adaptation of minority groups away from "straight-line theory"—that is, the process that culminates in the eventual absorption of the ethnic group into the larger culture and general population—are prejudice and discrimination.[10] Prejudice, often maintained through stereotypes, means avoidance; discrimination, often tied to legislation, leads to disadvantage.[11]

Gunnar Myrdal in 1944 used discrimination and the principle of cumulation to explain the plight of Black Americans in the 1930s.[12] Discrimination keeps the minority in a state of inequality—low income, poor housing, inferior education. This in turn is related to family disorganization and criminal and deviant behavior, which in turn leads the discriminator to justify more discrimination, which then leads to more deprivation, more disorganization, and more inequality. It should also be noted that the spiral does not operate exclusively on a downward path; it can also move upward, with racial discrimination progressively diminishing.

The cumulation process can also be seen in the historical development of Asian American communities. Prejudice and discrimination led to segregated housing and the exclusion of Asians from organizations and services of the dominant community. Therefore, Asians were forced to rely on their own resources—hospitals, jobs, insurance companies, social clubs—which led to segregated ethnic organizations and communities. These developments led in turn to cries about the unassimilability of Asians by the dominant community. But the situation can be reversed. Since World War II, the importance of ethnic community organizations has declined as opportunities in the dominant community increased for most established Asian American groups.

Generally, prejudice, because it is an attitude, is viewed as less damaging to a minority group than discrimination, although there is an assumed link between the two. Prejudice is much more widespread—can we control people's minds?—and therefore a difficult target to eradicate, whereas an attempt to control behavior, especially through legislation, is regarded as a more effective way of gaining equality.

Table 13.1 shows the responses by blacks, Hispanics, and Asians in Los Angeles regarding prejudice directed toward them. Among the groups, the Asians responded the most liberally; they perceived less prejudice from the white community than the other groups.

Table 13.2 shows the responses of the three groups to questions regarding reported instances of discrimination. Asians reported the highest

Table 13.1   Degree of Prejudice Directed Toward One's Racial or Ethnic Group (percent) (Los Angeles, 1984)

Degree of Prejudice Toward Respondent's Group	Race or Ethnicity of Respondent		
	Black	Hispanic	Asian
Most people are prejudiced	17	10	5
Some people are prejudiced	63	54	52
Most people are not prejudiced	21	36	42

Source: Bruce E. Cain and D. Roderick Kiewiet, *Minorities in California* (Pasadena: California Institute of Technology, 1986), p. III-115.

Table 13.2   **Personally Experienced Discrimination Reported by Blacks, Hispanics, and Asian Americans (percent) (Los Angeles, 1984)**

	Race or Ethnicity of Respondent		
Most Serious Discrimination Personally Experienced	*Black*	*Hispanic*	*Asian*
None	39	65	55
Social	19	16	30
Economic	42	19	15

Source: Bruce E. Cain and D. Roderick Kiewiet, *Minorities in California* (Pasadena: California Institute of Technology, 1986), p. III-114.

percentage of social discrimination and the lowest percentage of economic discrimination.

A more comprehensive overview of discrimination from a national perspective reported a wide number of incidents against Asian Americans:[13]

- Seattle: Shots fired into homes of Southeast Asian refugees
- New York: A Chinese woman pushed in front of a subway train
- California: The word *Jap* spray-painted on an Asian American legislator's garage door
- Houston: Comment by a public health official that Chinese and Vietnamese restaurants have "different standards of cleanliness"
- Los Angeles: Bumper stickers reading Toyota-Datsun . . . Pearl Harbor and Unemployment. Made in Japan.
- Davis, California: Fatal stabbing of a Vietnamese student by a white high school student
- Fort Dodge, Iowa: Laotian immigrant assaulted by a 23-year-old white male
- Massachusetts: At least twenty complaints concerning acts against Southeast Asian refugees in 1983
- Texas: Death of a white crab fisherman in a conflict between Vietnamese and local fishermen

Other incidents included vandalism of cars, misdemeanor assaults, graffiti, harassment, and intimidation. The most dramatic case was that of Vincent Chin, a 27-year-old American-born draftsman of Chinese ancestry. On the night of June 19, 1982, Chin went with three friends to a topless bar, the Fancy Pants Tavern, in the Detroit suburb of Highland Park, to celebrate his impending marriage. Some racial slurs were made by a 43-year-old automobile industry foreman, who thought that Chin was Japanese and somehow responsible for his unemployment (Japanese cars were outselling American-built cars at the time). A scuffle ensued, and all were asked to leave the night spot. Later that night, the white foreman and his 23-year-old stepson saw Chin in a fast-food restaurant, waited for him to leave, and while the stepson held Chin, the older man beat him with a baseball bat. Chin died four days later. Originally charged with second-degree murder, the white pair, in a plea bargain, were allowed to plead guilty to manslaughter. Wayne County Circuit Judge Charles Kaufman fined each man $3,780 and placed them both on three years' probation.

The Asian American community was outraged. The lenient sentences were interpreted by Asian Americans as an indication that they were unequal in the eyes of the law. The protests eventually forced an investigation, which produced a federal indictment of the older man for depriving Chin of his civil rights. Tried and found guilty, the prime assailant was sentenced to twenty-five years in prison in September 1984. That conviction was reversed on appeal. In April 1987—almost five years after the event—conflicting testimony and blurred memories of witnesses resulted in an acquittal of the killer on the federal charge. The issue in question was not the homicide but whether the motivation was "racial."

Table 13.3, based on FBI statistics on hate crimes for 1991, shows the suspected race of offenders and victims by race, ethnicity, religion, and sexual orientation. The highest offender category was "unknown" (43.3 percent), followed by whites (36.8 percent) and blacks (16.9 percent). Asians and Pacific Islanders constituted only 1 percent of the offenders.

In terms of race, the most common targets were blacks (35.5 percent), followed by whites (18.7 percent) and Asians and Pacific islanders (6 percent).

Responses to Difficulties

Although it is difficult to assess the reactions of all Asian Americans to the current racial climate, there is some evidence of disenchantment among immigrants in the Los Angeles area. Miles Corwin writes about some newcomers ready to "pack up and go back home," and others have already packed and left.[14] There are so many former Los Angeles residents in Seoul that they have formed a club to discuss readjusting to life in Korea. The 1993 riot in Los Angeles was one contributing factor, but many immigrants who had left white-collar jobs back home have found the less attractive jobs and racial tensions too much to handle. There were also complaints about the American educational system and the emphasis on the "bottom line" in American business. Fear, crime, and disillusionment had sullied the American dream.[15]

Linda Vista, a small community near San Diego, has gone through extreme demographic changes. What was once a primarily white community now houses newcomers who do not speak English, and the sights, sounds, and smells create an Asian ambience. Old-line residents feel that "their libraries, their stores, and their restaurants," no longer cater to their needs.

**Table 13.3   Suspected Race of Offenders in Hate Crimes and Hate Crime Bias
Motivations, 1991**

Suspected Race of Offender	Number of Incidents	Percentage of Incidents
White	1,679	36.8
Black	769	16.9
Native American	12	0.3
Asian/Pacific Islander	47	1.0
Multiracial	77	1.7
Unknown	1,974	43.3
Total incidents	4,558*	100.00

*A single incident may involve more than one offense.

Bias Motivation	Number	Percentage*
Race	2,963	62.3
Antiwhite	888	18.7
Antiblack	1,689	35.5
Anti-Native American	11	0.2
Anti-Asian/Pacific Islander	287	6.0
Antimultiracial	88	1.9
Ethnicity	450	9.5
Anti-Hispanic	242	5.1
Anti other ethnicity or national origin	208	4.4
Religion	917	19.3
Anti-Jewish	792	16.7
Anti-Catholic	23	0.5
Anti-Protestant	26	0.5
Anti-Islamic (Muslim)	10	0.2
Anti other religion	51	1.1
Antimultireligious	11	0.2
Antiatheist, antiagnostic, etc.	4	0.1
Sexual Orientation	425	8.9
Antihomosexual	421	8.9
Antiheterosexual	3	0.1
Antibisexual	1	0.0
Total	4,755	100.0

*Because of rounding, percentages may not add to totals.

Source: Asian Week, Jan. 15, 1993, p. 7. Based on FBI statistics.

But the newcomers indicate that once their children grow up, they do not wish to remain in Linda Vista.[16]

Broader Perspective

If we select a few headlines from other years—1924: "Congress Passes Law Denying Immigration of Asians"; 1942: "President Roosevelt Signs Executive Order 9066, Removing All Persons of Japanese Ancestry from the West Coast"—current anti-Asian actions take on a different coloration.

Current incidents reflect *isolate discrimination*—actions taken by individuals against other individuals.[17] This type of discrimination, which can be directly linked to prejudice, has minor societal impact, although it serves as a reminder to the minority group member that prejudice and discrimination have not been eliminated and that one must remain on guard. By contrast, the examples of 1924 and 1942 reflect *institutionalized discrimination*—actions taken by groups against other groups—which has far-ranging effects and is therefore much more damaging to the minority group. Of course, the distinction may mean little to the victims of current isolated attacks.

Isolate discrimination may not be as benign or minor in terms of societal effects when linked to power. A racially prejudiced individual in a position of power can influence policy and programs, even if only through negative votes or decisions. However, overall, the diminution of institutionalized discrimination can be regarded as an optimistic sign concerning the relationship between Asians and the dominant community, and one hopes that behavior on the isolate level will evolve in the same direction.

CIVIC ASSIMILATION

One of the last stages in the assimilationist perspective occurs when the ethnic minority no longer uses the ethnic variable in civic affairs. David Bell saw indications of this process in the political arena, although there still are, of course, Asian issues—immigration, redress for wartime mistreatment, and equal opportunity for disadvantaged Asians.[18] But Asian American politicians—outside of Hawaii—cannot run solely on an Asian American agenda; they must embrace wider platforms. The linkage to wider issues has kept Asian politicians from playing "typical minority politics." Similarly, Asian Americans are often excluded from affirmative action programs, and there are fears that they may become the targets of unofficial quotas.

THE ASIAN AMERICAN MODEL

From the data, we perceive certain patterns in the adaptation of Asians to the United States. Variables such as time of immigration, motives, and demographic factors—all relating to what the immigrants brought with them—are important, just as is the welcome that they received upon their arrival. But after their initial entrance, a number of adaptive patterns have emerged.

The two variables mentioned most often are assimilation and ethnic identity. The assimilation variable, as previously mentioned, encompasses integration into the schools, the workplace, and social groupings, as well as identification with the majority and marital assimilation. The ethnic identity dimension is essentially a pluralistic adaptation, focusing on the retention of ethnic ways. Figure 13.1 illustrates the model and the four types associated with the model.

Cell A: High Assimilation, Low Ethnic Identity

Cell A shows Asian Americans high in assimilation and low in ethnic identity. The individuals feel more American than ethnic; many members of the third generation and Asian Americans isolated from ethnic communities fall into this category. Language, lifestyles, and expectations are American; the ethnic language and culture are all but forgotten. High rates of marriage to non-Asians can be predicted; more females than males may belong to this category. Individuals who desire to become "American" no matter what the generation also fit into this cell.

Friendship and social patterns will also show a high proportion of non-Asian contacts. Friends will be from the majority culture; membership will be in dominant group organizations, such as fraternities and sororities.

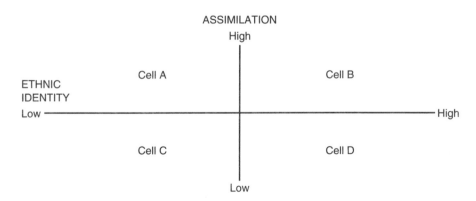

Figure 13.1   Assimilation Model

Ethnic identity, if present, will be primarily symbolic, involving occasional participation in ethnic holidays and festivals, the partaking of ethnic foods, or watching an ethnic movie now and then. But for Asian Americans in this category, the one inescapable fact is ethnic visibility, and reactions from the outside world force the retention of an ethnic identity, no matter how slight. Canadians currently apply the term *visible minority* to residents whose ethnicity is signaled by skin color.

Cell B: High Assimilation, High Ethnic Identity

The individuals who fit into this category will be similar in the assimilation category to those in Cell A, but will differ from those in the previous model by retaining a strong ethnic identity. Friendship patterns, membership in organizations, and interest show a strong bicultural perspective; the individual moves easily in and out of both cultures. Further, the person is knowledgeable about ethnicity and the ethnic culture and is comfortable with a strong ethnic identity. The category is a bicultural one; it may include some academics and some older individuals brought up with a multicultural perspective. The hyphenated Asian-American will fit under this category, although it will probably be difficult to maintain an even balance between the two.

Cell C: Low Assimilation, Low Ethnic Identity

This cell describes the alienated, the disenchanted, and the disillusioned. They have acquired very little of the American culture and are also uncomfortable with an ethnic identity. We see a small proportion of Asian Americans in this category.

Cell D: Low Assimilation, High Ethnic Identity

This cell includes a large number of newly arrived immigrants, as well as Asian Americans who have spent much of their lives in ethnic communities. The latter may have achieved a "functional level" of adaptation to the American culture but are more comfortable within the ethnic enclaves. Marriage will tend to be within the ethnic group; the person is more ethnic than American. Members of the first generation, especially those who emigrated at an advanced age, are likely to be in this category. Asian Americans who feel that the white society will never treat them as equals may also opt for a pluralistic adaptation.[19]

Variations in assimilation were observed by Marcus Lee Hansen, who saw a third-generation reawakening of ethnic identity—"what the second generation tries to forget, the third generation remembers."[20] For example, significant numbers of third- and fourth-generation Japanese Americans have enrolled over the years in the Education Abroad program of the University of California Tokyo Study Center, but few other manifestations of an ethnic revival are apparent. Perhaps it is not coincidental that the most observable examples occur among groups whose immigration has largely stopped.

The underlying assumption of assimilation theory is that the American mainstream has the power, the organization, and the resources that pull immigrant groups in its direction. It is incumbent on the less powerful to come to grips with the American culture, lest they remain outsiders looking in. At one time, the dominant society practiced a policy of selective exclusion. Asians were unwelcome, so there were modifications and delays in assimilation. It is no accident that the call for pluralism, for separate identities, and for a reevaluation of assimilationist models was led by ethnic groups who were excluded from equal participation in the society.

Now that exclusionary policies have been modified, it will be interesting to see if newer Asian immigrants, including American-born generations who have faced a minimal amount of institutionalized barriers, follow an assimilationist model.

As Gans indicated, the third and succeeding generations grow up without assigned roles or groups that anchor identity.[21] Ethnicity is no longer taken for granted. Most group members are acculturated participants in the mainstream; the primary, but still powerful, reminder of their "Asianness" remains their visibility. Other reminders, such as overt discrimination and the politics of exclusion, are no longer in vogue; ethnic organizations, especially those that stress civil rights and equality, have a difficult time attracting younger members without an ethnic "cause." One symptom of the progress of a group toward assimilation is the disappearance of ethnic organizations devoted to civil rights and equality; the existence of such groups, especially in Third World communities, indicates that much is yet to be achieved.

Studies focusing on the importance of social class in the Asian American communities are lacking. Even though many of the early immigrants would have been classified as lower-class in terms of income and education, their expectations were more middle-class—higher education for their children, saving for the future, ownership of land, starting their own business. Conversely, those who might have been classified as upper-class were not viewed as such by their peers in the dominant community. Views of class solidarity did not develop, especially across ethnic lines, so class consciousness in terms of social action to redress grievances was not a common phenomenon.

There is little question that social class and other status variables operate within each Asian community and that length of time in America is accompanied by an increased differentiation in income, education, mobility, housing, and lifestyle. Good marriages and good prospects are commonly defined in social-class terms; many parents search diligently for marital partners for their children in terms of good education, a good house in a good neighborhood, good family, and good income. The definition of desirability has even cut across ethnic boundaries—whereas in a previous era the question might have been "Is your fiancé Asian?" a more common question might now be "Is he a doctor?" Ethnic parents who deny the importance of such variables when judging others appear to have developed finely honed procedures to discover the "really eligible." And many are disappointed when their acculturated children marry for love, acquiring partners who lack the desired characteristics.

In conclusion, Asians, purveyors of the well-known Rashomon perspective—that views of reality are dependent on the position of the observer—provide a number of such perceptions. In business and economics, they are viewed as busy entrepreneurs, focusing on small businesses and the professions and generally doing well. In the mental health fields—psychiatry, psychology, counseling, and social work—Asian Americans are a cause of concern. They appear to have as many problems as others but do not avail themselves of professional services. For educators, Asian Americans are a source of delight—good, hardworking students—although the image is changing. To politicians, they are an unknown group, but one to be considered because of their growing numbers. For some frustrated Americans, Asian Americans are a convenient scapegoat—easy to stereotype, easy to blame.

In the final analysis, Bell is almost indisputably right in believing that immigrants, and specifically Asian immigrants, have been good for America.[22] Asian immigrants and their children have enriched and improved every field that they have entered. Their grocery stores provide fresh produce, their doctors enrich the health field, and their students enhance the quality of scholarship at our universities. But such credit should not be reserved solely for them—Asian Americans have followed the path that has been characteristic of other immigrant groups, and like those others, they have added much more to the society than they have taken away.

NOTES

1. Emory Bogardus, "A Race Relations Cycle," *American Journal of Sociology* 35 (1930): 612–617.

2. Robert E. Park, *Race and Culture* (New York: Free Press, 1950).

3. Michael P. Banton, *Racial Theories* (New York: Cambridge University Press, 1987).

4. Tamotsu Shibutani and Kian Kwan, *Ethnic Stratification* (New York: Macmillan, 1965).

5. Milton M. Gordon, *Assimilation in American Life: The Role of Race, Religion and National Origins* (New York: Oxford University Press, 1964).

6. Robert Blauner, *Racial Oppression in America* (New York: Harper & Row, 1972).

7. Michael Walzer, "Pluralism: A Political Perspective," in Stephan Thernstrom, ed., *Harvard Encyclopedia of American Ethnic Groups* (Cambridge, MA: Harvard University Press, 1980), pp. 781–787.

8. Philip Gleason, "American Identity and Americanization," in Thernstrom, *Harvard Encyclopedia*, pp. 31–58.

9. Lucie Cheng and Edna Bonacich, eds., *Labor Immigration under Capitalism: Asian Workers in the United States before World War II* (Berkeley: University of California Press, 1983).

10. Neil Sandberg, *Jewish Life in Los Angeles* (Lanham, MD: University Press of America, 1986), p. 134.

11. Harry H. L. Kitano, *Race Relations*, 4th ed. (Englewood Cliffs, NJ: Prentice Hall, 1991).

12. Gunnar Myrdal, *An American Dilemma* (New York: Harper, 1944).

13. U.S. Commission on Civil Rights, *Recent Activities against Citizens and Residents of Asian Descent* (Washington, DC: Government Printing Office, 1986).

14. Miles Corwin, "Packing Up and Going Back Home," *Los Angeles Times*, Mar. 4, 1993.

15. K. Connie Kang, "Fear of Crime Robs Many of Dreams in Koreatown," *Los Angeles Times*, June 21, 1993.

16. Beverly Beyette, "Linda Vista Asks, 'Whose Community Is This?'" *Los Angeles Times*, May 27, 1993.

17. Joe Feagin, *Racial and Ethnic Relations* (Englewood Cliffs, NJ: Prentice Hall, 1978).

18. David Bell, "The Triumph of Asian Americans," *New Republic*, July 15, 1985, pp. 24–31.

19. Herbert Gans, "Symbolic Ethnicity: The Future of Ethnic Groups and Cultures in America," in Norman Yetman, ed., *Majority and Minority* (Boston: Allyn & Bacon, 1985), pp. 429–442.

20. Marcus Lee Hansen, *The Problems of the Third Generation* (Rock Island, IL: Augustana Historical Society, 1938).

21. Gans, "Symbolic Ethnicity."

22. Bell, "Triumph of Asian Americans."

APPENDIX
Census Bureau Information on the Web

For the next several years information from the 2000 census will be appearing on the Census Bureau web site—*http://www.census.gov.*

There is also valuable information available about Asian Americans on the site of the Immigration and Naturalization Service: *http://www.ins.usdoj.gov/graphics/index.htm.*

The following, from pre-2000 Census data, gives an idea of the variety of information available on this extensive and ever-changing site.

THE ASIAN AND PACIFIC ISLANDER POPULATION
Claudette E. Bennett and Kymberly A. Debarros

The Asian and Pacific Islander Population Is Growing Rapidly

In 1996, the Asian and Pacific Islander population was estimated at 9.7 million, up from 7.3 million recorded in the 1990 census.[1] Since 1990, the Asian and Pacific Islander population has grown about 2 percent per year. Immi-

---

[1]The Current Population Survey (CPS) estimate, based on a sample, is subject to sampling and nonsampling errors. It is not controlled to independent estimates for this population. Estimates may differ because of different data collection and estimation procedures and sampling error. However, distributions of characteristics for the Asian and Pacific Islander population in the March 1996 CPS appear reasonable when compared with the 1990 census distribution. When comparing data for the Asian and Pacific Islander population for previous years, caution should be used.

gration to the United States accounted for much of this growth (about 86 percent); the balance was due to natural increase (births minus deaths). The Asian and Pacific Islander population accounted for 3.7 percent of America's population in 1996. By the year 2000, this population is projected to reach 12.1 million and represent about 4 percent of the total population.

The Asian and Pacific Islander population is heterogeneous and includes groups that differ in language, culture, and recency of immigration. Several Asian groups, such as the Chinese and Japanese, have been in this country for generations. In contrast, relatively few Pacific Islanders are foreign born. Hawaiians, of course, are native to this country.

With a median age of 29.8 years in 1996, the Asian and Pacific Islander population was younger than the non-Hispanic White population (median age of 36.5 years). This difference reflected the age structure of the two groups: 30 percent of the Asian and Pacific Islander population were under 18 years old, and 6.6 percent were 65 years old and over. In contrast, 24 percent of non-Hispanic whites were under 18 years, and 14 percent were 65 years and over.

A Majority of the Asian and Pacific Islander Population Lives in Just Three States

In 1996, 55 percent of the Asian and Pacific Islander population lived in the West, where this population represented 9 percent of the region's population. A majority (57 percent) of the Asian and Pacific Islander population lived in just three states: California, New York, and Hawaii.

The vast majority (94 percent) of the Asian and Pacific Islander population lived in metropolitan areas in 1996. Of these, one-half lived in the suburbs of metropolitan areas; a little less than one-half (45 percent) lived in the central cities of metropolitan areas. The Asian and Pacific Islander population represented 4 percent of the total population living in the suburbs and 5 percent of the total population living in the central cities.

Asian and Pacific Islander Families Were More Likely than Non-Hispanic White Families to Be Large

In 1996, the average size for both Asian and Pacific Islander families and non-Hispanic White families was about four people. About 74 percent of Asian and Pacific Islander families had three or more people, compared with 53 percent of non-Hispanic White families. In addition, Asian and Pacific Islander families were twice as likely to have five or more people as non-Hispanic white families (22 percent versus 11 percent).

Six in ten Asian and Pacific Islander families had related children under 18 years old, compared with 5 in 10 non-Hispanic White families. However, the two groups had a similar proportion of related children under 18 years old living with both parents (about 80 percent).

Educational Attainment Remains High for the Asian and Pacific Islander Population

In 1996, among the Asian and Pacific Islander population 25 years old and over, nearly 9 out of 10 men and about 8 out of 10 women had at least a high school diploma. However, high school completion rates varied widely among Asian and Pacific Islander groups. The 1990 census, the latest date for which statistically reliable data for the groups are available, showed that among Asians, the rate varied from 31 percent for Hmongs, who are among the most recent Asian immigrant groups, to 88 percent for Japanese, who have been in this country for several generations.

Within the Pacific Islander group, the proportion with at least a high school diploma ranged from 64 percent for Tongans to 80 percent for Hawaiians.

A lower proportion of Asians and Pacific Islanders 25 years and over than of comparable non-Hispanic Whites had at least a high school diploma in 1996 (83 percent versus 86 percent, respectively), although the difference in the percentages was relatively small. However, the proportion of the Asian and Pacific Islander population who completed college (42 percent) was almost twice that of the non-Hispanic White population (26 percent).

Asian and Pacific Islander men and women (46 percent and 37 percent, respectively) were more than 1½ times as likely to have a bachelor's degree than non-Hispanic white men and women (29 percent and 23 percent, respectively).

Researchers have suggested that past selective migration of more highly educated people from Asia and the Pacific Islands may have contributed to the high educational attainment of this group. However, the educational attainment of the native-born Asian and Pacific Islander population was also high. It is also important to note that the proportion completing high school and college varies greatly among the Asian and Pacific Islander groups.

Median Income Is Similar for Asian and Pacific Islander Families and for Non-Hispanic White Families

In 1995, the median income of Asian and Pacific Islander families ($46,360) was similar to that of non-Hispanic white families ($45,020). The median income of each group was also similar among families maintained by women with no spouse present (about $26,550) and among those maintained by men with no spouse present (about $38,820 for Asian and Pacific Islander families and $32,640 for non-Hispanic White families).

In 1995, median earnings of the Asian and Pacific Islander population 25 years old and over with a high school education who worked year round, full time ($21,120) were lower than those of the comparable non-Hispanic White population ($25,350).

Asians and Pacific Islanders with a bachelor's degree or more also had lower median earnings ($37,040) than comparable non-Hispanic whites ($42,050). Women with at least a bachelor's degree had similar earnings ($32,450 for Asians and Pacific Islanders and $34,250 for non-Hispanic Whites) (Figure A.1). Comparably educated Asian and Pacific Islander men, on the other hand, earned about $82 for every $100 earned by their non-Hispanic White male counterparts ($41,370 compared with $50,240).

Among the Asian and Pacific Islander population in 1995, men 25 years old and over who worked year round, full time had higher median earnings ($41,380) than comparable women ($32,450).

The Poverty Rate for Asian and Pacific Islander Families Is More Than Twice That for Non-Hispanic White Families

Despite higher educational attainment and a similar median family income, Asian and Pacific Islander families had a poverty rate (12 percent) double that for non-Hispanic White families (6 percent) in 1995. Eleven percent of Asian and Pacific Islander married-couple families and 4 percent of corresponding non-Hispanic White families lived in poverty (Figure A.2). There

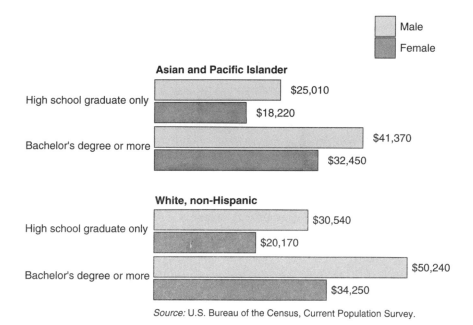

Source: U.S. Bureau of the Census, Current Population Survey.

Figure A.1   Median Earnings of Year-Round, Full-Time Workers 25 Years Old and Over, by Educational Attainment, Sex, and Race: 1995

was no statistical difference in the poverty rates for female householder families (26 percent for Asian and Pacific Islander and 22 percent for non-Hispanic White).

Overall in 1995, 14.6 percent of Asians and Pacific Islanders were poor, compared with 8.5 percent of non-Hispanic Whites.

For Further Information

See Current Population Reports, Series P20–503, *The Asian and Pacific Is-lander Population in the United States: March 1996* (Update) and tables on the Internet at *www.census.gov*.

CENSUS BUREAU FACTS FOR FEATURES*

Income and Poverty

Asians and Pacific Islanders had the highest median household income among the nation's race groups in 1997—$45,249. However, because Asian and Pacific Islander households were, on average, larger than White house-holds (3.17 people versus 2.58 people), their estimated income per house-hold member was lower ($18,569 compared with $20,093).

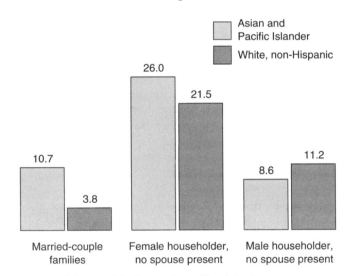

Source: U.S. Bureau of the Census, Current Population Survey.

Figure A.2. Poverty Rates, by Type of Family and Race of Householder: 1995 (In percent)

*A product of the U.S. Census Bureau's Public Information Office.

Both the number (1.5 million) and percentage (14.0 percent) of Asian and Pacific Islander individuals who were poor in 1997 were statistically unchanged from the previous year. For Asian and Pacific Islander families, the number and percent who were poor in 1997 were 244,000 and 10.2 percent, respectively.

Education

One of every two Asian and Pacific Islander adults ages 25 to 29 had attained a bachelor's degree or higher in 1997, contributing to that population's high percentage of college graduates. Comparatively, almost 1 in 3 Whites (29 percent), 1 in 7 African Americans (14 percent), and just over 1 in 10 Hispanics (11 percent) in the 25- to 29-year-old age group had at least a bachelor's degree.

Among all persons ages 25 and over in 1997, Asians and Pacific Islanders had the greatest proportion of college graduates of any racial or ethnic group, at 42 percent. This compared with 25 percent for Whites, 13 percent for African Americans, and 10 percent for Hispanics.

In 1996, non-Hispanic Asians and Pacific Islanders received 12 percent of the doctorates conferred by the nation's colleges and universities. This included 26 percent of those conferred in engineering, 22 percent each in mathematics and computer sciences, and 20 percent each in physical sciences (astronomy, physics, and chemistry) and biological sciences (biochemistry, botany, microbiology, physiology, and zoology).

Coming to America

In 1997, 24 percent, or 6.1 million, of the nation's foreign-born residents were Asians and Pacific Islanders. In addition, six in 10 Asians and Pacific Islanders in the United States were foreign-born.

China (including Hong Kong) and the Philippines were the leading countries of origin after Mexico for the nation's foreign-born residents in 1997, with each contributing 1.1 million.

Families

There were 2.2 million Asian and Pacific Islander families in 1997; of these, eight in 10 were married-couple families. Asian and Pacific Islander families are often large: 20 percent had five or more members, compared with 11 percent for non-Hispanic White families.

Asian and Pacific Islander children under 18 years of age were more likely to live with both parents (84 percent) that non-Hispanic white children (77 percent) in 1997.

In 1997, 58 percent of the nation's Asians and Pacific Islanders age 15 and over were married, 33 percent had never married, and 4 percent each were divorced and widowed.

Population Distribution

On July 1, 1998, an estimated 10.4 million Asians and Pacific Islanders lived in the United States, up 2.8 million from a total of 7.6 million on July 1, 1990. They comprised 3.8 percent of the total population in 1998, up from 3.0 percent in 1990.

Asians and Pacific Islanders had a higher rate of population growth between July 1, 1990 and 1998 than any other race or ethnic group: 37 percent.

The nation's Asian and Pacific Islander population is young, with an estimated median age on July 1, 1998, of 31.2 years, 4.0 years younger than the median for the U.S. population as a whole.

By 2020, according to middle-series population projections, the nation's Asian and Pacific Islander population is expected to reach 19.7 million (6.1 percent of the nation's total population).

In 1997, 55 percent of the nation's Asians and Pacific Islanders lived in the West and 95 percent resided in metro areas (49 percent in suburbs, 46 percent in central cities).

As of July 1, 1997, according to population estimates: California had more Asians and Pacific Islanders than any other state, 3.8 million. New York was a distant second (952,736), followed by Hawaii (748,748), Texas (523,972), and New Jersey (423,738).

The states with the highest concentration of Asians and Pacific Islanders were Hawaii (63 percent of the total population), California (12 percent), Washington (6 percent), and New Jersey and New York (5 percent each).

Los Angeles County, Calif., was the U.S. county with the highest number of Asians and Pacific Islanders (1.2 million). Honolulu County, Hawaii, was second (559,752), followed by Orange County, Calif. (344,330); Santa Clara County (San Jose), Calif. (343,387), and Queens County, N.Y. (317,893).

Between April 1, 1990, and July 1, 1997, according to population estimates: The number of Asians and Pacific Islanders residing in California jumped by 829,623, the largest increase of any state. Following California's lead were New York, which added 243,609 new Asian and Pacific Islander residents, Texas (192,544), New Jersey (146,714) and Florida (96,674).

Among counties, Los Angeles County, California, was No. 1 in Asian and Pacific Islander population increase, with a gain of more than 190,000. Neighboring Orange County, California, was No. 2, with 91,501. Others in the top five were Santa Clara County, California (76,905), Queens County, New York (75,220), and San Diego County, California (73,383).

Jobs

In 1997, among employed persons ages 16 and over, 38 percent of Asian and Pacific Islander men and 32 percent of women worked in managerial and professional specialty occupations (e.g., engineers, dentists, teachers, lawyers and reporters).

Languages

Between 1980 and 1995, the number of registrations in Japanese courses at U.S. colleges and universities almost quadrupled, from 11,500 to 44,700, while the number in Chinese courses more than doubled, from 11,400 to 26,500. Consequently, Japanese is now the fourth most popular foreign language course in U.S. colleges; Chinese is sixth. Furthermore, 42,300 of the nation's public high school students were enrolled in Japanese classes in fall 1994, up from 6,200 a dozen years earlier.

As of 1992, Chinese was tied with German as the third most common foreign language in which the nation's 17 million small businesses could conduct transactions: 2 percent could conduct them in Chinese. The leading foreign languages were Spanish and French.

SUGGESTIONS FOR FURTHER READING

The following works will serve as an introduction to many of the topics we have discussed in this book. Some, but not all, have been cited in the notes; most contain bibliographies.

RACE RELATIONS AND ACCULTURATION

Banton, Michael, *Racial and Ethnic Competition.* Cambridge: Cambridge University Press, 1983.
Blauner, Robert. *Racial Oppression in America.* New York: Harper & Row, 1972.
Daniels, Roger, and Harry H. L. Kitano. *American Racism: Exploration of the Nature of Prejudice.* Englewood Cliffs, NJ: Prentice Hall, 1970.
Glazer, Nathan. *We Are All Multiculturalists Now.* Cambridge, MA: Harvard University Press, 1997.
Gordon, Milton M. *Assimilation in American Life: The Role of Race, Religion and National Origins.* New York: Oxford University Press, 1964.
Kitano, Harry H. L. *Race Relations,* 4th ed. Englewood Cliffs, NJ: Prentice Hall, 1997.
White, Richard. "Race Relations in the American West," *American Quarterly* 38 (1986): 396–416.

HISTORIES OF IMMIGRATION

Daniels, Roger. *Coming to America: A History of Immigration and Ethnicity in American Life.* New York: HarperCollins, 1990.

Daniels, Roger. *Not Like Us: Immigrants and Minorities in America, 1890–1924.* Chicago: Ivan R. Dee, 1997.

Reimers, David M. *Still the Golden Door: The Third World Comes to America,* 2nd ed. New York: Columbia University Press, 1992.

ASIAN AMERICANS

Barkan, Elliott R. *Asian and Pacific Islander Migration to the United States: A Model of New Global Patterns.* Westport, CT: Greenwood Press, 1992.

Chan, Sucheng. *Asian Americans: An Interpretive History.* Boston: Twayne, 1991.

Friday, Chris. *Organizing Asian American Labor: The Pacific Coast Canned-Salmon Industry, 1870–1942.* Philadelphia: Temple University Press, 1994.

Lee, C. Lee, and Nolan W.S. Zane, eds. *Handbook of Asian American Psychology.* Thousand Oaks, CA: Sage Publications, 1998.

Okihiro, Gary Y. *Margins and Mainstreams: Asians in American History and Culture.* Seattle: University of Washington Press, 1994.

Saito, Leland K. *Race and Politics: Asian Americans, Latinos, and Whites in a Los Angeles Suburb.* Urbana: University of Illinois Press, 1998.

Takaki, Ronald T. *A Different Mirror.* Boston: Little, Brown, 1993.

Takaki, Ronald T. *Strangers from a Different Shore: A History of Asian Americans.* Boston: Little, Brown, 1989.

CHINESE AMERICANS

Chan, Sucheng. *This Bittersweet Soil: The Chinese in California Agriculture, 1860–1910.* Berkeley: University of California Press, 1986.

Daniels, Roger. *Asian America: Chinese and Japanese in the United States since 1850.* Seattle: University of Washington Press, 1988.

Ling, Huping. *Surviving on the Gold Mountain: A History of Chinese American Women and Their Lives.* Albany: State University of New York Press, 1998.

Lyman, Stanford M. *Chinese Americans.* New York: Random House, 1974.

McClain, Charles J., Jr. *In Search of Equality: The Chinese Struggle Against Discrimination in Nineteenth-Century America.* Berkeley: University of California Press, 1994.

Peffer, George Anthony. *If They Don't Bring Their Women Here: Chinese Female Immigration Before Exclusion.* Urbana: University of Illinois Press, 1999.

Salyer, Lucy. *Laws Harsh as Tigers: Chinese Immigrants and the Shaping of Modern Immigration Law.* Chapel Hill: University of North Carolina Press, 1995.

Tsai, Shih-shan Henry. *The Chinese Experience in America.* Bloomington: Indiana University Press, 1986.

Wong, K. Scott and Sucheng Chan, eds. *Claiming America: Constructing Chinese American Identities During the Exclusion Era.* Philadelphia: Temple University Press, 1998.

Yu, Renqui. *To Save China, To Save Ourselves: The Chinese Hand Laundry Alliance of New York.* Philadelphia: Temple University Press, 1992.

Yung, Judy. *Unbound Feet: A Social History of Chinese Women in San Francisco.* Berkeley: University of California Press, 1995.

Yung, Judy. *Unbound Voices: A Documentary History of Chinese Women in San Francisco.* Berkeley: University of California Press, 1999.

JAPANESE AMERICANS

Daniels, Roger. *Asian America: Chinese and Japanese in the United States since 1850.* Seattle: University of Washington Press, 1988.

Daniels, Roger. *Prisoners Without Trial: Japanese Americans in World War II.* New York: Hill & Wang, 1993.

Fiset, Louis. *Imprisoned Apart: The World War II Correspondence of an Issei Couple.* Seattle: University of Washington Press, 1997.

Kitano, Harry H. L. *Generations and Identity.* Needham Heights, MA: Ginn Press, 1993.

Kitano, Harry H. L. *Japanese Americans: Evolution of a Subculture,* 2nd ed. Englewood Cliffs, NJ: Prentice Hall, 1976.

Maki, T. Mitchell, Harry H.L. Kitano, and S. Megan Berthold. *Achieving the Impossible Dream: How Japanese Americans Obtained Redress.* Urbana: University of Illinois Press, 1999.

Matsumoto, Valerie J. *Farming the Home Place: A Japanese American Community in California, 1919–1982.* Ithaca, NY: Cornell University Press, 1993.

Okihiro, Gary. *Storied Lives: Japanese American Students and World War II.* Seattle: University of Washington Press, 1999.

Tamura, Linda. *The Hood River Issei: An Oral History.* Urbana: University of Illinois Press, 1993.

Takahashi, Jere. *Nisei/Sansei: Shifting Japanese American Identities and Politics.* Philadelphia: Temple University Press, 1997.

Van Sant, John E. *Pacific Pioneers: Japanese Journeys to America and Hawaii, 1850–1880.* Urbana: University of Illinois Press, 2000.

Yoo, David K. *Growing Up Nisei: Race, Generation, and Culture among Japanese Americans of California, 1924–1949.* Urbana: University of Illinois Press, 1999.

KOREAN AMERICANS

Barringer, Herbert R., and Sung-Nam Cho. *Koreans in the United States: A Fact Book*. Honolulu: University of Hawaii Press, 1989.

Choy, Bong-youn. *Koreans in America*. Chicago: Nelson Hall, 1979.

Hurh, Won Moo. *The Korean Americans*. Westport, CT: Greenwood Press, 1998.

Kim, Hyung-chan, ed. *The Korean Diaspora*. Santa Barbara, CA: Clio Press, 1977.

Patterson, Wayne, ed. *The Golden Mountain: The Autobiography of a Korean Immigrant, 1895–1960*. Urbana: University of Illinois Press, 1995.

Patterson, Wayne. *The Korean Frontier in America: Korean Immigration to Hawaii, 1896–1910*. Honolulu: University Press, 1988.

FILIPINO AMERICANS

Bulosan, Carlos. *America Is in the Heart*. Seattle: University of Washington Press, 1973.

Carino, Benjamin V. *The New Filipino Immigrants to the United States*. Honolulu: East-West Center, 1990.

Espiritu, Yen Le, ed. *Filipino American Lives*. Philadelphia: Temple University Press, 1995.

Posadas, Barbara M. *The Filipino Americans*. Westport, CT: Greenwood Press, 1999.

SOUTH ASIAN AMERICANS

Chandrasekhar, S., ed. *From India to America*. La Jolla, CA: Population Institute, 1982.

Daniels, Roger. *History of Indian Immigration to the United States:* New York: Asia Society, 1989.

Helweg, Arthur, and Usha M. Helweg. *An Indian Success Story: East Indians in America*. Philadelphia: University of Pennsylvania Press, 1990.

Jensen, Joan M. *Passage from India*. New Haven, CT: Yale University Press, 1988.

Leonard, Karen Isakson. *The South Asian Americans*. Westport, CT: Greenwood Press, 1997.

REFUGEE POLICY

Daniels, Roger. "American Refugee Policy in Historical Perspective," in J. C. Jackman and Carla Borden, eds. *The Muses Flee Hitler: Cultural Transfer* and Adaptation, 1930–1945. Washington, DC: Smithsonian Institution, 1983, pp. 61–77.

Haines, David W., ed. *Case Studies in Diversity: Refugees in America in the 1990s.* Westport, CT: Greenwood, 1997.

Loescher, Gil, and John A. Scanlan. *Calculated Kindness: Refugees and America's Half-Open Door, 1945 to the Present.* New York: Free Press, 1986.

Loescher, Gil, ed. *Refugees and the Asylum Dilemma in the West.* University: Pennsylvania State University Press, 1992.

SOUTHEAST ASIANS

Chan, Sucheng. *Hmong Means Free: Life in Laos and America.* Philadelphia: Temple University Press, 1994.

Freeman, James M. *Hearts of Sorrow: Vietnamese-American Lives.* Stanford, CA: Stanford University Press, 1990.

Haines, David W., ed. *Refugees as Immigrants: Cambodians, Laotians and Vietnamese in America.* Totowa, NJ: Rowman & Littlefield, 1989.

Hein, Jeremy. *From Vietnam, Laos, and Cambodia: A Refugee Experience in the United States.* New York: Twayne, 1995.

Tenhula, John, ed. *Voices from Southeast Asia: The Refugee Experience in the United States.* New York: Holmes & Meier, 1991.

Welaratna, Usha. *Beyond the Killing Fields: Voices of 9 Cambodian Survivors in America.* Stanford, CA: Stanford University Press, 1993.

PACIFIC ISLANDERS

Barkan, Elliott R. *Asian and Pacific Islander Migration to the United States: A Model of New Global Patterns.* Westport, CT: Greenwood, 1992.

Colbert, Evelyn S. *The Pacific Islands: Paths to the Present.* Boulder, CO: Westview Press, 1997.

Fuchs, Lawrence. *Hawaii Pono: A Social History of Hawaii.* New York: Harcourt, Brace, 1961.

Janes, Craig R. *Migration, Social Change, and Health: A Samoan Community in Urban California.* Stanford, CA: Stanford University Press, 1990.

Lind, Andrew. *Hawaii's People.* Honolulu: University of Hawaii Press, 1967.

Macpherson, Cluny, Bradd Shore, and Robert Franco, eds. *New Neighbors: Islanders in Adaptation.* Santa Cruz: University of California Press, 1978.

Index